Henry Jenner's Handbook of the Cornish language

Henry Jenner.

Henry Jenner's Handbook of the Cornish Language

Revised by

Michael Everson

and including three early articles
on Cornish by Jenner

evertype
2010

Published by Evertype, Cnoc Sceichín, Leac an Anfa, Cathair na Mart, Co. Mhaigh Eo, Éire. *www.evertype.com*.

First edition 1904, David Nutt, London.

A catalogue record for this book is available from the British Library.

ISBN-10 1-904808-37-9
ISBN-13 978-1-904808-37-4

Typeset in Baskerville by Michael Everson.

Cover design by Michael Everson.

The frontispiece photograph of Henry Jenner in retirement and the copy of his signature is published here by the kind permission of Mary Beazley. The signature was taken from Henry's own copy of the 1904 *Handbook*, marked "for lending".

Printed and bound by LightningSource.

DHÔ'M GWRÊG GERNÛAK
K. L. J.

Kerra ow Holon! Beniges re vo
Gans bennath Dew an dêdh a'th ros dhemmo,
Dhô whelas gerryow gwan pan dhetha vî,
Tavas dha dassow, ha dhô'th drovya dî.
En cov an dêdh splan-na es pel passyes;
En cov idn dêdh lowenek, gwin 'gan bês,
War Garrak Loys en Côs, es en dan skês
Askelly Myhal El, o'gan gwithes;
En cov lîas dêdh wheg en Kernow da,
Ha nŷ mar younk—na whekkah vel êr-ma
Dhemmo a dhîg genev an gwella tra,
Pan dhetha vî en kerh, en ol bro-na;
Dheso mî re levar dha davas teg,
Flogh ow empinyon vî, dho'm kerra Gwrêg.

GWAS MYHAL.

Scrîfes en agan Chŷ nŷ,
      Dawthegves dêdh Mîs Gorefan
           En Bledhan agan Arledh, 1904.

Table of contents

Preface to the 2010 edition

This new edition of Jenner's classic *Handbook of the Cornish Language* appears more than a century after the book's first publication. Now that the Cornish Revival has weathered many storms, it is well worth making Jenner's ground-breaking work available again, copies of the 1904 edition having become rare and expensive.

A useful way to have another look at Jenner's place in the Revival is to compare the contents of the 1904 *Handbook* with the three articles Jenner published between 1873 and 1877, near the beginning of his researches into Cornish. These articles are reproduced below as appendices to the main text. The orthographic system which Jenner used in 1904 was the culmination of many years of work, but it is important to notice that Jenner was aware *three decades earlier* of Alexander Melville Bell's 1865 "Visible Speech", and of Alexander John Ellis' 1867 "Palæotype" and 1871 "Glossic". Jenner's familiarity with these precursors of the International Phonetic Alphabet (IPA) is significant. It shows him to have had real phonetic training. It places his work in the context of modern linguistics.

And *linguist* is certainly the word which one must apply to Jenner. His achievement was truly remarkable. Synthesizing the texts, the description in Edward Lhuyd's 1707 *Archaeologia Britannica*, Edwin Norris' 1859 *Sketch of Cornish Grammar*, Robert Williams' 1865 *Lexicon Cornu-Britannicum*, and Frederick Jago's 1882 *English-Cornish Dictionary*, Jenner sorted it all out: he devised a system which was practical enough to use to begin to revive the language. He uses an orthography that supports Late Cornish while still retaining a connection to the orthographic forms of the Middle Cornish scribal tradition. Jenner's Cornish *looks* Cornish. I wager that the scribes of Glasney could have read it, and that Jordan and Tregear and the author of *Bewnans Ke* would likewise have found it to be familiar. And his spelling partakes of *tota Cornicitas*: it can write Middle and Late Cornish without linguistic compromise.

Jenner's orthography provides a good, clear relationship between sound and spelling without diverging drastically from that of the traditional texts. He used diacritical marks for precision where necessary. His phonology is for the most part sound; he recognized the earlier phonemes /y/ and /ø/ by the way they had unrounded to /i/ and /e/ in Late Cornish. He endeavoured to describe the reduction of unstressed syllables to schwa using the symbols ŏ and ŭ. His section on grammar is wide-ranging and largely reliable. Jenner appears to regard the differences between Middle Cornish and Late Cornish as being more apparent than real; his work is generally free of the unwarranted purism of some later Revivalists. Of particular interest is his belief that it was undesirable to try to reconstruct a "foreign" accent based on "scientific affectation". He recognized that the contact between Cornish and English must have led to similarities in phonology, and held that the sound and intonation of the English spoken in Cornwall should have a proper and positive influence on the pronunciation of Revived Cornish.

This re-edition is not a mere facsimile. I have added phonetic transcriptions in the IPA, to assist the modern reader in under-standing exactly which sounds Jenner was recommending.* Jenner's Cornish spellings have been kept as he wrote them, except where a typographical error or omission had rendered his intention obscure. Breton spellings, however, have been updated to modern orthography.

---

* Two characters used here, [ɨ] and [ʉ], are not used in the IPA proper; the Oxford English Dictionary uses them for reduced [ɪ] (*schwi*) and reduced [ʊ] (*schwu*). See Note 31 on page 52.

PREFACE TO THE 2010 EDITION

The book being newly typeset has benefited from some changes for the modern reader. Chapter headings and subsections within chapters have been numbered as sections for ease of citation. It will be seen that some of the numbers are rather long, but in fact they do reflect the complex net of nested, numbered, and lettered paragraphs with which Jenner structured his work. Biblical references use European digits rather than Roman, and standard references ("Matthew 2:1–20" rather than "*St Matthew* ii. 1–20"). Hypothetical forms are prefixed with an *asterisk as is now standard practice. Editorial comments of my own are given in {curly brackets}.

From time to time one encounters negative assessments by modern readers who have criticized Jenner for some of his social comments. It is true: today's reader will find some of Jenner's remarks to be what we now consider to be politically incorrect, indeed rather embarrassing. It must be remembered that the book was published at a time when such ideas were commonplace. This does not make them accurate or admirable; it is a reason, not an excuse. The most extreme of such comments have been moved to footnotes—where they can be safely ignored by the reader whose interests are merely linguistic.

I would like to give my thanks to Mary Beazley for encouraging me so wholeheartedly to re-publish the work of her Uncle Harry. I am most grateful to my colleagues Eddie Climo, Owen Cook, Thomas Leigh, Christian Semmens, Craig Weatherhill, and Nicholas Williams for their proofreading, and for many useful comments on Jenner's text and on my editorial additions. The responsibility for any lurking typographical or interpretative errors remains mine.

Michael Everson
Westport, Co. Mayo
January 2010

Preface to the 1904 edition

This book is principally intended for those persons of Cornish nationality who wish to acquire some knowledge of their ancient tongue, and to read, write, and perhaps even to speak it. Its aim is to represent in an intelligible form the Cornish of the later period, and since it is addressed to the general Cornish public rather than to the skilled philologist, much has been left unsaid that might have been of interest to the latter, old-fashioned phonological and grammatical terms have been used, a uniform system of spelling has been adopted, little notice has been taken of casual variations, and the arguments upon which the choice of forms has been based have not often been given.

The spelling has been adapted for the occasion. All writers of Cornish used to spell according to their own taste and fancy, and would sometimes represent the same word in different ways even in the same page, though certain general principles were observed in each period. There was a special uncertainty about the vowels, which will be easily appreciated by those who are familiar with Cornish English. Modern writers of all languages prefer consistent spelling, and to modern learners, whose object is linguistic rather than philological, a fairly regular system of orthography is almost a necessity. The present system is not the phonetic ideal of "one sound to each symbol, and one symbol for each sound," but it aims at being fairly consistent with itself, not too difficult to understand, not too much encumbered with diacritical signs, and not too startlingly different from the spellings of earlier times, especially from that of Lhuyd, whose system was constructed from living

Cornish speakers. The writer has arrived at his conclusions by a comparison of the various existing spellings with one another, with the traditional fragments collected and recorded by himself in 1875, with the modern pronunciation of Cornish names, with the changes which English has undergone in the mouths of the less educated of Cornishmen, and to some extent with Breton. The author suggests that this form of spelling should be generally adopted by Cornish students of their old speech. The system cannot in the nature of things be strictly accurate, but it is near enough for practical purposes. Possibly there is much room for controversy, especially as to such details as the distribution of long and short vowels, the representation of the Middle Cornish *u, ue, eu* sometimes by *î*, sometimes by *ê*, and sometimes by *eu* or *ew*, or of the Middle Cornish *y* by *i, e*, or *y*, or occasionally by an obscure *ă, ŏ*, or *ŭ*, and it is quite likely that others might arrive at different conclusions from the same evidence, though those conclusions might not be any the nearer to the sounds which the Cornishmen of the seventeenth and eighteenth centuries really did make. As for grammatical forms, it will be seen that the writer is of opinion that the difference between Middle and Modern Cornish was more apparent than real, and that except in the very latest period of all, when the language survived only in the mouths of the least educated persons, the so-called "corruptions" were to a great extent due to differences of spelling, to a want of appreciation of almost inaudible final consonants, and to an intensification of phonetic tendencies existing in germ at a much earlier period. Thus it is that inflections which in the late Cornish often seem to have been almost, if not quite, inaudible, have been written in full, for that is the author's notion, founded on what Middle Cornishmen actually did write, of what Modern Cornishmen were trying to express. For most things he has precedents, though he has allowed himself a certain amount of conjecture at times, and in most cases of difficulty he has trusted, as he would advise his readers to do, to Breton rather than to Welsh, for the living Breton of to-day is the nearest thing to Cornish that exists.

Why should Cornishmen learn Cornish? There is no money in it, it serves no practical purpose, and the literature is scanty and of no great originality or value. The question is a fair one, the answer is simple. Because they are Cornishmen. At the present day Cornwall, but for a few survivals of Duchy jurisdictions, is legally and practically a county of England, with a County Council, a County Police, and a Lord-Lieutenant all complete, as if it were no better than a mere Essex or Herts.[1] But every Cornishman knows well enough, proud as he may be of belonging to the British Empire, that he is no more an Englishman than a Caithness man is, that he has as much right to a separate local patriotism to his little Motherland, which rightly understood is no bar, but rather an advantage to the greater British patriotism,[2] as has a Scotsman, an Irishman, a Welshman, or even a Colonial; and that he is as much a Celt and as little of an "Anglo-Saxon" as any Gael, Cymro, Manxman, or Breton. Language is less than ever a final test of race. Most Cornishmen habitually speak English, and few, very few, could hold five minutes' conversation in the old Celtic speech. Yet the memory of it lingers on, and no one can talk about the country

---

1 Cf. "Ista sunt nomina corrodiorum et pensionum *in Anglia et Cornubia* quæ sunt in dono Regis Angliæ" {'The following are the names of the grants and payments *in England and Cornwall* which are in the gift of the King of England.'} Harl. MS 433, f. 335, temp. Ric. iii.

2 The Bretons of to-day {1904} habitually speak of Brittany as "*notre petite patrie*" {'our little fatherland'} and France as "*notre grande patrie*" {'our great fatherland'}, and none have fought and died for France more bravely than these. As soldiers (and still more as sailors) they are to France what the Highlanders are to Britain, and avenge the atrocities of 1793 in the same noble fashion as that in which the Gaels have avenged the horrors of Culloden and its sequel. Loyalty is in the blood of Celts, whether to clan, or to great or little Fatherland.

itself, and mention the places in it, without using a wealth of true Cornish words. But a similar thing may be said of a very large proportion of Welshmen, Highlanders, Irishmen, Manxmen, and Bretons.

Omnia Græce,

Quum sit turpe magis nostris nescire Latine.

{ 'Everything is Greek,

when it is more shameful to be ignorant of Latin.'}

The reason why a Cornishman should learn Cornish, the outward and audible sign of his separate nationality, is sentimental, and not in the least practical, and if everything sentimental were banished from it, the world would not be as pleasant a place as it is.

Whether anything will come of the Cornish part of the Celtic movement remains to be seen, but it is not without good omen that this book is published at the "Sign of the Phœnix."

A few words of comprehensive apology for the shortcomings of this handbook. When the writer was asked by the Secretary of the Celtic-Cornish Society to undertake a Cornish grammar, which was the origin of this book, it was more than twenty years since he had dropped his Cornish studies in favour of other and more immediately necessary matters. Much of what he once knew had been forgotten, and had to be learnt over again, and the new grammar was wanted quickly. There must needs be, therefore, inaccuracies and inconsistencies, especially with regard to the spelling, which had to be constructed, and he is conscious also that there are at least two living men, if no more, who could have made a far better book. Of either of these two, Dr Whitley Stokes and Professor Joseph Loth, Doyen of the Faculty of Letters in Rennes University, who probably know more about Cornish between them than any one else ever did, the writer may well say, as John Boson of Newlyn said of Keigwin two centuries ago, "*Markressa an dean deskez fear-na gwellaz hemma, ev a venja kavaz fraga e owna en skreefa-*

composter, etc."[3] For, indeed, even in that same *skreefa-composter* is there much scope for argument, and Boson's "et cetera" stands for a good deal besides.

It is not given to a grammar-writer to strive after originality. If he did so, he would probably not be the better grammarian. The writer therefore has no hesitation in acknowledging to the full his many obligations to previous workers on the subject. To Lhuyd and Pryce, to Gwavas, Tonkin, Boson, and Borlase he owes much (and also, parenthetically, he thanks Mr John Enys of Enys for lending him the Borlase MS). But it is to the workers of the second half of the nineteenth century, living or departed, that he owes most, and especially to Dr Edwin Norris, Dr Whitley Stokes, Professor Loth, Canon Robert Williams, and Dr Jago. Of the works of these writers he has made ample use, though he has not necessarily agreed with them in every detail.

The well-known work of Edwin Norris has been of the greatest value in every way, and the copious examples given in his "Sketch of Cornish Grammar" have frequently saved the writer the trouble of searching for examples himself. Dr Whitley Stokes's editions of two dramas and a poem have been of the greatest assistance, the notes to the *St Meriasek* being especially valuable in collecting and comparing the various forms of irregular verbs, etc. Without Canon Williams's Lexicon nothing could have been done, and though some amount of friendly criticism and correction has been given to it by Dr Stokes and Professor Loth, neither of whom, of course, really undervalues the Lexicon in the least, no one can fail to appreciate that excellent work. Professor Loth's articles are mostly on details. A more general work from his hand is much to be desired, and every Cornish student must look forward to the forthcoming volume of his *Chrestomathie Bretonne*, which will contain

---

3 "If that learned wise man should see this, he would find reason to correct it in orthography, etc." —*Nebbaz Gerriau.*

the Cornish section. It would have been better for the present work if its author could have seen that volume before writing this. But Professor Loth's articles in the *Revue Celtique* have been full of suggestions of the greatest value. Dr Jago's English-Cornish Dictionary has also been most useful. In a somewhat uncritical fashion, he has collected together all the various forms and spellings of each word that he could find, and this rendered it possible to make easily comparisons which would otherwise have given a good deal of trouble. Even the somewhat unconventional lexicographical arrangement of the book has had its uses, but, if one may venture an adverse criticism, it was a pity to have followed Borlase in including without notice so many Welsh and Breton words for which there is no authority in Cornish. It is on this account that the work needs to be used with caution, and may at times mislead the unwary.

The author begs to thank very heartily Mr E. Whitfield Crofts ("Peter Penn" of the *Cornish Telegraph*) for his great service in making this handbook known among Cornishmen.

Perhaps a subject in connection with Cornish which may be of greater general interest than anything else is the interpretation of Cornish names. It is for this reason that a chapter embodying shortly some general principles of such a study has been added, and for those who would try their hands at original verse composition in Cornish a chapter on the principles of Cornish prosody has also been given. The composition of twentieth-century Cornish verse has already begun. Dr C. A. Picquenard of Quimper, well known as a Breton poet under the title of *Ar Barz Melen*, has produced several excellent specimens, Mr L. C. R. Duncombe-Jewell published the first Cornish sonnet in *Celtia* in 1901, and the present writer has contributed a sonnet and translations of the Trelawny Song and the National Anthem to the *Cornish Telegraph*, besides writing two Christmas Carols, one in *Celtia* and one printed separately, and the dedication of this book, which, he may remark, is not meant for a sonnet, though it happens to run to fourteen lines.

The writer had originally intended to add some reading lessons, exercises, and vocabularies, but it was found that the inclusion of these would make the book too large. He hopes to bring out shortly a quite small separate book of this character, which may also include conversations, and he has in preparation a complete vocabulary, though he has no idea as to when it will be finished.

Part 1

The history of the Cornish language and literature

1.1. The story of the Cornish language

There have been seven Celtic languages—not all at once, of course—and indeed it is possible that there may have been more; but seven are known to have existed. One other may have been a Celtic speech, or it may have been something pre-Celtic, but of it we know too little to judge.

The Celtic languages belong to the type known as Aryan or Indo-European, the language of the higher or white races whose original habitat was once taken to have been near or among the Himalayas, but is now located with much less exactness than heretofore. To this class belong the Sanscrit, with its multitude of Indian derivatives; the Persian, ancient and modern; the Greek, the Latin with all its descendants, the Lithuanian, the Slavonic, the Teutonic and Scandinavian, the Albanian and the Celtic.[4]

---

4 {Jenner's paragraph continues on here at some length. Its content—including the reference to "the higher or white races"—is of its time, but the ideas it contains are mistaken and wholly unacceptable in 2009. The text is reproduced here, only because it appeared in the first edition.}

It is not to be supposed that the possession of an Aryan language is necessarily a proof of the possession of Aryan blood. In many cases the conquering white race imposed its language on the aborigines whom it subjugated and enslaved. This must have been very much the case in Britain, and it is probable that the lower classes of a great part of England, though they now speak a language of mixed Teutonic and Latin origin, as they once spoke Celtic, are largely the descendants, through the slaves successively of Britons, Romans, and Saxons, and the "villains" or *nativi* of

The Celtic languages are subdivided into two branches, representing two separate immigrations, about which little is known for certain, except that they happened a very long time ago. These are:

1. The Goidelic (or Gaelic), consisting of the three languages, or properly the three dialects, known as the Gaelic of Ireland, of the Scottish Highlands, and of the Isle of Man. It has been said, with some truth, that these three are as far apart as three dialects of the same language can well be, but are not sufficiently far apart to be counted as three distinct languages. Until the first half of the eighteenth century the written Gaelic of the Scottish Highlands differed from that of Ireland scarcely more than the written English of London differs from that of New York. Even now, though the use of the sixth and seventh century Latin minuscules, which

the Norman manorial system, of the aboriginal palæolithic "cave" man, and have far less in common with the Anglo-Saxon, the Celt, or any other white man than they have with the Hottentot, the Esquimaux, the Lapp, or the Australian "blackfellow." This is particularly the case in what was once the forest-covered district of middle England. There, no doubt, when there was any fighting to be done, the aboriginal hid in the woods until it was all over, and only then came out to share in the spoil and the glory and the drinks; while the white man, whether Briton, Saxon, or Norman, went out to fight, and not infrequently to be killed. A survival, perhaps, of the unfittest was the result, which may account for some of the peculiar characteristics of the Midland lower classes. That the successive changes of masters were matters of little or no importance to the enslaved aboriginal, while a life of servitude was intolerable to the free white man, may account for the fact that the labouring classes of Devon, Cornwall, Somerset, Wales, and the Welsh border are of a type infinitely superior in manners, morals, and physique to the same class in the Midlands, because they now consist almost entirely of the descendants of the free Britons who were driven westward rather than submit to the overwhelming invasion of the Teutonic tribes. Thus it is that probably, except for a certain Silurian (or Iberian) element in South Wales, which descends from the higher or fighting sort of pre-Aryan, and a surviving aboriginal element in parts of Ireland, the natives of what are known as the "Celtic" parts of these islands are more purely Aryan than any except the upper and upper middle classes of the so-called "Anglo-Saxon" districts of Britain. And of the Celtic parts of Britain, the Highlanders of Scotland and the Cornish are probably of the most unmixed Aryan or white race.

people choose to call "Irish" letters, has been dropped in Scotland, any one who can read the one dialect will have little difficulty in reading the other. Manx adopted in the seventeenth century an attempted, but not very successful, phonetic spelling, based partly on Welsh and partly on English,[5] and therefore looks on paper very different from its sister languages; but it takes a Gaelic-speaking Highlander of intelligence a very short time to get to understand spoken Manx, though spoken Irish (except the Ulster dialect) is more difficult to him. Possibly Pictish, if it was Celtic at all, which is uncertain, was of the Gaelic branch, for we find but little of any language difficulty when St Columba and his fellow-missionaries, whose own speech certainly was Gaelic, were evangelizing among the Picts. But the absence of such mention proves very little, for Christian missionaries, from Pentecost onwards, have not infrequently made light of the linguistic barrier, and we really know next to nothing about Pictish.

2. The Brythonic (or British), consisting of Welsh, Cornish, and Breton. These may be said to be as near together as three separate languages can well be, but to have drifted too far apart to be accounted three dialects of the same language. The place of Cornish, linguistically as well as geographically, is between Welsh and Breton, but though in some points in which Welsh differs from Breton, Cornish resembles the former, on the whole it approaches more nearly to the latter. Probably Cornish and Breton are both derived from the language of the more southern, while Welsh represents that of the more northern Britons.[6] Of course Cornish, like Welsh, has been influenced to some extent by English, while the

5 {Modern research indicates that Manx spelling is in origin Middle Scots.}
6 The Britons of the Kingdom of the North (Cumberland and Strath-clyde) probably spoke the progenitor of Welsh, which they perhaps brought south with them, displacing the South British in Gwynedd and Powys, and later in South Wales, when they also drove out the Goidelic intruders.

foreign influence on Breton has been French. It is probable that the ancient Gaulish, certainly a Celtic language, belongs to this branch.

The seven Celtic languages, then, are Irish, Albanic (or Scottish), and Manx Gaelic, Welsh, Cornish, Breton, and Gaulish, and it is possible that Pictish must be added to these.

Though a philologist has much to say on the points of resemblance between the Goidelic and Brythonic branches, and though no one who studies both can fail to be struck by their affinity in vocabulary, in grammar, and even in idiom, the speakers of different branches—a Welshman and a Highlander, for instance—are no more mutually intelligible than an Englishman and a German would be, if as much so. The three sets of Gaels, however, can understand one another with considerable difficulty, and Irish priests have been known to preach sermons (with but moderate success) in the Catholic parts of the Highlands. But though there has been for some time a Welsh mission of some sort of Nonconformists in Brittany (with doubtless a very limited following), it is said that the missionaries, though they learnt Breton easily, were greatly disappointed with the extent to which at first they could understand the Bretons or make themselves understood. Simple things of everyday life might be asked for in Welsh, and a Breton might "average" what was said, but no sort of conversation could be held, though any one who knew both Welsh and Breton might make himself understood at some length by a mixed audience, if he very carefully picked his phrases; it would not, however, be good Welsh or good Breton. But the same would only apply in a far less degree to Cornish, for Cornish is very much nearer to Breton than Welsh is.[7] The divergence is increased by the tendency of all the Celtic languages, or, indeed, of all languages, to

---

7 In September 1903, at the end of the Congress of the *Union Régionaliste Bretonne* at Lesneven in Finistère, the present writer made a speech in Cornish, perhaps the first that had been made for two hundred years,

subdivide into local dialects. Thus the Irish of Munster, of Connaught, and of Ulster must be mutually intelligible only with great difficulty; the dialect of Munster, by reason of the difference of the stress accent, being especially divergent. There is growing up now, with the Irish revival, what may be called a Leinster dialect, founded on the literary language, with peculiarities of its own. The Scottish Gaelic has at least four marked dialects: Northern, spoken in Sutherland, part of Caithness, and Ross; Western, spoken in Inverness-shire and Argyle and in the Islands; and the rather broken-down dialects of Arran and of Perthshire, but the speakers of these are not very unintelligible to one another. Even Manx has a tendency to a "north side" and a "south side" dialect. Welsh has two fairly well marked dialects, of North Wales and South Wales, and the Welsh of Glamorgan, once the classical form of the language, before the Cardiganshire Welsh of the translation of the Bible superseded it, is now tending to be a broken-down form of South Welsh. But all these spoken dialects of Welsh are kept together and their tendency to divergence is greatly checked by the existence of a very clearly defined spelling, grammar, and standard of style in the book language of what is far and away the most cultivated and literary of all the Celtic tongues. Breton has four well-defined dialects, those of Leon, Treguier, Cornouailles, and Vannes, besides the broken-down Breton of the Croisic district, the Vannes dialect differing from the others as much as Cornish does, and curiously resembling Cornish in some of its peculiarities. Here there is no one literary standard, but each of the four dialects has its own, though it is generally held, rightly or wrongly, that the Leonais dialect is the best, and the Vannetais the worst. An examination of the names of places in West Cornwall gives some

---

and rather to his astonishment he was fairly well understood by the Bretons. It is true that all were educated men, but only one of them had studied Cornish.

indication that there was a slight difference of dialect between the Hundred of Kerrier, or perhaps one should rather say the peninsula of Meneage, and the Hundred of Penwith, but it amounted to very little, and the evidence is very scanty.

The difference between Cornish and its two sisters is not very easy to define in a few words. There are differences of phonology, vocabulary, and grammatical forms. In phonology the most marked difference from both is the substitution of *s* or *z*, with a tendency, intensified in later Cornish, to the sound of *j* or *ch*, for *d* or *t* of Welsh and Breton. Cornish agrees with Breton in not prefixing a vowel (*y* in Welsh) to words beginning with *s* followed by a consonant, and its vowel sounds are generally simpler and less diphthongalized than those of Welsh. It agrees with Welsh in changing what one may call the French *u* sound into *î* (English *ee*) {[y] > [i]}, going apparently further than Welsh in that direction, while Breton still retains the *u*. Like Welsh, it retained the *th* and *dh* sounds {[θ], [ð]} which Breton, in nearly all its dialects, has changed into *z*, though these in Cornish, like the guttural *gh*, and *v* or *f* {[x], [v], [f]}, showed a tendency to drop off and become silent, especially as finals. In vocabulary Cornish follows Breton more closely than Welsh, though there are cases where in its choice of words it agrees with the latter, and cases in which it is curiously impartial. An instance of the last is the common adjective 'good'. The ordinary Welsh word is *da*, though *mad* (Gaelic *math*) does exist. In Breton *mad* is the regular word, though *da* is used as a noun in the sense of satisfaction or contentment (*da eo gant-han* 'good is with him' = 'he is pleased'). In Cornish *da* and *mas* are used about equally. As an instance of the first, *bras*, which in Welsh means 'fat, gross', is the more common Cornish and Breton word for 'large' or 'great', though *mêr* (*mur*, *meur*) in Cornish, and *meur* in Breton, the equivalents of the Welsh *mawr*, are also used. In grammatical forms Cornish almost invariably in cases where Welsh and Breton differ follows the latter, but, as in vocabulary, it sometimes has also ways of its own.

Except for the existence of Cornish names in the Bodmin Gospels, and in Domesday Book and one or two early charters, and of the Cornish vocabulary in the Cottonian Library, the earliest mention of the Cornish as differentiated from any other British language that has been as yet discovered occurs in Cott. MS Vesp. A. xiv, in the British Museum (the volume in which the said vocabulary is included), in a Latin life of St Cadoc. This speaks of St Michael's Mount being called, "in the idiom of that province," *Dinsol* (or 'the Mount of the Sun').

Giraldus Cambrensis, writing in the latter part of the twelfth century, says: "*Cornubia vero et Armorica Britannia lingua utuntur fere persimili, Cambris tamen propter originalem convenientiam in multis adhuc et fere cunctis intelligibili. Quæ, quanto delicata minus et incomposita magis, tanto antiquo linguæ Britanniæ idiomati, ut arbitror, est appropriata.*"[8]

In the fifteenth-century cartulary of Glasney College, belonging to Mr Jonathan Rashleigh of Menabilly, an old prophecy is quoted: "*In Polsethow ywhylyr anethow, in Polsethow habitaciones seu mirabilia videbuntur.*"[9] This is supposed to date before the foundation of the college in 1265.

In a letter of 1328-9 from John de Grandisson, Bishop of Exeter, 1327-1369, to Pope John XXII, the writer speaks of Cornwall as looking on the south upon Vasconia [Gascony] and Minor Britannia [Brittany];[10] "*Cujus lingua ipsi utuntur Cornubici.*"[11] And in

---

8 *Descript. Cambr.*, vi. {'Cornwall and Brittany speak almost the same language, still in many ways and almost in all intelligible to the Welsh because of the original resemblance. Which language, inasmuch as it is less delicate and more unformed, is to that degree, I believe, like the ancient speech of Britain.'}

9 {'In Posethow wonders or miracles will be seen'. For the erroneous *habitaciones*, compare *annedhow* 'dwellings' with *annethow* 'wonders'.}

10 *Cf.* "Where the great vision of the guarded mount
           Looks toward Namancos and Bayona's hold."

11 {'The language of which/of whom the Cornish themselves speak.'}

another letter in the same year to certain cardinals he says: "*Lingua, eciam, in extremis Cornubie non Anglicis set Britonibus extat nota.*"[12] With this comes another passage in the Register of Bishop Grandisson, quoted by Dr Oliver in his *Monasticon Diœcesis Exoniensis* (p. 11), which, in an account of the submission of the parish of St Buryan to the bishop, after a certain quarrel between them, states that a formal submission was made by the principal parishioners in French and English (the names are given, thirteen in number), and by the rest in Cornish, interpreted by Henry Marseley, the rector of St Just, and that after this the bishop preached a sermon, which was interpreted by the same priest for the benefit of those members of the congregation who could only speak Cornish. These records are to be found in Mr Hingeston Randolph's edition of the Grandisson Registers, and in these and other fourteenth-century Exeter registers there are several allusions to the obligations of hearing confessions and propounding the Word of God in Cornish.

But until the time of Henry VIII we have no trustworthy information about the state or extent of the language. It is highly probable, from the number of places still retaining undoubtedly Celtic names, and retaining them in an undoubtedly Cornish form, that until at least the fifteenth century the Tamar was the general boundary of English and Cornish; though there is said to be some evidence that even as late as the reign of Elizabeth, Cornish was spoken in a few places to the east of the Tamar, notably in the South Hams. Polwhele, however, limits the South Hams use of Cornish to the time of Edward I, and we know from the English Chronicle that when Athelstan drove the "Welsh" out of Exeter in 936, he set the Tamar for their boundary.[13] In the reign of Henry

---

12 {'Also in the remote parts of Cornwall there is a language known to the Britons, not to the English.'}

13 {The copy of the 1904 *Handbook* in the possession of Craig Weatherhill has what appears to be a pencilled margin note in Morton Nance's handwriting on this page. The note reads: "'The Cornish Language

VIII we have an account given by Andrew Borde in his *Boke of the Introduction of Knowledge*, written in 1542. He says, "In Cornwall is two speches, the one is naughty Englysshe, and the other is Cornysshe speche. And there be many men and women the which cannot speake one worde of Englysshe, but all Cornyshe." He then gives the Cornish numerals and a few sentences of ordinary conversation. These are much mixed with English, and were, no doubt, such as might have been heard on the borders of Devon, for he probably did not penetrate very far, being doubtless deterred by the impossibility of obtaining drinkable beer—a circumstance which seems to have much exercised his mind in describing Cornwall. These numerals and sentences are, as far as is known, the earliest specimens of printed Cornish, earlier by a hundred and sixty-five years than Lhuyd's Grammar, though Dr Jago, quoting from Drew and Hutchins, who had evidently never seen this book, Dr Davies's *Llyfr y Resolusion* of 1632, or Gibson's edition of Camden's *Britannia* of 1695, says that there is no evidence that anything was ever printed in Cornish before Lhuyd.

The Reformation did much to kill Cornish. Had the Book of Common Prayer been translated into Cornish and used in that tongue, two things might have happened which did not—the whole language might have been preserved to us, and the Cornish as a body might have been of the Church of England, instead of remaining (more or less) of the old religion until the perhaps unavoidable neglect of its authorities caused them to drift into the outward irreligion from which John Wesley rescued them.[14] But it is said by Scawen and by Bishop Gibson in his continuation of

---

was current in a part of the South Hams in the time of Edward I. Long after this it was common on the banks of the Tamar.' Hitchens and Drew, *History of Cornwall*, 1824, p. 2."}

14 Clarendon's account of the Cornish troops in the Great Rebellion gives the impression that there was no lack of piety among them at that time.

Camden's *Britannia*, that they *desired* that the Prayerbook might not be translated, and, though the statement is disputed, it is quite possible that the upper classes, who spoke English, did make some such representation, and that the bulk of the population in Cornwall, as elsewhere, had no wish for the Reformed Service-book in any language; for there were churches in Cornwall in which the old Mass according to the Use of Salisbury was celebrated as late as the seventeenth century, notably in the Arundel Chapel in St Columb Church, as may clearly be inferred from the inscription on the tomb of John Arundel and his wife, the latter of whom died in 1602.

It is asserted by Carew, Polwhele, Davies Gilbert, Borlase, and others, that in the time of Henry VIII Dr John Moreman, the parson of Menheniot, was the first to teach his parishioners the Creed, Lord's Prayer, and Commandments in English, these having been "used in Cornish beyond all remembrance." This same Dr Moreman is mentioned in the petition (or rather *demand*) presented to Edward VI by the Cornwall and Devon insurgents, in favour of the old form of worship. One paragraph of this is as follows: "We will not receive the new service, because it is but like a Christmas game. We will have our old service of Matins, Mass, Evensong, and Procession as it was before; and we the Cornish, *whereof certain of us understand no English*, do utterly refuse the new service."

In the early part of the reign of Elizabeth, during the course of the many discussions on church matters, a number of articles were drawn up, to judge by their general tone, by the extreme Protestant party, and a copy of these, taken from a MS in Corpus Christi College, Cambridge, occurs in Egerton MS 2350, f. 54, in the British Museum. They are entitled "Articles drawn out by some certaine, and were exhibited to be admitted by authority, but not so admitted", and their date, to judge by accompanying letters, etc., is about 1560. The last article is "A punishment for such as cannot say the Catechisme", and in it there occurs the following sentence: "Item that it may be lawfull for such Welch or Cornish children as can speake no English to learne the Præmises in the Welch tongue or Cornish language."

In the same reign, but somewhat later, a report on England, addressed to Philip II of Spain by an Italian agent, speaks thus of Cornwall: "*Li hauitanti sono del tutto differenti* di parlare, *di costume et di leggi alli Inglesi; usano le leggi imperiali cosi como fa ancola li Walsche loro vicini; quali sono in prospettiva alla Irlanda et sono similmente tenuti la maggior parte Cattolici.*"[15] However, since the agent insists that the Severn divides Cornwall from England, he can hardly have known much about the country. The report occurs among a number of Spanish state papers in Add. MS 28,420, in the British Museum.

In Carew's *Survey of Cornwall*, written about 1600, we read, however, that the language had been driven into the uttermost parts of the Duchy, and that very few were ignorant of English, though many affected to know only their own tongue. It seems, however, from what he says further on, that the *guaries*, or miracle plays, were then commonly acted in Cornish, and that the people flocked to them in large numbers, and evidently understood them. Carew adds that the principal love and knowledge of the language died with one "Dr Kennall, the civilian", probably John Kennall, D.C.L., Archdeacon of Oxford. Carew gives the numerals and a few other specimens of the language.

In a survey of Cornwall, by John Norden, entitled *Speculum Magnæ Britanniæ, pars Cornwall*, addressed to James I, the following account of the language is given. "The Cornish people for the moste parte are descended of British stocke, though muche mixed since with

---

15 {'The inhabitants are completely different *in terms of language*, customs, and laws compared to the English; they are subject to imperial laws just like their neighbours the Welsh; they are facing toward Ireland and are similarly for the most part Catholic.'}

the Saxon and Norman bloude, but untill of late years retayned the British speache uncorrupted as theirs of Wales is. For the South Wales man understandeth not perfectly the North Wales man, and the North Wales man little of the Cornish, but the South Wales man much. The pronunciation of the tongue differs in all, but the Cornish is far the easier to be pronounced." Here he goes on to compare the sound of it with the Welsh, to the disadvantage of the latter.... "But of late the Cornishmen have much conformed themselves to the use of the English tongue, and their English is equal to the best, especially in the Eastern partes; even from Truro eastward is in a manner wholly Englishe. In the west parte of the county, as in the Hundreds of Penwith and Kerrier, the Cornishe tongue is mostly in use, and yet it is to be marvelled that though husband and wife, parents and children, master and servauntes, doe mutually communicate in their native language, yet there is none of them but in manner is able to converse with a stranger in the English tongue, unless it be some obscure persons that seldom converse with the better sort."

In 1630 Sir John Dodridge in his *History of the Ancient and Modern estate of the Principality of Wales, Duchy of Cornwall, and Earldom of Chester*, says: "The people inhabiting the same [i.e. Cornwall] are call'd Cornishmen, and are also reputed a remanent of the Britaines... they have a particular language called Cornish (although now much worn out of use), differing but little from the Welsh and the language of the Britaines of France."

In 1632, Dr John Davies, the well-known Welsh lexicographer, published a Welsh translation of the *Booke of Christian Exercise* of Robert Parsons the Jesuit, under the title of *Llyfr y Resolusion*. In it he gives a Cornish version of the Lord's Prayer and Creed, the earliest extant, and evidently translated from Latin, not from English.

In the same year appeared a play called *The Northern Lass*, by Richard Brome. In this occurs an opprobrious sentence of Cornish, put into the mouth of a Cornishman bearing the absurd name of

"Nonsence", and addressed to a Spaniard who had no English, on the argument that Cornwall being the nearest point of Britain to Spain, Cornish might possibly approach nearer to Spanish than English did.

The next mention of Cornish we find in a diary of the Civil War, written by Richard Symonds, one of the Royalist army in Cornwall in 1644 (Brit. Mus., Add. MS 17,052). He gives a short vocabulary of common words, together with four short sentences. To these he appends the following note:

"The language is spoken altogether at Goonhilly, and about Pendennis and the Land's End they speak no English. All beyond Truro they speak the Cornish language."

Much about the same time William Jackman, the vicar of St Feock, near Falmouth, chaplain of Pendennis Castle during its siege by the rebel troops, was in the habit of using Cornish for the words of administration of Holy Communion, because the old people did not understand English. The Cornish words asserted to have been used by him were printed in Hals's History of Cornwall in 1750, though they do not occur in all copies of that scarce book.

In 1662 and 1667 John Ray, in his *Itinerary*, mentions one Dickon Gwyn (his real name was Dick Angwin), of St Just, as the only man who could write Cornish. Ray adds that few of the children could speak it, "so that the language is like in a short time to be quite lost."

This is probably the "Sieur Angwin" mentioned in a valuable little treatise on the Cornish language by John Boson of Newlyn, of which more later. This little tract, entitled *Nebbaz Gerriau dro tho Carnoack* (or "A few words about Cornish"), is only known from a copy which formerly belonged to the late Mr W. C. Borlase. It was written about the year 1700, and according to it the Cornish-speaking district was then "from the Land's End to the Mount and towards St Ives and Redruth, and again from the Lizard to Helston and towards Falmouth," but the language had decreased very much within the writer's memory.

It is recorded by Dr Borlase that Cheston Marchant, who died at Gwithian in 1676 aged 164 (!), could speak nothing but Cornish.

Writing in the latter part of the reign of Charles II., William Scawen, a Cornish antiquary, gives a long account of the state of the language in his time, in a treatise in which he laments the decline thereof, accounting for it by no less than sixteen elaborate reasons. This treatise, *Antiquities Cornu-Britannick*, was abridged by Thomas Tonkin, the Cornish historian, and the abridgment was printed in 1777, and again by Davies Gilbert at the end of his history. A copy of the full form of it in Tonkin's beautiful hand-writing, a much more elaborate work, is in Add. MS 33,420 in the British Museum. According to this, the inhabitants of the western promontories of Meneage and Penwith were in the habit of speaking the language, so much so that the parson of Landewednack, Mr Francis Robinson, used to preach in Cornish down to the year 1678, that being the only tongue well understood by his parishioners. Scawen mentions the MSS of the aforesaid "Anguin," as he spells him, and laments their destruction. He also speaks of a "Matins" (possibly a Primer, or Hours of our Lady) in Cornish, which had belonged to "Mr Maynard."[16]

In Bishop Gibson's edition of Camden's *Britannia*, published in 1695, there is a short account of the Cornish Language, and the Lord's Prayer and Creed, the same versions as those given by Scawen, are given as specimens. According to Gibson the language was confined to two or three western parishes, and was likely to last a very little longer. He mentions the *Poem of the Passion*, the *Ordinalia*, and the *Creation* as the only books existing in the language.

---

16 Probably the well-known Sir John Maynard, whose MSS are now in Lincoln's Inn Library. He represented a Devon constituency at one time.

The next authority is that excellent Celtic scholar, Dr Edward Lhuyd, who published his *Archæologia Britannica* in the year 1707. He gives the following list of the parishes in which the language was spoken: St Just, Paul, Buryan, Sennen, St Levan, Morva, Sancreed, Madron, Zennor, Towednack, St Ives, Lelant, Ludgvan, and Gulval, and along the coast from the Land's End to St Keverne (this would also include St Hillary, Perran Uthno, Breage, Germoe, Mullion, Gunwalloe, Ruan Major and Minor, Landewednack, Grade, and St Keverne), adding that many of the inhabitants of these parishes, especially the gentry, do not understand it, "there being no need, as every Cornishman speaks English." There is a letter of Lhuyd's to Henry Rowlands, author of *Mona Antiqua Restaurata* (1723), printed at the end of that work, in which similar information, dated 1701, is given. Lhuyd in this letter relates his adventures in Brittany, and remarks on the closeness of Cornish to Breton.

Then the language quickly receded, until, in 1735, there were left only a few people at Mousehole, Paul, Newlyn, St Just, and other parishes along the coast between Penzance and the Land's End who understood it. It was about this time that Gwavas and Tonkin finished their collections on the subject, and the language they found seemed to them a most irregular jargon—a peculiarity of which was a striking uncertainty of the speakers as to where one word left off and another began.

In the early part of the eighteenth century there was a little coterie of antiquaries at Penzance and the neighbourhood, who had busied themselves much with the remains of the old language. The patriarch of these was old John Keigwin of Mousehole, the translator of the *Poem of the Passion* and the play of *The Creation*. He was born in 1641, and died in 1710, and, according to Lhuyd and Borlase, his knowledge of Cornish was "profound and complete." However, that did not prevent him from making some extraordinary mistakes in his translations, which should perhaps be set down to the archaic form of the language with which he had to deal. He seems to have been a considerable if rather pedantic linguist, being accredited with an acquaintance with Latin, Greek, French, and even Hebrew, and in a translation into Cornish of the letter of King Charles to the people of Cornwall, he made use of his Hebrew knowledge when he failed to remember the exact Cornish word, writing "milcamath" for "war" {Hebrew מלחמת *milḥamaṭ*}. Among the other members of this little party may be mentioned William Gwavas, John Boson and his brother Thomas, Thomas Tonkin the historian, Oliver Pender, and last (as probably the youngest) Dr William Borlase, the author of the well-known History of Cornwall. It does not seem that any of these, except Keigwin, troubled themselves much about Cornish literature, but they did good service in the way of preserving words, proverbs, colloquial sentences, etc., and seem to have found great enjoyment in translating various passages of Scripture, songs, etc., into the Cornish that was current in their own day. These being spelt more or less phonetically (as far as the writers knew how to do so), and therefore varying a good deal in orthography, are now of great value in determining the sound of the latest Cornish.

When Lhuyd was at work upon his Cornish Grammar, he received considerable assistance from Keigwin, Gwavas, and Tonkin, and a vocabulary and collection of Cornish fragments compiled by the last two under the title of *Archæologia Cornu-Britannica* were afterwards printed by Dr William Pryce in 1790, with Lhuyd's Grammar, *under his own name*, with the same title.[17] This fraud, if it really deserves so harsh a name, was exposed by Prince L. L. Bonaparte, into whose hands the original MS of some of it fell; but though it certainly was not right of Pryce to act in this

---

17 In Tonkin's notes to Carew's *Survey* (Lord de Dunstanville's edition) passages which occur in Pryce are referred to pages of "my *Archæologia Cornu-Britannica*."

manner, he does deserve some credit for having published the vocabulary at all, and the service that he did in so doing may be the better estimated by a knowledge of the fact that it was very considerably through the medium of Pryce's publication that Dr Edwin Norris obtained the acquaintance with Cornish necessary to enable him to bring out his valuable edition of the early Cornish dramas. It is strange that so much abuse has been heaped upon Pryce, while Davies Gilbert has escaped with comparative freedom, in spite of a villainously careless edition of a number of scraps of Cornish (printed at the end of his edition of the play of *The Creation*), gathered entirely from Tonkin's MS, the Gwavas MS, or the Borlase MS, and inserted, with notes and all, without a word of acknowledgment, and in such a manner as to lead one to think that the translation and notes at any rate were his own doing. Pryce certainly took the trouble to correct his proofs, and Davies Gilbert could hardly have attempted to do so. Moreover, if Pryce's preface be read carefully, it will be seen that he by no means claims the whole credit for himself, but gives plenty of it, though perhaps not enough, to Gwavas, Tonkin, Lhuyd, and Borlase. The impression left by the preface is that Pryce was a more or less intelligent editor who added a little of his own, the amount of which he exaggerated.

In 1746 Captain (afterwards Admiral) the Hon. Samuel Barrington, brother of Daines Barrington the antiquary, took a sailor from Mount's Bay, who spoke Cornish, to the opposite coast of Brittany, and found him fairly able to make himself understood. In 1768 Daines Barrington himself writes an. account of an interview with the celebrated Mrs Dolly Pentreath, popularly, but erroneously, supposed to have been the last person who spoke the language. He also contributed to *Archæologia*, in 1779, a letter received in 1776, written in Cornish and English, from William Bodener, a fisherman of Mousehole, who according to Polwhele died in 1794. The writer states that not more than four or five people in his town, and these old folk of eighty years of age, could speak Cornish. But

19

Barrington says that he received information that John Nancarrow of Market-Jew, aged only forty in 1779, could speak it. Dolly Pentreath died in 1777; but Pryce, in the preface to his book of 1790, part of which is his own, though one knows not how much of it to believe, and Whitaker, vicar of Ruan-Lanihorne, in his Supplement to Polwhele's *History of Cornwall* (1799), mention that two or three people were still living who were able to speak Cornish, though this was only hearsay evidence.[18]

In his *History of Cornwall*, vol. v (1806), the Rev. R. Polwhele speaks of one Tompson, an engineer of Truro, whom he met in 1789, the author of the well-known epitaph on Dolly Pentreath, and says that he knew more Cornish than ever Dolly Pentreath did. But Polwhele did not think that at the time he wrote there were two persons living who could really converse in Cornish for any length of time. Some years ago the present writer came upon a letter in the British Museum addressed to Sir Joseph Banks, and dated 1791, the author of which mentions his own father as the only living man who could speak Cornish. Unluckily the reference to the letter has been lost, and there is so much Banks correspondence in the British Museum that it is almost impossible to find it again. But the statement is by no means conclusive, and

---

18 {The copy of the 1904 *Handbook* in the possession of Craig Weatherhill has what appears to be a pencilled margin note in Morton Nance's handwriting on this page. The note reads::

"Coth Doll Pentreath cans ha deau
Marow ha kledyz ed Paul plêaw
Na ed en Egloz, gan pobel brâs
Bes ed Egloz-hay coth Dolly es.

Old D. P. aged 102 (*No!*)
Deceased & buried in Paul parish
Not in the church with people great & high
But in the Churchyard doth old Dolly lie".}

there were probably several other "last living men" going on at once, and certainly John Tremethack, who died in 1852 at the age of eighty-seven, must have known a good deal of Cornish, some words of which he taught to his daughter, Mrs Kelynack of Newlyn, who was living in 1875. There was also George Badcock, the grandfather of Bernard Victor of Mousehole, who taught a certain amount of Cornish to his grandson, who was living in 1875, when the present writer saw him.

Then it is considered that Cornish, as a spoken language, died out. The process was gradual, though perhaps rather rapid at the last, and, as far as is generally known, the old tongue finally disappeared in the earlier half of the nineteenth century. Words and sentences, and even such things as the Creed and Lord's Prayer were handed on, some of them to our own day. The mother-in-law of the present writer, Mrs W. J. Rawlings (*née* Hambly) of Hayle, who died in 1879 at the age of fifty-seven, had learnt to repeat the Lord's Prayer and Creed in Cornish when she was a child at school at Penzance, but unluckily had quite forgotten them in later life. In 1875 Mr and Mrs John Kelynack, Mrs Soady, Mrs Tregarthen, and Captain Stephen Richards, all of Newlyn, and Mr Bernard Victor of Mousehole handed on to the Rev. W. S. Lach Szyrma, then vicar of Newlyn, and to the present writer the tradition of the numerals and a few words and sentences, which may be found in a paper contributed by the present writer to the *Transactions of the Philological Society* in 1876, and a few years later Dr Jago received some of the same tradition. Thus it may be said that so long as any of these three are alive, a faint flicker of living Cornish remains, even if there is no verity in the weird legends of the survival of more as an esoteric language among the peasantry and the mining and fishing folk of the West. But even if the spoken Cornish be dead, its ghost still haunts its old dwelling, for the modern English speech of West Cornwall is full of Celtic words, and nine-tenths of the places and people from the Tamar to the Land's End bear Cornish names.

Mr Hobson Matthews in his *History of St Ives, Lelant, Towednack, and Zennor*, has an interesting chapter on Cornish. He gives reasons for supposing that the language survived in St Ives, Zennor, and Towednack even longer than in Mounts Bay, and states that the families of Stevens and Trewhella were among the last to keep it up in Towednack. He also mentions one John Davy, who was living in 1890 at Boswednack in Zennor (a hamlet between the Gurnard's Head and Zennor Churchtown), who had some traditional knowledge of Cornish, knew the meanings of the place-names in the neighbourhood, and "could converse on a few simple topics in the ancient language." Unless Mr Matthews, whose judgment one would trust in such a matter, actually heard him do so, the last statement is not easy to believe.

1.2. The literature and other remains of the Cornish language

The following is a list, in order of date, of the known remains of Cornish from the earliest times to the end of the eighteenth century.[19] There may be others of very early date, which have been hitherto classified as old Welsh or Breton, such as the Lament for Geraint, King of Devon, generally attributed to Llywarch Hen, and certain glosses in Latin MSS.

1.2.1. *The Manumissions in the Bodmin Gospels* (Add. MS 9381, in the British Museum). The MS is of the tenth century, and belonged to St Petrock's Priory of Black Canons, originally Benedictine, at Bodmin. At the beginning and end are manumissions of serfs from whose names about two hundred Cornish words may be gathered. These have been printed in the *Revue Celtique* (vol. i. p. 332), with notes by Dr Whitley Stokes.

1.2.2. *The Cottonian Vocabulary* (Cott. MS Vesp. A. xiv, in the British Museum). {Now called the *Old Cornish Vocabulary*, OCV.} This forms part of a MS of the end of the twelfth century, and consists of about seven pages, preceded by a calendar containing many Celtic names, and followed by lives of Welsh and Cornish saints. The words are classified under various headings, such as heaven and earth, different parts of the human body, birds, beasts, fishes, trees, herbs, ecclesiastical and liturgical terms, and at the

---

19 {The Treagear homilies (the longest prose text in Cornish which we have) and the verse play *Bewnans Ke* were unknown in Jenner's time.}

end occur a number of adjectives. It has been printed by Zeuss in his *Grammatica Celtica*, by Dr Norris with the *Ordinalia*, and has been incorporated into Canon Williams's Cornish Lexicon. Many of the words in it were incorporated by Dr John Davies in his Welsh Dictionary, as coming from what he calls the *Liber Landavensis*, and a quotation from the Life of St Cadoc in the same MS is spoken of in Camden's *Britannia* as coming from the Book of Llandaff. The MS evidently bore that name for a time. It is probable, from certain mistakes in it, that the vocabulary is a copy of an earlier one, in which the letters *p* and *þ* of the Saxon alphabet were used.

Of about the same date as this manuscript was a composition in Cornish, of which the original is lost, except a few words. This was a *Prophecy of Merlin*, which only exists in a translation into Latin hexameters by John of Cornwall, who in his notes gives a few words of the original, which are certainly Cornish. Like many of the so-called Merlin prophecies, this relates to the struggle between Stephen and the Empress Matilda, but it contains local Cornish allusions of great interest. The only known MS is one of the fourteenth century, in the Vatican.

1.2.3. The single sentence, *In Polsethow ywhylyr anethow*, in the Cartulary of Glasney College. If the writer of the history of the foundation of the college is correct, this prophecy, 'In Polsethow [the Pool of Arrows, the old name of Glasney] shall be seen habitations', is older than the foundation in 1265. It is therefore the oldest known complete sentence of Cornish, and is interesting as containing the inflected passive *whylyr*. There is an abstract of the cartulary, by Mr J. A. C. Vincent, in the 1879 volume of the *Journal of the Royal Institution of Cornwall*, and this sentence is given there, with an explanatory note by the late Mr W. C. Borlase. The original belongs to Mr Jonathan Rashleigh of Menabilly.

1.2.4. On the back of a charter in the British Museum (Add. Charter 19,491) the present writer discovered in 1877 a fragment of forty-one lines of Cornish verse. {Now called simply *The Charter*

Fragment, CF.} The writing was very faint, indeed the MS had passed through other and by no means incompetent hands without this precious endorsement being noticed, and the finder might have missed it too had he not been deliberately looking for possible Cornish words on the backs of a number of charters relating to St Stephen-in-Brannel, after he had finished the necessary revision of the cataloguing of these documents. The date of the document is 1340, but the Cornish writing on the back is somewhat later, perhaps about 1400. The language and spelling agree with those of the *Poem of the Passion* and the *Ordinalia,* and the exact metre is not found anywhere else. The speaker (it may be a part in some play) offers a lady to some other person as a wife, praises her virtues, and then gives the lady some rather amusing advice as to her behaviour to her future husband, and how to acquire the position attributed in Cornish folklore to the influence of the Well of St Keyne and St Michael's Chair. A copy of these verses was printed in the *Athenæum* in 1877, but, as the writer admits, his readings were not at all good, for the writing was very faint. Dr Whitley Stokes, who had the advantage of working on a photograph, which brought out many letters which were invisible in the original, published an amended version in the *Revue Celtique.*

1.2.5. *The Poem of Mount Calvary,* or *The Passion.* {Now called *Pascon agan Arluth,* PA.} There are five MSS of this in existence. One is in the British Museum (Harl. 1782), and is probably the original, said to have been found in the church of Sancreed. It is a small quarto, on rough vellum, written very badly in a mid-fifteenth-century hand, and embellished with very rude pictures. Of the other copies, two are in the Bodleian, an incomplete and much "amended" one in the Gwavas collection of Cornish writings in the British Museum, with an illiterate translation by William Hals, the Cornish historian, and one is in private hands. It has been twice printed, once with a translation by John Keigwin of Mousehole, edited by Davies Gilbert in 1826, and by Dr Whitley Stokes for the

Philological Society in 1862. There is very little in this poem beyond a versified narrative of the events of the Passion, from Palm Sunday to Easter morning, taken directly from the four Gospels, with some legendary additions from the Gospel of Nicodemus and elsewhere, preceded by an account of our Lord's fasting and temptation. The metre consists of eight-lined stanzas (written as four lines) of seven-syllabled lines. There are two hundred and fifty-nine of these stanzas.

1.2.6. *The Ordinalia.* These consist of three dramas collectively known under this title. The first play, called *Origo Mundi*, begins with the Creation of the World, the Fall of Man, Cain and Abel, etc.; this being followed by the building of the Ark and the Flood, the story of the temptation of Abraham closing the first act. The second act gives us the history of Moses, and the third represents the story of David and of the building of Solomon's Temple, curiously ending with a description of the martyrdom of St Maximilla as a Christian (!) by the bishop placed in charge of the temple by Solomon. The second play, *Passio Domini*, represents the Temptation of Christ, and the events from the entry into Jerusalem to the Crucifixion; and this goes on without interruption into the third play, *Resurrectio Domini*, which gives an account of the Harrowing of Hell, the Resurrection, and the Ascension, with the Legend of St Veronica and Tiberius, and the death of Pilate. As in the *Poem of the Passion*, the pseudo-Gospel of Nicodemus and other legendary sources are drawn upon. {Still called collectively the *Ordinalia*; individually *Origo Mundi*, OM; *Passio Domini*, PD; *Resurrectio Domini*, RD.}

But running through the whole and interwoven with the Scriptural narrative comes the beautiful and curious Legend of the Cross. The legend, most of which is in the dramas, is this. When Adam found himself dying, he sent his son Seth to the Gates of Paradise to beg of the angel that guarded them the oil of mercy, that his father might live. The angel let him look into Paradise, where he saw many strange and beautiful foreshadowings of things that should be upon the earth; and the angel gave him three seeds from the Tree of Life, and he departed. When he came to where his father was, he found that he was already dead, and he laid the three seeds in his mouth, and buried him therewith on Mount Moriah; and in process of time the three seeds grew into three small trees, and Abraham took of the wood thereof for the sacrifice of Isaac his son; and afterwards Moses' rod, wherewith he smote the rock, was made from one of their branches. And soon the three trees grew together into one tree, whereby was symbolized the mystery of the Trinity; and under its branches sat King David when Nathan the Prophet came to him, and there he bewailed his sin, and made the *Miserere* Psalm {Psalm 51}. And Solomon, when he would build the Temple on Mount Sion, cut down the tree, which was then as one of the chiefest of the cedars of Lebanon, and bid men make a beam thereof; but it would in no wise fit into its place, howsoever much they cut it to its shape. Therefore Solomon was wroth, and bid them cast it over the brook Cedron as a bridge, so that all might tread upon it that went that way. But after a while he buried it, and over where it lay there came the Pool Bethesda with its healing powers; and when our Lord came on earth the beam floated up to the surface of the pool, and the Jews found it, and made thereof the Cross whereon Christ died on Calvary.

The metres of these plays are various arrangements of seven and four-syllabled lines, of which more anon in the chapter on prosody. There are three MSS of this Trilogy in existence. 1. The Oxford MS of the fifteenth century, from which the others were copied, and from which Dr Edwin Norris edited the plays in 1859. 2. Another Oxford MS, presented to the Bodleian by Edwin Ley of Bosahan about 1859, with a translation by John Keigwin. The copy of the text is older by a century than the translation. 3. A copy in the library of Sir John Williams, Bart., of Llanstephan, Carmarthenshire, with an autograph translation by Keigwin. This was Lhuyd's copy.

1.2.7. *The Life of St Meriasek.* {Now called *Beunans Meriasek*, BM.} This play, the MS of which was written by "Dominus Hadton"[20] in the year 1504, as appears by the colophon, was discovered by Dr Whitley Stokes some thirty-two years ago among the MSS of the Peniarth Library, near Towyn in Merioneth. It represents the life and death of Meriasek, called in Breton Meriadec, the son of a Duke of Brittany, and interwoven with it is the legend of St Sylvester the Pope and the Emperor Constantine, quite regardless of the circumstance that St Sylvester lived in the fourth century, and St Meriasek in the seventh. The play contains several references to Camborne, of which St Meriasek was patron, and to the Well of St Meriasek there. It is probable that it was written for performance at that town. The language of the play is later than that of the *Ordinalia*, the admixture of English being greater, while a few of the literal changes, such as the more frequent substitution of *g* (soft) for *s*, and in one instance (*bednath* for *bennath*) the change of *nn* to *dn*, begin to appear. The grammar has not changed much, but the use of the compound and impersonal forms is more frequent, and the verb *menny* has begun to be more commonly used as a simple future auxiliary. The metres are much the same as those of the *Ordinalia*. The spelling is rather more grotesque and varied. But, since this play (or combination of plays) is to a large extent {based} on local Cornish and Breton, rather than on conventional Scriptural lines, it has an interest, full of mad anachronisms as it is, which is not to be found in the Biblical plays. Some passages are of considerable literary merit, and a good deal of early Cornish and Breton history is jumbled up in it, and yet

---

20 {Nance reads *Rad. Ton*, that is, for *Radulphus* or *Ricardus Ton*. There was a priest Dominus Ricardus Ton at Crowan, near Camborne, in 1537. See P. Beresford Ellis, *The Cornish Language and its Literature* (London and Boston: Routledge & Keegan Paul, 1974), p. 41.}

remains to be worked out, for Dr Whitley Stokes's excellent edition of 1872 does not go very much into historical side questions. It is unlucky that this play was not discovered until after the publication of Canon Williams's Lexicon, but his own interleaved copy of the Lexicon, with words and quotations from *St Meriasek*, is in the possession of Mr Quaritch of Piccadilly, and Dr Stokes has published forty pages of new words and forms from the same play in *Archiv für Celtische Lexicographie*.

1.2.8. The Cornish conversations in Andrew Borde's *Booke of the Introduction of Knowledge*, printed in 1542. These consist of the numerals and twenty-four sentences useful to travellers. They were evidently taken down by ear, and appear in a corrupted form. Restored texts, agreeing in almost every detail, were published by Dr Whitley Stokes in the *Revue Celtique*, vol. iv, and by Professor Loth in the *Archiv für Celtische Lexicographie* in 1898.

1.2.9. In Carew's *Survey of Cornwall*, 1602, are the numerals up to twenty, with a hundred, a thousand, and what is meant for ten thousand, but is really something else. There are also ten words compared with Greek, a dozen phrases, some more words, and the Cornish equivalents of twelve common Christian names.

1.2.10. *The Creation of the World, with Noah's Flood*, by William Jordan of Helston, A.D. 1611. {CW.} The construction of this play is very like that of the first act of the *Origo Mundi* (the metres are substantially the same), and the author has borrowed whole passages from it; but as a whole Jordan's play possesses greater literary merit, and there are many additions to the story in it, and much amplification of the ideas and dialogue. Occasionally sentences of several lines in English are introduced, and it is curious to note that whenever this is the case, they are given to Lucifer or one of his angels, and in such a manner as to seem as if the author meant to imply that English was the natural language of such beings, and that they only spoke Cornish when on their good behaviour, relapsing into their own tongue whenever they became more than ordinarily excited or vicious. Five complete copies of this play are known, two of which are in the Bodleian, one in the British Museum (Harl. MS 1867), and two are in private hands (one bound up with the MS of *The Passion* already mentioned). Besides these there is a fragment in a similar hand to that of the complete Museum copy (certainly not that of John Keigwin, who translated the play in 1693 at the request of Sir Jonathan Trelawny, then Bishop of Exeter, though it has his translation on the opposite pages to the text) in the Gwavas collection in the British Museum. In a list of books published in *Welsh* (as it is expressed), given in one of Bagford's collections for a History of Printing (Lansdowne MS 808, in the British Museum), mention is made of this play. No date is given, but the names of the books are arranged chronologically, and this comes between one of 1642 and one of 1662. The play has been printed (with Keigwin's translation) by Davies Gilbert in 1827, and with a translation by Dr Whitley Stokes in the Philological Society's volume for 1864. Of William Jordan, the writer, nothing is known whatever. He may have been merely the transcriber, and it is possible that the transcription may be connected with that revival of Cornish patriotism which seems to have happened in the early seventeenth century.

1.2.11. *Nebbaz Gerriau dro tho Carnoack* ('A few words about Cornish'), by John Boson of Newlyn. The only known MS of this little tract in Cornish and English was formerly among the MSS of Dr William Borlase in the possession of his descendant, Mr W. C. Borlase. The present writer had it in his possession for a short time in 1877 or 1878, and copied about half of it, but returned it to Mr Borlase, who wanted it back, and it was then printed in the 1879 volume of the *Journal of the Royal Institution of Cornwall*. At the time of the sale of Mr Borlase's library, this tract, which when the present writer last saw it used to live between the pages of Dr Borlase's MS Collections on Cornish, did not appear, and its present ownership is unknown. It is in the handwriting of the Rev. Henry Usticke,

Vicar of Breage (died 1769), and in the Gwavas MS in the British Museum there are several pieces in the same hand. As a copy of Boson's original it is rather inaccurate, but Boson wrote by no means a clear hand. It is of great interest as the composition of one who, though he was brought up to speak English, as he himself says, had acquired a thorough knowledge of Cornish as it was spoken in his day, without having even looked at any of the literary remains of the language. He was also a man of general education, and in this tract and in his letters is rather fond of airing his Latin. Very little is known of him except that he was the son of Nicholas Boson and was born at Newlyn in 1655 and died some time between 1720, the date of his last letter to Gwavas, and 1741, the date of the death of the latter, who is recorded to have received a copy of verses in Cornish found among Boson's papers after his death. The date of the *Nebbaz Gerriau* is unknown, but it mentions a little book called *The Duchess of Cornwall's Progress*, which the author says that he wrote "some years past" for his children, refers (though not by name) to John Keigwin, who died in 1710, as being still alive, and does not mention Lhuyd's Grammar, published in 1707, so that we may infer that the date is somewhere about 1700. *The Duchess of Cornwall's Progress*, which had at least thirty pages (for he refers to the thirtieth page), was probably in English, with a few passages in Cornish, which Dr Borlase, who had seen two copies of it, transcribed into his Cornish Collections. Judging from his letters and from this tract, John Boson was a man of considerable intelligence, and one about whom one would like to know more, and his Cornish writings are of more value than those of the somewhat pedantic Keigwin.

1.2.12. *The Story of John of Chy-an-Hur*. {Now called *Jowan Chy an Horth*, JCH.} This is a popular tale of some length, of a labouring man who lived at Chy-an-Hur, or the Ram's House, in St Levan,[21]

---

21 {The site of Chy-an-Hur (*Chyanhor* in c. 1840 Tithe Apportionment) is now occupied by a thatched cottage called Mount Whistle.}

and went east seeking work, and of what befell him. It is the *Tale of the Three Advices*, found in many forms. It appears first in Lhuyd's Grammar, printed in 1707, where it has a Welsh translation. Lhuyd says that it "was written about forty years since," which dates it *circ.* 1667. Part of it, undated, but in the hand of John Boson, occurs with an English translation in the Gwavas MS (Brit. Mus., Add. MS 28,554). This, as appears by a note on the back of the first leaf, was written out for Gwavas's instruction in Cornish. The spelling is altogether different from Lhuyd's. Another copy in Cornish of Lhuyd's spelling, with an English translation, is in the Borlase MS, copied from the lost MS of Thomas Tonkin, with some corrections by Dr Borlase. It was printed with Lhuyd's Welsh and an English version, in Pryce's *Archæologia Cornu-Britannica* {ACB} in 1790, and by Davies Gilbert at the end of his edition of Jordan's *Creation*, 1827, in Cornish and English. The English versions of Borlase, Pryce, and Davies Gilbert are substantially the same, and are probably Tonkin's. An English version, translated from Lhuyd's Welsh, but pretended to be from Cornish, was printed in *Blackwood's Magazine* in 1818, and again in an abridged and expurgated form in Mr J. Jacob's collection of Celtic Fairy Tales in 1891. There is a much amplified version of the story in English in William Botterell's *Traditions and Hearthside Stories of West Cornwall*, published at Penzance in 1870, and a short and rather foolish one in Hunt's *Popular Romances of the West of England*, 1865, 1871, 1881. The language is a good specimen of the latest Cornish. The same story is given as an Irish folk-tale in an early volume of *Chambers's Journal*.

1.2.13. The Preface to the Cornish Grammar in Lhuyd's *Archæologia Britannica.* {AB.} This consists of two and a quarter folio pages of close print, and is written in the Cornish of his own day. It is the work of a foreigner, but is nevertheless very well done. A not very good translation, probably the work of Tonkin and Gwavas, is given by Pryce, and reprinted by Polwhele in the fifth volume of his History.

1.2.14. The rest of the remains of Cornish consist of a few songs, verses, proverbs, epigrams, epitaphs, maxims, letters, conversations, mottoes, and translations of chapters and passages of Scripture, the Lord's Prayer, the Creed, the Ten Commandments, King Charles's Letter, etc. They are found in the Gwavas MS (Brit. Mus., Add. MS 28,554), a collection made by William Gwavas, barrister-at-law, and ranging in date from 1709 to 1736; in the Borlase MS of the date of about 1750, in the handwriting of Dr William Borlase, Rector of Ludgvan, formerly in the possession of his descendant, the late W. C. Borlase, F.S.A., M.P., but now belonging to Mr J. D. Enys, of Enys; in Pryce's *Archæologia Cornu-Britannica*, 1790, and in Davies-Gilbert's editions of the *Poem of the Passion* and Jordan's play of *The Creation*, published respectively in 1826 and 1827. Those in the Borlase MS (except a few from a work of John Boson), and those printed by Pryce and Davies Gilbert, were probably taken from the Gwavas MS and from Tonkin's MSS. There is also one epitaph dated 1709 in Paul Church, an epitaph on Dolly Pentreath, which does not appear ever to have been inscribed on her tomb, and the letter of William Bodenor in 1776.

These fragments may be classified as follows:

1.2.14.1. *SONGS AND POEMS*.

1.2.14.1.1. Lhuyd's Elegy on William of Orange, 1702. Sixty-three lines of verse in rhyming triplets, in modern Cornish, with occasional archaic turns. A copy occurs in the Gwavas MS; it was printed by Pryce, with a Latin version, as part of a correspondence between Lhuyd and Tonkin, and by Polwhele in his fifth volume, with the same correspondence. There is a copy with an English version by John Keigwin in the library of Sir John Williams, Bart, of Llanstephan.

1.2.14.1.2. A song beginning "*Ma leeas gwreage, lacka vel zeage*", a series of moral platitudes on married life and the bringing up of children, by James Jenkins of Alverton, near Penzance (died 1710). This consists of five stanzas of five or six lines each. There is a complete copy in the Gwavas MS, and a copy wanting one line in the Borlase MS, and this incomplete version, with a translation, has been printed by Pryce and Davies Gilbert. A note in Pryce says that Tonkin had it from Lhuyd and again from Gwavas, whose is the translation. It is in idiomatic late Cornish, in rather wild spelling.

1.2.14.1.3. Song on James II and William of Orange, by John Tonkin of St Just, a tailor, who appears to have been a solitary Whig in a nation of Jacobites, as with very few exceptions the Cornish certainly were. It begins, *"Menja tiz Kernuak buz galowas,"* and consists of fourteen four-lined stanzas of modern Cornish, probably composed in 1695, to judge by the historical allusions. It is in the Gwavas MS only, and has never been printed.

1.2.14.1.4. A song of moral advice by the same writer, beginning *"Ni venja pea a munna seer,"* and consisting of seven four-lined stanzas, only one of which, beginning *"An Prounter ni ez en Plew East,"* has been printed (from the Borlase MS) in the *Journal of the Royal Institution of Cornwall* for 1866. The complete song is in the Gwavas MS, and has never been published.

1.2.14.1.5. A song beginning *"Pelea era why moaz, moz, fettow, teag"* (Where are you going, fair maid? he said). This consists of six four-lined stanzas, the second and fourth lines of each stanza being the burthen:

> *"Gen agaz bedgeth gwin* (or according to Borlase, Tonkin, and Gwavas, *pedn du*) *ha agaz blew mellyn"* ('With your white face, or black head, and your yellow hair') and

> *"Rag delkiow sevi gwra muzi teag"* ('For strawberry leaves make maidens fair').

The song was sung by one Edward Chirgwin or Chygwin, "brother-in-law to Mr John Groze of Penzance, at Carclew, in 1698," as a note by T. Tonkin says. Whether it was translated from English or whether the Cornish is the original does not appear.[22]

---

22 {It is now clear that an English version must have preceded this

The story is not quite the same (or quite so scrupulously "proper") as the English nursery version. There is a copy in the handwriting of Chirgwin in the Gwavas MS, and one copied from Tonkin's MS in the Borlase MS. It was printed by Pryce in an amended form, and by Polwhele.

1.2.14.1.6. A song on the curing of pilchards (not a very poetical subject) by John Boson. Twenty-six lines of rhyming couplets beginning "*Me canna ve war hern gen cock ha ruz*" ('I will sing, or my song is, of pilchards with boat and net'), and describing the process of bringing the fish ashore and putting them into bulks and making "fairmaids" of them. There is a copy with a translation in the Borlase MS, which was printed in the *Journal of the Royal Institution of Cornwall* for 1866, and Davies Gilbert printed it at the end of his edition of Jordan's Creation in 1827, but without any translation.

1.2.14.2. *VERSES AND EPIGRAMS.*

1.2.14.2.1. Nine short sayings in verse, printed in Pryce and Davies Gilbert, and copied by Borlase from Tonkin. The first, "*An lavar goth ewe lavar gwir*," etc., occurs also in Lhuyd.

1.2.14.2.2. Epigram on the verdict in the suit of Gwavas *v.* Kelynack, respecting tithes of fish. Eight lines by W. Gwavas. It occurs in the Gwavas and Borlase MSS, and in Pryce and Polwhele.

1.2.14.2.3. "To Neighbour Nicholas Pentreath," by Gwavas. Six lines. In the Borlase MS, and in Pryce and Polwhele.

1.2.14.2.4. "Advice from a friend in the country to his neighbour who went up to receive £16,000 in London," by John Boson. In the Borlase MS, and in Pryce and Polwhele. Eight lines.

1.2.14.2.5. "On a lazy, idle weaver." In the Gwavas and Borlase MSS, and in Pryce and Polwhele. Six lines.

Cornish one; indeed, a profusion of versions of this song, called in English "Dabbling in the Dew", among other names, has sprung up.}

1.2.14.2.6. "Verses on the Marazion Bowling-Green." In the Gwavas and Borlase MSS, and in Pryce and Polwhele. Six lines by Gwavas.

1.2.14.2.7. "Advice to Drunkards." Four lines, by Gwavas. In the Gwavas and Borlase MSS, and in Pryce and Polwhele.

1.2.14.2.8. A Cornish riddle. Five lines. In the Gwavas and Borlase MSS, and in Pryce, Gilbert, and Polwhele.

1.2.14.2.9. "Advice to all men." Written by Gwavas to form part of his own epitaph. Four lines.

1.2.14.2.10. "Another" [of the same sort], three lines, also by Gwavas.

1.2.14.2.11. "A concluding one," four lines, also by Gwavas. These last three, copied from the same page of the Gwavas MS, all occur also in the Borlase MS, and in Pryce, Gilbert, and Polwhele.

1.2.14.2.12. "A Fisherman's Catch" given by Captain Noel Cator of St Agnes to T. Tonkin, 1698. In the Borlase MS, and printed in the *R. I. C. Journal*, 1866, and in Mr Hobson Matthews's History of St Ives, Lelant, Towednack, and Zennor.

1.2.14.2.13. Six lines of moral advice, found among the papers of J. Boson after his death, and given to Gwavas. In the Borlase MS, and *R. I. C. Journal*, 1866.

1.2.14.2.14. Certificate of Banns from W. Drake, Rector of St Just, to Thos. Trethyll, Vicar of Sennen. Two versions, one in the Gwavas MS and one in Pryce, the latter being also in the Borlase MS. Drake died in 1636.

1.2.14.2.15. Verses on a silver hurling ball given to W. Gwavas. Seven lines by Thos. Boson, 1705. In the Gwavas MS. Unpublished.

1.2.14.2.16. Three couplets of verse, and a short piece of prose from J. Boson's *Duchess of Cornwall's Progress*. In the Borlase MS. Unpublished.

1.2.14.2.17. Prophecy, attributed to Merlin, of the burning of Paul, Penzance, and Newlyn. Two lines. In the Borlase MS, and often printed in Cornish histories and guide-books.

1.2.14.2.18. Elegy on the death of James Jenkin of Alverton. Four verses of three lines each, by John Boson, 17 Feb. 1711~1712. In the Gwavas MS. Unpublished.

1.2.14.3. *PROVERBS, MOTTOES, AND MAXIMS.*

1.2.14.3.1. From Scawen. Fourteen proverbs. In the Borlase MS; printed in the edition of Tonkin's abridgment of Scawen's *Antiquities Cornu-Britannick*, 1777, and in Davies Gilbert's History, and in his edition of the *Poem of the Passion*. Also in *R. I. C. Journal*, 1866, with sixteen others from the Borlase MS.

1.2.14.3.2. Mottoes of the families of Gwavas, Harris of Hayne,[23] Glynne, Tonkin, Godolphin, Boscawen, Polwhele, Noye, and Willyams of Carnanton. All except those of Glynne, Noye, and Willyams are printed in Pryce. All but Glynne and Willyams occur in Davies Gilbert's edition of Jordan's *Creation*, and the Willyams motto, though it occurs as a Cornish phrase in Pryce's preface and in the Gwavas and Tonkin MSS, is only found as a motto in pedigree books and on the sign-board of the inn in Mawgan Churchtown. The Glynne motto, *"Dre weres agan Dew"* ('Through the help of our God'), is given, with an incorrect translation, in Mr Hobson Matthews's History.

1.2.14.3.3. Mottoes for bowls, occurring in the Gwavas MS, and some in Davies Gilbert's edition of *The Creation*.

1.2.14.3.4. Maxims, proverbs, etc., about thirty in number, in the Borlase MS, in Pryce, and in Davies Gilbert's edition of *The Creation*, under the title of "Sentences in vulgar Cornish." Some of them are also in the Gwavas MS.

---

23 The motto of Harris of Hayne, *"Car Dew dres pub tra"* is mentioned in Boson's *Nebbaz Gerriau*, and is part of stanza 23 of the *Poem of the Passion*.

1.2.14.4. *CONVERSATIONS AND PHRASES.*

1.2.14.4.1. About seventy sentences, in the Borlase MS, in Pryce, and in Davies Gilbert's edition of *The Creation*, under the title of "Things occurring in common discourse." There are some additional ones in the Borlase MS.

1.2.14.4.2. About a hundred and fifty phrases, sentences, and idioms, copied by Dr Borlase from Lhuyd's MSS. Some, but by no means all, are in Lhuyd's Grammar.

1.2.14.4.3. A considerable number of similar phrases scattered throughout Borlase's Cornish Vocabulary at the end of his History of Cornwall. These are to be found, evidently copied from the Vocabulary, in a manuscript which belonged in 1777 to Henry Brush of Carnaquidn Stamps (on the road from Penzance to Zennor), which place belonged to William Veale of Trevaylor, who married the daughter of Gwavas. The MS is now in the possession of a descendant of Henry Brush.

1.2.14.4.4. A few expressions and phrases scattered through the Gwavas MS, in the letters of Boson, and in letters and notes of Gwavas.

1.2.14.5. *EPITAPHS.*

1.2.14.5.1. On James Jenkins, by John Boson, 1711~1712, in the Gwavas MS. Four lines. The Borlase MS, quoting the very letter in which it occurs, says that it is on John Keigwin, which is a mistake.

1.2.14.5.2. On John Keigwin, by John Boson, 1715. In the Gwavas MS. Four lines.

1.2.14.5.3. On Captain Stephen Hutchens, in Paul Church, 1709. The only Cornish inscription in any church. Probably by John Boson. Two lines. Frequently printed in guide-books, etc.

1.2.14.5.4. On William Gwavas, by himself. In the Gwavas MS, and in Pryce, Polwhele, and Davies Gilbert. Partly in English. These four are also in the Borlase MS, and are printed in the *R. I. C. Journal*, 1866.

1.2.14.5.5. On Dolly Pentreath, by —— Tompson of Truro, engineer. Printed by Polwhele, and later in Blight's *Week at the Land's End*, and other guide-books. A variant occurs in John Skinner's *Journal of a Tour in Somerset, Devon, and Cornwall*, 1797, in Add. MS 28,793, f. 62, in the British Museum.

1.2.14.6. *LETTERS.*

1.2.14.6.1. William Gwavas to Oliver Pender, 11th August 1711. Partly in Cornish.

1.2.14.6.2. Oliver Pender to W. Gwavas, 22nd August 1711. Mostly in Cornish.

1.2.14.6.3. John Boson to W. Gwavas, 5th April 1710. Nearly all in Cornish.

1.2.14.6.4. An unsigned letter, including a version of the "Old Hundredth." Partly in rhyme.

1.2.14.6.5. Note, addressed apparently to one going to America, by William Gwavas, 1710, on the back of a copy of the Creed in Cornish. These five are in the Gwavas MS, and have never been printed.[24]

1.2.14.6.6. Letter of William Bodenor to the Honble. Daines Barrington, 3rd July 1776. Printed in *Archæologia* (vol. v, 1779), in "Uncle Jan Treenoodle's" *Specimens of Cornish Provincial Dialects*, 1846; in a paper on the Cornish Language by the present writer in the *Transactions of the Philological Society*, 1873, and in *Archiv für Celtische Lexicographie*, with notes and emendations by Professor Loth, in 1898.

---

24 {The third and fourth have been published in Oliver J. Padel, ed. 1975. *The Cornish Writings of the Boson family*. Redruth: Institute of Cornish Studies. ISBN 0-903686-09-0. The first, second, and fifth have been published in Alan M. Kent & Tim Saunders. 2000. *Looking at the Mermaid: a reader in Cornish literature 900–1900*. London: Francis Boutle. ISBN 1-903427-01-0.}

1.2.14.7. *TRANSLATIONS.*

1.2.14.7.1. *Passages of Scripture.*

Genesis 1. Two versions, one by John Boson and one probably by John Keigwin. Both are in the Gwavas MS. One, Boson's, with his name to it, is in the Borlase MS. Boson's was printed by D. Gilbert at the end of his edition of the *Poem of the Passion*, and in a much revised form by Canon Williams at the end of his Lexicon. Keigwin's version was printed by D. Gilbert at the end of his edition of Jordan's *Creation*. There are many verbal variations from the Gwavas copies in the printed editions.

Genesis 3, translated by William Kerew, in the Gwavas MS. Published by Professor Loth in the *Revue Celtique*, April 1902.

Matthew 2:1-20, translated by W. Kerew, in the Gwavas MS. Published in the *Revue Celtique*, April 1902.

Matthew 4, also by W. Kerew, in the Gwavas MS. Published in the *Revue Celtique*, April 1902.

The last three were copied from a MS of Matthew Rowe of Hendra in Sancreed, by H. Usticke.

Proverbs 30:5, 6.

Psalms 2:11; 7:11; 35:1, 2

These are in the Gwavas MS, probably translated by W. Gwavas himself. Unpublished.

Psalm 100, of the Sternhold and Hopkins version, literally translated line for line, followed by an unsigned letter partly in rhyme. In the Gwavas MS. Unpublished.

1.2.14.7.2. *The Lord's Prayer.*

There are ten versions extant besides the modern one of Canon Williams.

1. In John Davies's *Llyfr y Resolusion* (a translation of Robert Parsons's *Book of Christian Exercise*), printed in 1632, and again in 1684. Translated from the Latin.

2. In Scawen's *Antiquities Cornu-Brittanick*, circ. 1680. Printed in Tonkin's abridgment in 1777. The same version is given in

Bishop Gibson's additions to Camden's *Britannia* in 1695, and by Polwhele.

3, 4. Two versions in John Chamberlayne's *Oratio Dominica in diversas linguas versa*, 1715, one of which is evidently meant for the version in Scawen and Camden.

5, 6. Two versions by John Keigwin, one said to be in Ancient Cornish and the other in Modern. Both are in the Gwavas and Borlase MSS, and were printed by Pryce and D. Gilbert.

7, 8. Two versions, one by John and one by Thomas Boson, in the Gwavas MS. Unpublished.

9, 10. Two versions by W. Gwavas, in the Gwavas MS. Unpublished. One of these, nearly identical with Keigwin's Modern, is said in a note to have been collected from J. Keigwin, Thomas Boson, Captain Thomas Tonkin, Oliver Pender, James Schollar, and T. Tonkin.

The first four are without the ἐκφώνησις at the end. All except the first are from the English. {Jenner means *doxology*, not *ecphonesis*.}

1.2.14.7.3. *The Apostles' Creed.*

1. In the *Llyfr y Resolusion*, 1632, 1684.

2. In Scawen and in Gibson's Camden.

3. In Hals's *History of Cornwall.*

4, 5. By John Keigwin, one in the Gwavas MS and both in the Borlase MS, and printed by Pryce and D. Gilbert.

6. By Thomas Boson, in the Gwavas MS. Unpublished.

7, 8. By William Gwavas, in the Gwavas MS. Unpublished.

There is a modern revised version in Williams's Lexicon.

1.2.14.7.4. *The Ten Commandments.*

1, 2. By John Keigwin, one in the Gwavas MS, and both in the Borlase MS, and in Pryce and D. Gilbert. One of these in a revised form is in Williams's Lexicon.

3. In the Gwavas MS, but without name. Unpublished.

4. By John Boson, in the Gwavas MS. Printed with notes by Professor Loth in vol. xxiv of the *Revue Celtique*.

5. By William Kerew, in the Gwavas MS. Printed with the preceding.

6. By T. Boson, in the Gwavas MS. Unpublished.

7. By W. Gwavas, in the Gwavas MS. Unpublished.

1.2.14.7.5. *The Words of Administration of Holy Communion.*

These are stated to be the words used by William Jackman, Vicar of St Feock. They occur in Hals's History.

1.2.14.7.6. *King Charles I's Letter to the People of Cornwall.*

This is a translation by John Keigwin of the Letter of Thanks from the Martyr King to the People of Cornwall for their loyalty in 1643, still to be seen in many churches in the Duchy. It occurs in the handwriting of Keigwin in the Gwavas MS, and in Dr Borlase's hand in the Borlase MS. It has been misprinted, with notes by the present writer (who had no opportunity of revising the proofs), in the Rev. A. Cummings's *History of Cury and Gunwalloe*, 1875, and Mrs Dent's *Annals of Winchcombe and Sudeley* (the place from which the original Letter is dated), 1877.

1.2.14.8. *GRAMMARS AND LEXICA.*

The following grammatical and lexicographical pieces belong more or less to the living period of Cornish:

1.2.14.8.1. Lhuyd's *Cornish Grammar*, printed in his *Archæologia Britannica* in 1707, and reprinted by Pryce in 1790.

1.2.14.8.2. Lhuyd's *Cornish Vocabulary*. The unpublished MS belongs to Sir John Williams, Bart., of Llanstephan, Carmarthenshire. Most of the words in it are to be found in Borlase's and Pryce's Vocabularies (see below). They were collected partly from the Dramas, partly from the Cottonian Vocabulary, and partly from living people.

1.2.14.8.3. *The Gwavas Vocabulary*. This is a short vocabulary of the latest Cornish (extending from A to O) in the Gwavas MS. The words were incorporated into Borlase's Vocabulary.

1.2.14.8.4. *The Hals Vocabulary*. This is a fragment (A to C) in the Gwavas MS. It is fantastic and of little value.

1.2.14.8.5. *The Borlase Vocabulary*, compiled from the MSS of Lhuyd, Gwavas, and Tonkin, from Lhuyd's *Archæologia*, from oral tradition, and from other sources. The original MS is in the Borlase Collection, now belonging to Mr J. D. Enys, and it was printed at the end of Dr Borlase's *Antiquities Historical and Monumental of Cornwall* in 1754, and again, revised, in 1769. It is a copious vocabulary, but is rendered rather less valuable by the inclusion of a large number of Welsh and Breton words, gathered chiefly from other parts of Lhuyd's *Archæologia*, or from John Davies's Welsh Dictionary.

1.2.14.8.6. *Pryce's Vocabulary*, or rather that of Gwavas, Tonkin, and Pryce. Printed, with Pryce's edition of Lhuyd's Grammar, at Sherborne in 1790. Some of this vocabulary was collected from the literary remains of Cornish, but a very large part was compiled from living tradition, not much by Pryce himself, but by Gwavas and Tonkin.

Though some of these have been used by Canon Williams in his *Lexicon Cornu-Britannicum*, by Dr Whitley Stokes in his Supplementary Cornish Glossary (*Transactions of the Philological Society*, 1868–9), and still more in Dr Jago's English-Cornish Dictionary, they have not been thoroughly exhausted yet, and a good many more words may be collected from them, as also from the attempted interpretations of place-names in Pryce's book and in the Gwavas MS.

.

Part 2

The grammar
of the Cornish language

2.0. Introductory note

The Cornish language divides very naturally into three periods: (1) Ancient, (2) Middle, (3) Modern.

1. The Ancient period is only represented by the Cottonian Vocabulary, which, though a MS of the twelfth century, is probably a copy of a much earlier one, by perhaps a few glosses, and by the names in the Bodmin Gospels. It has no extant literature.

2. The Middle period is that of the Add. Charter fragment, the *Ordinalia*, the *Poem of the Passion* (fifteenth century), the *Life of St Meriasek* (1504), and to some extent of the play of *The Creation* (1611), though the last is partly transitional. Judging from the few words preserved in John of Cornwall's twelfth-century translation of a prophecy of Merlin, the lost original of that was perhaps in an early form of Middle Cornish.

3. The Modern period begins with the few sentences in Andrew Borde's book (1542), and continues to the end.

As the whole of the extant literature of Middle Cornish is in verse,[25] it gives us little help as regards the colloquial Cornish even of its own period, and judging from Andrew Borde's sentences, only some forty years later than the *St Meriasek* and seventy years earlier than Jordan's play, Middle and Modern Cornish must have

---

25 {The Treagear Homilies in late Middle Cornish had not yet been discovered in Jenner's day.}

overlapped one another a good deal. It is probable that those who wrote verse would continue to use archaic forms long after they had been dropped in prose and in conversation. But the difference between Middle and Modern Cornish is not really very great, and comes to very little more than a difference of spelling, an uncertainty about the final letters of certain words, and a tendency to contractions, elisions, and apocopations in words, which, though recognized in their fuller form in the spelling of Middle Cornish verse, may have been nearly as much contracted, elided, and apocopated in Middle Cornish conversation. Dr Whitley Stokes points out in his edition of Jordan's *Creation* certain changes, and though the language of that play is substantially Middle Cornish, the spelling is largely of the pre-Lhuydian popular Modern Cornish sort. Among these changes are the following:

1. The final *e* becomes *a*. [This is perhaps only a question of spelling, and need not imply a difference of sound. Probably a sound as of the German final *e* is intended.][26] {The sound is [ə].}

2. *th* and *gh* have become mute, and are often interchanged. [In Modern Cornish *th* is often omitted, or represented by *h*.] {Middle Cornish [θ], [ð], and [x] may weaken to [h] or be lost (in medial and final position).}

3. *m*, *n*, become respectively *bm*, *dn*. [Probably the sounds existed long before they were recognized in spelling.][27] {The sounds are [ᵇm] and [ᵈn].}

4. *s* becomes frequently a soft *g* (*j*). [This *j* sound also may have existed long before it was written as a *g* or *j*. The *s* of the earlier MSS was probably never intended to represent in these cases a

---

26 The remarks added here in [square brackets] are those of the present writer. {That is, they are Jenner's comments on Stokes. The remarks added here in {curly brackets} are those of the present editor.}

27 {It is worth nothing that Jenner believed that pre-occlusion existed before it appeared in spelling. Many hold the same view today.}

true *s*. Dr Stokes might also have mentioned the similar cases of *she* being used where the older MSS write *sy* for the second person singular.] {The sound [s] often becomes [dʒ]; Jenner's observation of *she/sy* could posit [s] > [ʃ] (?> ([ʒ]) > [dʒ]. More likely Jenner was taking *s* to mean [z], in which case he posits [z] > [ʒ] > [dʒ] with [ʒ] represented by *sh*. The most probable scenario explaining the alternation of [z] and [dʒ] recognizes dialectal variation as far back as the Old Cornish period, one dialect's /d/ having an assibilated allophone [dz] which became [z] in eastern Middle Cornish, and the other having a more palatalized allophone [dʑ] which became [dʒ] in western Middle Cornish, not really written until later Middle and Late Cornish.}

The apparent changes of vowel sounds in the still later Cornish, more fully discussed further on, are mostly these:

1. *a* long {[æː]} sometimes becomes *aw* {[ɒː]}, especially before *l*, *n*, or *r*, and occasionally as a final; *a* short {[æ]}, under similar circumstances, becomes *o* short {[ɔ]}.[28]

2. *u*, with (approximately) the French sound of that letter {[yː]}, becomes *ee* (*î*) {[iː]}, or else *ew*, as in the English word *dew*. {[juː]; nowadays it would seem more likely that the pronunciation for this is [iʊ].}

3. *eu*, *ue*, with the French sound of *eu*, or the German *ö* {[øː]}, becomes *e* (= *ay* in *may*) {[eː]}.

4. *y* of Middle Cornish, perhaps pronounced as *î* {[ɪ]}, but sometimes obscurely, like the primary sound of the Welsh *y* {[ʌ] or [ə] (likely not [ɨ])}, often became short *e* {[ɛ]}.

5. An open long *y*, which may have been sounded *ee* (*î*) in Middle Cornish, often later became *ei* (or as *i* in *mine*), though

---

28 {Jenner did not have the benefit of phoneme theory, but the change here describes the result of the appearance of a new Late Cornish phoneme /ɒ/, [ɒː] when long and [ɔ] when short.}

there are inconsistencies in this respect, showing that the change was not universal. {In final position orthographic <y> [iː] often diphthongizes to [ɔɪ]. Jenner's English *mine* here is evidently Cornish English [mɔɪn], not R.P. [maɪn].}

6. In a considerable number of cases short *o* {[ɔ]} became the "obscure vowel," *o* of *London* or *u* of *until* {Jenner means [ə] though in English the stressed form is [ʌ], a vowel which does not occur in Cornish}.

It does not follow that these were very distinct changes between Middle and Modern Cornish. Possibly the change in sound was a good deal less than on paper, and consisted in intensifying earlier changes. The Middle Cornish system of spelling looks very like an inheritance from an earlier time still.

The grammatical changes were few, and, except for a diminishing use of pronominal suffixes, those, like the new preterite of *gwîl* 'to do' were chiefly false analogies, or else imitations of English. But it is to be remembered that a great proportion of the remains of Modern Cornish consists of translations and a few original compositions by persons whose own language was English, who had in some cases learnt Cornish very imperfectly. This would apply to most of the translations of passages of Scripture, to Lhuyd's Preface (though, of course, *his* own language was Welsh), and to Gwavas's attempts. The really valuable specimens are the writings of Boson, Bodenor's Letter to Daines Barrington, some of the Gwavas MS letters and songs, and the story of John of Chy-an-Hur. These, written by men who spoke Cornish fluently and had no theories and often no knowledge of philology, probably represent what people really spoke in the seventeenth and eighteenth centuries. That faintness and even silence of final letters, which seems to have been a characteristic of Cornish as it is of French, was the cause that, in writing as phonetically as they knew how, these practical speakers of Cornish often omitted the ends of words, and made it seem as though their verbs had largely lost their inflections. Words were spelt alike which should have been differentiated—it was as though one should spell *avais*, *avait*, *avez*, and *avaient* all alike {for [ave]}, and words were run together that should have had at least apostrophes between them; but the grammar was not always as broken-down as it looks, and by a comparison with the older remains of Cornish it is not difficult to restore approximately the proper spelling. The Cornish represented in Lhuyd's writings has tended to confuse some things. Lhuyd was a Welshman, and is constantly trying to run off into Welsh, and he had for his teacher John Keigwin, who thought that he understood the Cornish of the medieval dramas, but was often mistaken. Probably had a resuscitated medieval Cornishman read the dramas aloud to Keigwin, he would have understood them quite as well as the ordinary English board-school[29] boy would understand St Paul's Epistles in the Authorized Version, read by a revived Jacobean divine; but the spelling and the medieval handwriting, which he could not always read, put him out terribly, and some very weird forms and words are the result. Also Keigwin had, or thought he had, a knowledge of Hebrew and Greek, which he uses on occasions with dire results. Far be it from any Cornish student to undervalue the usefulness of Keigwin. But for him, and for Gwavas and Tonkin, the work of reconstruction would have been much more difficult than it is, and these writers undoubtedly preserved a great deal of most valuable matter that otherwise would have been lost, but their work needs to be used with great caution, and the translations and original compositions which they produced do not always represent quite fairly the late forms of the language.

---

29 {"Board-school" is both an archaic term for "boarding school" and a term for "a school under the management of a School-board, as established by the Elementary Education Act of 1870" (OED).}

2.1. Spelling and pronunciation

2.1.1. On the pronunciation in general.

In simple Cornish words of more than one syllable the stress accent is generally, though not universally, on the last but one.[30] The vowel of this syllable has usually its plain, clear *long* or *short* sound. The vowels of the unaccented syllables are usually *obscure* in the case of two of the broad vowels (*a, o*), and *short* in the case of the thin vowels (*e, i, y*) and of *u*, unless they are combinations of two vowels, in which case they are always long; but *e* in a final unaccented syllable is also generally *obscure*.[31] The *obscure* vowel is the sound of *u* in the English word *until*, or *o* in *London*, and there is

---

30 In compound words the accent is always on the qualifying part, and if that is a monosyllable and comes last, the accent is therefore on the last syllable. This is common in place-names.

31 {Jenner has in this section identified a distinction which seems to have been overlooked by most researchers until relatively recently. In 1995 in *Cornish Today*, Nicholas Williams suggested that Late Cornish forms like *Cornowok* suggested *o-coloured schwa*; in January 2007 I posted about *i-coloured schwa* and *a-coloured schwa* on one of the Cornish internet discussion lists. In July 2008 I suggested to the Spellyans group that a three-way distinction *tavas* ['tævɔz] 'tongue'; *gwelys* ['gwɛlɨs] 'seen' (cf. *gwelas* ['gwɛlɔs] 'saw'), *arlùth* ['ɑɹlʉθ] to the Spellyans discussion list. It was not until September 2008, when I began preparing this edition of the *Handbook* that I realized that Jenner's description here (distinguishing *a/o, e/i/y, u*)—made a century ago—is of the same nature as a description of three varieties of schwa, realized as [ɔ], [ɨ], and [ʉ] (sometimes known as *schwa, schwi*, and *schwu*). See also §2.1.2.3}

very little, if any, difference in sound between the obscure *a, e, o,* and *u*.[32] When this sound occurs, as it occasionally does, on an accented syllable, or anywhere where it might be mistaken for a plain sound, it is written, according to the spelling of this book, *ă, ŏ,* or *ŭ.* In words of one syllable ending in a consonant the vowel is generally to be taken as *short,* unless it is marked long (*â, ê, î, ô, û,ŷ*), or is a combination of two vowels. In monosyllables ending in a vowel, that vowel usually has its *long* sound, but as Cornish is largely accented in ordinary conversation by *sentences* (as is the case in Gaelic, and to a considerable extent in English), many monosyllables are slurred over with no accent (as *enclitics* or *proclitics,* according to whether they follow or precede the word on which they depend), and with more or less of the *obscure* vowel. The modern Cornish intonation of English is probably a very fair guide to the intonation of Cornish.[33]

The consonants, especially *f, v, dh, th,* are rather more lightly sounded than in English.[34] Any peculiarities of sound will be given under each consonant.

During the period in which the existing remains of Cornish literature were written, that is, between the twelfth and the middle of the eighteenth century, the spelling was very unsettled. There were at least six different systems, if no more.

1. That of the Cotton Vocabulary. {OCV.}

2. That of the *Ordinalia,* with a sub-variety in that of the *Poem of the Passion.* {OM, PC, RD; PA.}

---

32 {In phonetic transcription one now distinguishes stressed [ʌ] as in ['lʌndən] and unstressed [ə] as in [ən'tɪl].}

33 It seems likely that in the very peculiar intonation of Zennor, Morvah, Towednack, and the country part of St Ives the true intonation of Cornish may be best preserved. But this is mere conjecture.

34 {Perhaps "lightly" means "lenis", in which case Jenner posits the consonants to be realized as [ʃ ɣ ð θ], and so on.}

3. That of the *St Meriasek.* {BM.}

4. That of Jordan's *Creation.* {CW.}

5. That of Boson, Keigwin, and other seventeenth and eighteenth century writers.

6. That of Lhuyd.

Not only did different writers differ from one another, but various ways of representing the same sound were used by the same writer. The earlier spelling shows a certain amount of Welsh, old English, and old French affinities; the latest is evidently modelled on modern English, which does not suit it very well, and the transition from one to the other is not very abrupt. It is the object of the present book to represent the probable pronunciation of Modern Cornish by a system fairly consistent in itself, but not too startlingly divergent from those adopted by previous writers (or from that of Breton, where coincidence occurs), and not too much encumbered with diacritical signs. It is to some extent a following of Dr Edward Lhuyd, whose system, though rather clumsy and unnecessarily puzzling in places, was on the whole very good and of great value.

2.1.2. The vowels.

Simple: *a, â, e, ê, i, î, o, ô, ŏ, u, û, ŭ, y, ŷ.*

Compound: *aw, ei, ey, ew, oi, oy, ou, ow.*

2.1.2.1. *SIMPLE VOWELS.*

2.1.2.1.1. *a*, short, as *a* in *man*. Before *l* and *r* it is generally sounded as *o* in *not*. {[æ]; [ɔl], [ɔɹ].[35]}

2.1.2.1.2. *â*, long {[æ:]}, the lengthened sound of *a* short, *not* as the English broad *a* in *father* {'fɑðə(ɹ)}, or long *a* in *mane* {mem}, but as a broad *a* is commonly sounded in Cornish English. Thus *bâ* would have something between the sound of the English word *bare*

35 {Jenner's "not" is [nɔt], and the transcriptions are given here as [ɔl] and [ɔɹ]. Nowadays it would seem more likely that this should be considered a lower allophone [ɑ] of the phoneme /æ/ in words like *carr* [kaɹ]; for the Late phoneme /ɒ/ see §2.1.2.1.2 and footnote 23.}

(of course without the *r* trilled at all {[bɛ:(ɹ)]}) in the mouth of a correct speaker, and the actual sound of the bleat of a sheep.[36]

In some words, and especially before a liquid followed by a consonant, *a* tends to be sounded as *aw* {[ɒ:]} or short *o* {[ɔ]}. Thus *âls* 'cliff', *gwander* 'weakness', *wartha* 'upper' are sounded *awls*, *gwonder*, *wortha* or *worra*, and *brâs* 'great' is sounded *brawz*. {[ɒ:lz], ['gwɔndɔɹ], ['wɔɹθə]~['wɔrə], [bɹɒ:z].[37]}

In unaccented syllables *a* represents nearly the sound of *u* in *until*, or, as a final, the English sound of *a* at the end of proper names, such as *Vienna, Maria,* etc., which is more or less the final *e* of German, *meine, deine,* etc., or perhaps the *e* of the French words *le, de, me,* etc. {[ə].}

2.1.2.1.3. *e*, short {[ɛ]}, as *e* in *men, pen,* etc.

2.1.2.1.4. *ê*, long {[e:]}, as *ai* in *main*, *ay* in *say*.[38]

2.1.2.1.5. *i*, short {[ɪ]}, as *i* in *in, pin,* etc.

2.1.2.1.6. *î*, long {[i:]}, as *ee* in *seen,* etc.

2.1.2.1.7. *o*, short {[ɔ]}, as *o* in *on*.

2.1.2.1.8. *ô*, long, as *aw* in *dawn*, not as *o* in *bone*. {[ɔ:], not [o:] (or [oʊ]?) or R.P. [əʊ].}[39]

2.1.2.1.9. *ŏ*, obscure, as *o* in *London, ton,* etc. {[ə] or back-coloured [ɵ]; Jenner does not distinguish this from [ʌ] (see footnote 27).}

---

36 The modern Cornish pronunciation of the word "trade", in its local and rather contemptuous sense of "ropes' ends, dead mice, and other combustibles" (as a Cornishman once defined it), shows the sound of this vowel fairly well.

37 {Nowadays it would seem more likely that *âls* and *brâs* have the Late phoneme /ɒ/ and *gwadn, gwander,* and *wartha* have the lower allophone of /æ/ following *w* and before *r*: ['gwɑn]~['gwɑᵈn], ['gwɑndɔɹ], ['wɑɹθə]~['wɑrə].}

38 Care must be taken in this case to avoid that *ŷ* sound given to the English *a* in London twang (*e.g.* lȳdy {['laɪdi]} for lady).

39 {Note that in 2.1.2.1.2 and 2.1.2.1.8 Jenner does not distinguish *brâs* 'great' [bɹɒ:z] from *ros* 'rose' [ro:z] or *dauns* 'dance' [dɔns] from *dons* 'they come' [do:ns].}

2.1.2.1.10. *u*, short {[ʊ]}, as *u* in *full*.

2.1.2.1.11. *û*, long {[uː]}, as *oo* in *fool*.

2.1.2.1.12. *ŭ*, obscure {[ə] or back-coloured [ɵ]}, as *u* in *until*.

2.1.2.1.13. *ŷ*, long, as *i* in *mine*. {[ɔɪ], as with a Cornish accent; not as in standard English [aɪ].}

2.1.2.1.14. *y*, short, as *y* in *carry*, *marry*, etc. This is used chiefly as an unaccented final in a word of more than one syllable. {[ɪ]~[i].}

In the case of the letter *y*, there is a variation of sound in such monosyllables as *nŷ*, *whŷ*, *jŷ*, *hŷ* under certain circumstances. In this system of spelling the circumflex is omitted when these words are enclitic. {Nowadays it would seem likely that the pronunciation is [iː] or [ɔɪ] under stress (Jenner's *ŷ*), and [i] when unstressed in absolute auslaut (Jenner's *y*).}

2.1.2.2. *COMPOUND VOWELS*.

Of these, *aw*, *ai*, *ei*, *ay*, *ey*, *ou*, are only repetitions of the simple vowels *ô*, *û*, and *ŷ*. The other four[40] have sounds not otherwise represented.

2.1.2.2.1. *aw* has the same sound as *ô* {[ɔː]}. It is very rarely used. {Nowadays it would seem likely that long /o/ is [oː], and that to distinguish [oː] from [ɔː] one may write *au* for this sound, reserving *aw* for [aʊ].}

2.1.2.2.2. *ai*, *ay*, *ei*, *ey*, have nearly the same sound as *y*, rather more diphthongalized. {Evidently Jenner means [ɔɪ], or perhaps [eɪ]. Nowadays it would seem likely that there are three diphthongs to distinguish, which can be written *ai* [eː]~[eɪ], *ay* [aɪ], and *ey* [ɔɪ].}

---

40 {Or five, as Jenner lists *eu*, *ew*, *oi*, *oy*, and *ow*. Jenner does not seem to recognize a diphthong [eʊ], though as his focus is toward the later spectrum of the language, original [eʊ] would often have merged with either [iʊ] or [oʊ]. Nowadays it would seem likely that there are seven diphthongs to distinguish, which can be written *ay* [aɪ], *ey* [ɔɪ], *oy* [ɔɪ], *aw* [aʊ], *ew* [eʊ], *ow* [oʊ], and *yw* [iʊ]. the other "compound vowels" are *ai* [eː], *au* [ɔː], *ou* [uː].}

2.1.2.2.3. *eu, ew* have the sound of *ew* {[ju:] (in narrow transcription [i̯u:])} in the English word *dew*, the usual English long *u*. This sound is also represented in Cornish by *y* consonant followed by *u*, as in the word *yu* 'is' which has exactly the sound of the English personal pronoun *you*. {Nowadays it would seem more likely that the sound is [iʊ] (narrowly [iy̯]), and that this should be preferred to [ju:], though [ju:] is widespread in the revived language.}

2.1.2.2.4. *oi, oy* have the sound of *oy* {[ɔɪ], narrowly [ɔɪ̯]} in *boy*.

2.1.2.2.5. *ow* has two sounds—(1) as an unaccented final, as *o* {[oʊ]} in *bone*. This is also its sound when it occurs without any consonant, in the possessive pronoun *ow* 'my' and the participle particle *ow*; (2) in other cases it sounds as *ou* {[u:]} in *you*, and rarely as *ow* {[aʊ]} in *now*. {Nowadays it would seem likely that one should distinguish *ow* [oʊ] (with a range of reduced forms when unstressed) and *aw* [aʊ].}

2.1.2.2.6. *ou* has the same sound as *û* {[u:]}, and as the second sound of *ow* {*ow* being [aʊ], this would be [ʊ]}. It is the regular symbol for that sound in Breton, and very commonly in the Cornish dramas, where, as in Breton, *u* commonly represented, approximately, the French *u* {[y]}, which later became *î* {[i:]} or *ew* {[iʊ]}.[41]

2.1.2.3. *GENERAL REMARKS ON THE VOWELS.*

In the Middle Cornish manuscripts the vowels are represented in various ways, and there is a special uncertainty about unaccented and obscure vowels.

---

41 {Jenner is describing the change of Middle Cornish /y/ to Late Cornish /i/; while Jenner does not specify the environment in which *u* became *î* or *ew*, nowadays it seems likely that when stressed (usually in absolute auslaut) [y:] broke to [iʊ].}

Vowels were sometimes lengthened by doubling, or by adding a *y*, and rarely, until Jordan's *Creation*, by adding a mute *e* after the closing consonant; but often quantity was not indicated at all.

Long *î* (*ee* in *see* {[iː]}) was more often than not represented by *y*, but, as in Welsh, *y* not infrequently represented the obscure vowel (*u* in *unfit* {[ʌ]~[ə]}), and often a sound which later became a short *e*, but in unaccented syllables was, as is not unusually the case in English, more of the nature of the obscure vowel {[ə]}, or perhaps something between that and a short *i* {[ə] > [ɨ] < [ɪ]}. Indeed all unaccented vowels tend to become obscure, very much as they do in English, and hence are variously expressed.

The *u* of the earlier MSS probably once represented approximately the French *u* or the German *ü* {[y]}, the *u* of Devon and East Cornwall English {[ʏ]}, or the *ao* of Scottish Gaelic {[uː]}, not exactly the same sounds, but very near to each other. As in Greek *v* and Welsh *u*, this sound approached nearer and nearer to *i* {[iː]} (*ee* in *seen*), until in Cornish it ceased to be recognized as having any *u* sound in it at all. In Welsh it is still written as *u* {North Welsh [ɨ]}, and in carefully spoken Welsh is quite distinguishable from *î*. In Breton the sound is still approximately that of the French *u* {[y]}. In some words in Cornish this sound became *ew* {[juː]} (as in the English word *few*) and rarely *u* {[uː]} (*oo* in *moon*), but generally it became *î* {[iː]} (English *ee*).[42]

What was once the sound of the French and Breton *eu* or the German *ö* {[øː]~[œ]}, was represented in the MSS by *u, eu, ue*. Later this became *ê* {[eː]~[ɛ]} (*ay* in *may*). Thus, *dueth* or *duth* 'came' became *dêth*; *luen, leun* 'full' became *lên*; *due* 'comes' became *dê*; *mur, meur* 'great' became *mêr*.[43] This change is found occasionally as early as the *Poem of the Passion*. The rhythm shows that *ue* and *eu*

---

42 The combination *ao* in Irish is pronounced *î*. Thus *caol* 'narrow' is *cül* in the Highlands and *kîl* in Ireland. {Scottish Gaelic [kʰuːɫ], Irish [kɰiːlʲ].}

43 {[døːθ] > [deːθ], [løːn] > [leːn], > [døː] > [deː], [møːɹ] > [meːɹ].}

form only one syllable. In the case of *lues* {[lyɔz]} (= *luas*) 'many', which later became *lîas* {[liɔz]} (or *leeas*), the rhythm shows that the *u* and *e* did not form a single vowel. Occasionally, as in the second person plural of certain tenses, *eu* of the early MSS became *ew* {[eʊ]}, which it was probably intended to represent, but was often confused with *ou* {[uː]} (= *û* or *oo*).[44]

The sound of *ô* or *aw*, as it certainly became in later Cornish, was represented by *e, o, oy, a, oa, ao, au, aw*. The tendency to pronounce *a* as *aw* or short *o* before *l, n, r*, doubled or followed by a consonant, and sometimes single, is very marked in the spelling of late Cornish, and in the present pronunciation of placenames. There is no evidence of its age in Cornish; but it is very common in English and Irish, though unknown in standard Welsh or Breton.

There seems no doubt, by the same evidence, that a long *y* of older Cornish often became *i*, as in the English word *mine* {[iː] > [ɔɪ]}. Vulgarly, as with the English long *i*, it sometimes even became *oy*. Boson writes *choy* for *chy* 'house', but Lhuyd writes it *tshȳi* or *tshei* {[tʃɔɪ], [tʃeɪ]}, which last is its usual modern sound in place-names. *Nȳ* 'we', *whȳ* 'you', *jȳ* 'they', and *hȳ* 'she', are written *nei, huei, dzhei, hei*, by Lhuyd, and Jenkins of Alverton, using the earlier form of the third person plural, written *y* in the Dramas, spells it *eye*. Yet there are cases where the older pronunciation is retained, and probably this was always the case when the words were enclitic. Professor Loth has pointed out a similar change in

---

44 The word *bewnans* 'life' formed from the root *bew*, was often written *bownans* in late Cornish and probably pronounced *boonans* {original ['beʊnɔns] > ['boʊnɔns] > ['buːnɔns]}. Similarly *bowjy* (= *bewgh-chȳ*) 'cow-house', must have been *bewjy* {original ['beʊdʒi] > ['boʊdʒi] > ['buːdʒi]}. This last, which is one of the surviving Cornish words, has its *ow* at present sounded as in *now*. This change has happened not infrequently in place-names. {It is not clear how Jenner gets from ['buːdʒi] to ['baʊdʒi]; it is too late for the Great Vowel Shift.}

the Quiberon sub-dialect of Vannetais Breton, and that in some of the same words.

In the unscientific spelling of the seventeenth and eighteenth centuries, that is to say, in the system of every one except Lhuyd, and occasionally of Gwavas and Tonkin when they followed Lhuyd, the English values of the period were often given to the letters; but the following were vowel symbols in general use:

For	*â*	of the present system,	*a, aa*	Lhuyd	*â.*
"	*a*	"	*a, u, e, o*	"	*a.*
"	*ê*	"	*ea*	"	*ê.*
"	*e*	"	*e, i*	"	*e.*
"	*î*	"	*ee*	"	*î, ŷ.*
"	*i*	"	*i*	"	*i.*
"	*ô, aw*	"	*oa, o, aw, au, ao*	"	*v, ô*
"	*o*	"	*o*	"	*o.*
"	*ŏ, ŭ, ă*	"	*o, u, a, e*	"	*ẏ.*
"	*û, ou*	"	*u, oo, ou*	"	*ụ, û.*
"	*ow*	"	*ô, ow, ou, au*	"	*oụ, o, ô.*
"	*u*	"	*u, oo*	"	*u.*
"	*ew, yu, eu*	"	*ew, yu, yw*	"	*iụ, yụ, eụ.*
"	*ŷ, ei, ay*	"	*y, ei, ay*	"	*ei, y, ẏi.*
"	*y*	"	*y, i, e*	"	*y, i.*

A final *e* mute was often used to lengthen a vowel, as in English. Many names of places and persons retain this *e* mute at the present day, and when the preceding vowel is *a*, educated persons generally give it the sound of the English long *a* in *mane* {[mein]}, but that is a change analogous to the modern vulgarism of pronouncing *clerk* as *clurk* instead of *clark*.[45] The proper sound of the Cornish *â* is still

---

45 {Of this "vulgarism" the OED says: "The pronunciation (klɑːk) is evidenced in the south of England from the 15th c.; cf. *bark, hark, dark,*

heard in such words in the mouths of the peasantry {[æː]}. Compare such a name as *Polglaze* in the two pronunciations {[pɔl'qlæːz], [pɔl'gleɪz]}.

2.1.3. The consonants.

Simple: *b, c, d, f, g, h, j, k, l, m, n, p, q, r, s, t, v, w, y, z.*

Compound: *bm, ch, dh, dn, gw, gh, ng, qw, sh, th, wh, zh, gwl, gwr, qwr, wl, wr.*

2.1.3.1. *SIMPLE CONSONANTS.*

2.1.3.1.1. *b* has the same sound {[b]} as in English.

2.1.3.1.2. *c* is always hard, being used only before *a, o, u*. The same sound before *e, i, y* is represented by *k*. {[k].}[46]

2.1.3.1.3. *d* before *a, o, u* is usually hard, as in English, but, as in Gaelic, before *e, i, y* it has a sound approaching to *j*, or like *di* in *soldier*. In the MSS a soft *g* was often written for *d* in such cases. It is a common change in many languages. Cf. the Italian *oggi* 'today', for the Latin *hodie*. {[d], palatalized [dʲ] ~ [dʒ].}

2.1.3.1.4. *f* has the same sound {[f]} as in English. In the MSS it is often confused with *v*. As a final it is very lightly sounded. {[ɸ]}

2.1.3.1.5. *g* is always hard {[g]}, as in *get, go*. The soft *g* {[dʒ]}, as in *gin*, is here represented by *j*, but in the MSS *g* was often used for it.

2.1.3.1.6. *h* has two degrees of sound. As an initial it is rather more lightly sounded than in English, except when it is a mutation of *c* (see §2.2), when it is more strongly sounded. Then, and when it occurs in the middle of a word, it represents in a lighter form the

---

etc., from earlier *-er*; also *serjeant, hearth, Cherwell, Hertford*, and the 15–17th c. *clargy*. The dialects, esp. the northern, have retained the *e*, as Sc. (klɛrk, klerk). In U.S. the pronunciation is (klɜːk); 'of late this has become somewhat frequent in London and its neighbourhood'."}

46 {Jenner does not mention the practice common in the medieval texts of writing [s] as *c* before front vowels. This seems to be an oversight on his part.}

guttural *c'h* of Breton, the *ch* of German, Welsh, and Gaelic, or the guttural *gh* of older English. At the end of a word this is to be written *gh*. It is a smooth guttural, as in Scottish Gaelic, without the rasping sound which it has in colloquial Welsh or in German. {[h], [x].}

2.1.3.1.7. *j* is sounded {[dʒ]} as in English. It generally represents what was once written *s*. Lhuyd writes *dzh* for this sound, and the MSS often represent it by *g*.

2.1.3.1.8. *k* is generally only used before *e, i, y*, or as a final. It has the same sound as in English. It often happens in grammatical inflections that a broad root vowel is changed to a thin one. In such cases if the preceding letter is a *c* it must be changed to *k*. {[k].}

2.1.3.1.9. *l* has the ordinary English sound {[l]}. Sometimes a double *l* of earlier Cornish was written *lh* (*telhar* 'place', for *teller*). This may perhaps represent the aspirated *ll* of Welsh {[ɬ]}, or (as in Portuguese) the *l mouillé* (as *li* in *valiant*) {[ʎ]}. {Nowadays *ll* is interpreted variously as a tense [ɬ] or [l̩] or a weakly geminate [lˑ] (not fully long [lː]) or as *lh*, a devoiced [l̥] or aspirate [lʰ].}

2.1.3.1.10. *m* has usually the same sound {[m]} as in English. When it follows a *short* vowel in an *accented syllable* or a *monosyllable*, it has a peculiar sound as though a *b* were prefixed to it, or as though the speaker had a slight cold in the head {[ᵇm]}. This *b* was frequently written in the later MSS, and in the mouths of less educated persons the *b* supplanted the *m* altogether. Thus *lemmyn* 'now' became successively *lebman* and *lebban*. The vanishing of the *m* altogether did not occur in monosyllables, and it is undesirable to imitate it in other words. In the system of spelling adopted in this book, the *b* will be written in cases where it was habitually written in later Cornish, but even when it is not written it is always to be sounded in the case of *short* vowels in *accented* syllables or *monosyllables*.

2.1.3.1.11. *n* is usually sounded {[n]} as in English. When it follows a *short* vowel in an *accented* syllable or in a *monosyllable*, a *d* sound (analogous to the *b* sound with *m*) precedes it {[ᵈn]}. This *d* is often written in the later MSS, and will be used in this book in cases where it is regularly found in later Cornish, but it is to be pronounced even where it is not written. In words of more than one syllable[47] the *d* often supplanted the *n* (e.g. *henna* 'that' became successively *hedna* and *hedda*), and monosyllables were sometimes made into dissyllables by it (e.g. *pen*, *pedn*, *pedden*); but both of these are vulgarisms not to be imitated.

2.1.3.1.12. *p* is sounded {[p]} as in English.

2.1.3.1.13. *q* is sounded as in English, and is always followed by *w* {[kw]}. It is generally used in an initial mutation (see §2.2) of *gw*, but occurs occasionally, followed by *w*, as a radical sound.

2.1.3.1.14. *r* has the same sound as in correct English, that is to say, it is very slightly heard when followed by a consonant or at the end of a word, unless the next word begins with a vowel, but, as in English, it often influences the preceding vowel. Its full sound is trilled, not guttural.[48]

2.1.3.1.15. *s* is the most puzzling of the consonants. It had probably four or five different values in the MSS, and might represent *s*, *z*, *sh*, *zh*, *j* {[s], [z], [ʃ], [ʒ], [dʒ]} according to circumstances. As an initial, or before *c*, *k*, *f*, *l*, *m*, *n*, *p*, *q*, *r*, *t*, *w*, it was generally *s*, as in *so* {[s]}; as a final, and before *b*, *d*, *g*, *j*, *v*, it was normally *z* or as *s* in *rose* {[z]}. But between two vowels in the same word, or coming after another consonant and followed by a vowel, or as a final followed by a word beginning with a vowel and closely

---

47 The word *en* 'in' in quite late Cornish, was apparently sounded *et*, which is a solitary case of the disappearance of *n* in a monosyllable.

48 {This description is imprecise enough, but nowadays it seems likely that an adequately authentic pronunciation can be achieved by using the alveolar approximant [ɹ] initially, medially, and following consonants, and the alveolar tap [ɾ] intervocalically. This does seem to be consistent with Jenner's description. His final comment means that the sound is [ɹ]~[ɾ] not French or Breton [ʁ].}

connected grammatically with its predecessor, it had commonly the sound of *j* {[dʒ]}, so much so that *g* soft was often substituted for it, and there are cases where even an initial *s* must have meant *sh* or *zh* {[ʃ] or [ʒ]}. Thus we find *cowsesow* 'speeches' written *cowgegyow*, *carensa* 'love' *carenga* (for *carenja*), and in place-names, though we find *Nanskeval*, *Nanspean*, *Nanswidn* when the epithet begins with a consonant, when it begins with a vowel we find *Nanjizel* (= *Nans isal* 'the lower valley'[49]). Sometimes in late Cornish the definite *j* sound so completely superseded the *s* or *z*, that it or its equivalent, *g* soft or *dzh*, was always written for it, and in such cases it is written *j* in the present system of spelling, but in other cases the best rules will be to pronounce *s*:

2.1.3.1.15.1. As an initial; before *c*, *k*, *f*, *l*, *m*, *n*, *p*, *q*, *r*, *t*, *w*; or when doubled, as *s* in *so* {[s]}.

2.1.3.1.15.2. As a final, except when the next word, grammatically connected, begins with a vowel; or before *b*, *d*, *g*, *j*, *v*, as *z* or *s* in *rose* {[z]}.

2.1.3.1.15.3. Between two vowels in the same word; after another consonant and followed by a vowel; or as a final followed by a grammatically connected word, such as an epithet, beginning with a vowel, as *j* {[dʒ]}.

For the last rule compare Mrs Gamp's pronunciation of English (in *Martin Chuzzlewit*).[50] There seems to have been an inherent

---

49 {*Nanjizel* was *Nansusal* in 1302, suggesting that the qualifier is not *isal*, 'low' but perhaps *usel*, 'howling', as the valley directly faces the prevailing southwest winds.}

50 {Mrs Gamp says things like "dispoged", "fiery furnage", "Jonadge's belly", where [z] or [s] becomes [dʒ]. On 14 May 1922 a *New York Times* article wrote that philologist Ernest Weekley of the University of Nottingham had written on Gamp's dialect; it said that Weekley had noted "the nautical 'to forge' (ahead) for earlier 'to force', an example of an pronunciation which may have been much more prevalent than one would conclude from mere spelling."}

tendency to the *j*, *sh*, or *zh* sounds in every Cornish *s*,[51] but especially in those which represent a *d* or *t* of Welsh and Breton. The writer is aware that this is a very inadequate discussion of the question, but he does not wish to be unduly intricate, or to enter into a deep phonetic explanation. Those who would study the question more minutely are referred to an article by Professor J. Loth in vol. xviii. of the *Revue Celtique*.

2.1.3.1.16. *t* before *a*, *o*, *u* is hard {[t]}, as in English, but before *e*, *i*, *y* has a sound approaching to that of *ch* {[tʃ]} in *church*, or to *ti* {[ʃ] in words ending in *tion*}. Sometimes *ch* is written and fully pronounced where a *t* was formerly written. Thus *chy* 'house' was formerly *ty*, and in the eighteenth century *tí* 'thou' was pronounced and often written *chee*.

2.1.3.1.17. *v* is sounded {[v]} as in English, but is often nearly inaudible at the end of a word, unless the next word begins with a vowel. Thus *ev* 'he' is often written *e* in later MSS.

2.1.3.1.18. *w*, except in compound vowels, is always a consonant, and has the same sound {[w]} as in English. For its sound before *l* and *r* see §2.1.3.2.10. {For its sound before *h* see §2.1.3.2.8.}

2.1.3.1.19. *y* consonant is sounded {[j]} as *y* consonant in English, or as *j* in German. It is always consonant when it precedes a vowel, unless it is written *ŷ*, when it is a vowel, as in such words as *crŷes*, *tŷak*, etc. {['kɪɔɪɔz], ['tɔɪɔk].}

2.1.3.1.20. *z* is only used as an initial, but it is seldom used at all. The sound {[z]} is that of an English *z*.

2.1.3.2. *COMPOUND CONSONANTS. {DIGRAPHS.}*

2.1.3.2.1. *bm*, *dn* represent respectively the sound of *m* and *n* after a short vowel in an accented syllable or monosyllable (see §2.1.3.1.10 and §2.1.3.1.11). There is no vowel sound between the two letters {[ᵇm], [ᵈn]}.

---

51 *Cf.* the *s* or *z* of *azure*, *treasure*, *sure*, *pleasure*, *sugar*, in English.

2.1.3.2.2. *ch* is always sounded {[tʃ]} as in *church*. It usually represents a former *t*, or else occurs in borrowed English words.

2.1.3.2.3. *dh* is sounded {[ð]} as *th* in *thy*, *the*, etc., the Welsh *dd*, the Old English and Icelandic *ð*, the Modern Greek *δ*. In the MSS it is represented by *th* or *ʒ*. Lhuyd writes it *ð*.[52]

2.1.3.2.4. *th* (written *τ* by Lhuyd) is sounded {[θ]} as *th* in *thin*, *thick*, etc., the Welsh *th*, the Old English and Icelandic *þ*, the Greek *θ*. At the end of a syllable, especially after *r*, the sounds of *dh* and *th* are very light and tend to become inaudible, and are often represented by *h*, or omitted altogether. Thus, *gwartha*, *porth*, *barth*, *lowarth*, *gordhya*, *gortheb*, *kerdh* often appear as *gwarha*, *gwarra*, *por*, *barh*, *lowar*, *lowarh*, *gorria*, *gorreb*, *kerr*. Thus also, *Porthgwartha* (in St Levan), is now written *Porthgwarrah* and pronounced nearly *Pergworra*.[53]

2.1.3.2.5. *gh* is used at the end of words for the strong or guttural *h* {[x]}. Lhuyd writes a Greek *χ* for this sound.

2.1.3.2.6. *ng* (written by Lhuyd with an inverted Irish *g*, *ᵹ*) has the sound of *ng* in *singer*, not as in *finger* or *manger*. {[ŋ], not [ŋg] or [ndʒ].}

---

52 Dr Whitley Stokes, in a paper of additions to Williams's Cornish Lexicon (Philol. Soc. 1868), gives it as his opinion that the *th* of the MSS should not be written *dh* at the end of a word, and that Williams, in doing so, was wrongly following Welsh analogy. But there is an evident tendency in *late* Cornish to end words in *z* for *s*, *v* for *f*, *g* for *k*, and a considerable number of words which Williams ends in *dh* end in the corresponding *z* in Breton, so that one is more inclined to follow Williams in this matter, though there is a good deal to be said both ways. {Nowadays it seems most likely that it was common for final consonants to be voiced in stressed syllables, but unvoiced in unstressed syllables, as in *mab* 'son', *methewnep* 'drunkenness'; *wheg* 'sweet', *carrak* 'rock'; *mog* 'smoke', *gallosek* 'powerful'; *dov* 'tame', *warnaf* 'on me'; *badh* 'boar', *nowyth* 'new'.}

53 {In fact, *Porthgwarra* does not contain the element *gwartha* 'higher', upper', but *gorwedhow* 'wooded slopes' (*Porthgorwethau* 1387).}

2.1.3.2.7. *sh* has the same sound {[ʃ]} as in English. It is only used in a few words of English derivation.

2.1.3.2.8. In *wh* the *h* is always sounded. This combination represents the Welsh *chw*. Lhuyd writes it *hu̜*. {Voiceless [ʍ]; the Welsh is [xw].}

2.1.3.2.9. *zh* has the broader sound of *sh*, or that of the French *j*. {[ʒ].}

2.1.3.2.10. In *gwl*, *gwr*, *qwr*, *wl*, *wr* there is a very light but quite audible sound of *w* before the *l* or *r*. So light is the *w* that it was often omitted in the MSS. Thus *gwlasketh* 'kingdom', *gwrîg* 'did' and the mutation *wrîg* were sometimes written *glasketh*, *grîg*, *rîg*. But this was incorrect. {Evidently [gʷl], [gʷɹ], [kʷɹ], [ʷl], [ʷɹ], though in the revived language these often, though not always, simply as [gl], [gɹ], [kɹ], [l], [ɹ].}[54]

These directions for pronunciation must needs be only approximate. The exact phonetics are not attainable. The pronunciation of Cornish place-names forms something of a guide to the old sounds, only one must be careful not to be misled by the modern tendency to pronounce words as they are spelt according to the English values of letters, and one must also remember that there is no settled system of place-name orthography.

---

54 Here Jenner offers a few more linguistic musings which are both mistaken and inappropriate:

There must have been among Cornish speakers a tendency to a somewhat blurred sound of certain letters, as though there were an obstruction of some sort in their vocal organs, not altogether unlike that attributed on the stage and in fiction, with some foundation in fact, to the Hebrew race. This is shown by the tendency to turn *s* and *z* into *sh* and *zh*, and to insert *b* before *m*, and *d* before *n*. In the English spoken in Cornwall at the present day this tendency has quite disappeared, and the pronunciation, though not always the same as the standard English, is remarkably crisp and clear. Readers are solemnly warned against attempting to base or support any theories of Jewish or even of Phœnician influence in Cornwall on the above coincidence.

2.2. The initial mutations

In all the Celtic languages there are certain partly grammatical and partly phonetic changes of the first letters of words, which are called by various names, the most convenient of which is *initial mutations*. These changes take place in Cornish when words beginning with the letters *P*, *C* or *K*, *T* or *Ch*, *B*, *G*, *D* or *J*, and *M* are preceded by certain adjectives, prepositions, pronouns, particles, etc., which stand in some governing or qualifying relation to them. Words beginning with other letters, except occasionally *F* and *S*, do not change their initials. Very similar changes are often made in the case of the second halves of compound words.

The mutable letters, *P*, *C* or *K*, *T* or *Ch*; *B*, *G*, *D* or *J* form two classes, with mutual relations to one another. A third class, related to the other two, is formed of *F* or *V*, *H*, *Dh*, and *Th*. Of these last *F* and *H* are the only ones that can occur as primary or unchanged initials. Of these

P, *C* or *K*, and *T* or *Ch* are called *tenues* or thin (or hard) letters.

B, *G*, and *D* or *J* are called *mediæ* or middle (or soft).

F or *V*, *H*, *Dh*, and *Th* are called *aspirates*.

One set of *tenuis*, *media*, and *aspirate* is called *labial* (or lip letters), a second is called *guttural* (or throat letters), a third is called *dental* (or teeth letters), from the parts of the mouth most used in forming them.

The labials are:

Tenuis, *P*; *Media*, *B*; *Aspirate*, *F* or *V*.

The gutturals are:

Tenuis, C or *K*; *Media, G*; *Aspirate, H.*

The dentals are:

Tenuis, T or *Ch*; *Media, D* or *J*; *Aspirate, Th* or *Dh.*

There is no difficulty in perceiving that the letters forming each of these classes are closely related to one another; in most languages they are interchangeable under certain conditions, and the changes in the Celtic languages called *initial mutations* are based upon these relations, though the method, rules, and arrangement of these changes differ in the six languages, as do also the names by which they are known.

In Cornish (as in Breton) the general principle is that (1) the *tenuis* changes under some circumstances into the *media*, and under others into a form of the *aspirate*; and that (2) the *media* changes to a form of the *aspirate* under some circumstances, and into the *tenuis* under others; but that (3) the conditions which change the *tenuis* into the *media* change the *media* into the *aspirate*: while those which change (4) the *tenuis* into the *aspirate* leave the *media* unchanged; and those which change (5) the *media* to the *tenuis* leave the *tenuis* unchanged.

In this book we shall call the original or radical condition of a word its FIRST STATE.

Thus *Pen* 'a head', *Car* 'a friend', *Tâs* 'a father', *Blew* 'hair', *Gras* 'grace', *Dên* 'a man', *Mab* 'a son', are in their first state.

The change of the *tenuis* to the *media*, or a radical *media* to an *aspirate*, we call the SECOND STATE.

Thus, the same words in their second state are *Ben, Gar, Dâs, Vlew, 'ras, Dhên, Vab.*

The change of the *tenuis* to the *aspirate* we call the THIRD STATE.

Thus, for the first three words the third state is *Fen, Har, Thâs.*

The other four, beginning with *mediæ* or *m*, have no third state.

The change from the *media* to the *tenuis* we call the FOURTH STATE. It is commonly called *provection*.

69

Thus, the fourth state of *Blew*, *Gras*, and *Dên* (the words beginning with *tenues* or *m* having no fourth state) is *Plew*, *Cras*, *Tên*.

[It is to be noted, however, that none of these three words, being nouns, would be likely to be subjected to this last change in any real construction, for the fourth state is used almost exclusively with *ow*, the particle of the present participle of verbs, with the conjunctions *a* and *mar* 'if', and *maga* 'as', sometimes with the verbal particle *y* or *e*, and sometimes with the adverbial particle *en*, so that it is generally applied to verbs and adjectives.]

The following is a table of changes:

P has two changes, to *B* (second state), and *F* (third state).

C (or *K*)[55] has two changes, to *G* (second state) and *H* (third state).

T (or *Ch*)[56] has two changes, to *D* (or *J*)[56] (second state) and *Th* (third state).

B has two changes, to *V* (second state) and *P* (fourth state).

G has two changes, omitted or changed to *W* (second state) and *C*[55] or *K* or *Q* (fourth state).

D has two changes, *Dh* (second state) and *T* (fourth state).

M has one change, to *V* (second state).

Occasionally in a few words *F* changes in the second state to *V*, and in one case to *H*. *S* rarely changes to *Z*. There is one change of *D* to *N* (like what is called the nasal mutation in Welsh). This is in the word *dôr*, 'earth' which after the article *an* is *nôr*.

In the following tables cases of the use of mutations are shown. It is to be noted that *e* 'his' is one of the words which govern the second state, and *ow* 'my' the third state, and *agan* 'our' the first

---

55 *C* before a broad vowel, *k* before a thin vowel, and *q* before a *w*. {By "broad vowel" Jenner means "back vowel" and by "thin vowel" he means "front vowel".}

56 The *ch* and *j* are used for an earlier *t* and *d* in a few words, through intensification of the thin sounds of the latter. See §2.1.3.1.

state, while the particle *ow* of the present participle governs the fourth state.

Examples of the use of the first, second, and third states:

	First State	Second State	Third State
Tenues	*agan pen* 'our head'	*e **b**en* 'his head'	*ow **f**en* 'my head'
	agan car 'our friend'	*e **g**ar* 'his friend'	*ow **h**ar* 'my friend'
	agan tâs 'our father'	*e **d**âs* 'his father'	*ow **th**âs* 'my father'
Mediæ	*agan blew* 'our hair'	*e **v**lew* 'his hair'	*ow blew* 'my hair'
	agan gras 'our grace'	*e '**r**as* 'his grace'	*ow gras* 'my grace'
	agan golow 'our light'	*e **w**olow* 'his light'	*ow golow* 'my light'
	agan dên 'our man'	*e **dh**ên* 'his man'	*ow dên* 'my man'
	agan mab 'our son'	*e **v**ab* 'his son'	*ow mab* 'my son'

Examples of the use of the fourth state:

	First State	Fourth State
Tenues	*palas* 'to dig'	*ow palas* 'digging'
	cara 'to love'	*ow cara* 'loving'
	kelmy 'to bind'	*ow kelmy* 'binding'
	terry 'to break'	*ow terry* 'breaking'
Mediæ	*bewa* 'to live'	*ow **p**ewa* 'living'
	gŏrra 'to put'	*ow **c**ŏrra* 'putting'
	gwelas 'to see'	*ow **q**welas* 'seeing'
	dôs 'to come'	*ow **t**ôs* 'coming'
	môs 'to go'	*ow môs* 'going'

There are a few irregular mutations. Rarely a *B* after the adverbial particle *en* changes to *F* instead of *P*, e.g. *en frâs* 'greatly' from *brâs*, sometimes an *M* after the same particle changes to *F*, sometimes an initial *G* becomes *Wh*, not *C* or *K*, for the fourth state, and in the MSS there are other exceptional changes. The mutations are very irregularly written even in the best MSS. Sometimes a word is written in its first state when it ought to be in one of the other states, and sometimes mutations are made when they ought not to be, but probably the writers used them correctly enough in speaking, without perhaps clearly recognizing the changes as they made them.

The rules for the use of the initial mutations will be given, as occasion occurs, throughout the book, and they will be tabulated at the end, where they will require less explanation than they would if they were given now.[57] But this chapter should be thoroughly learnt and understood before going any further, as these changes are a very important part of Cornish grammar, and a habit should be formed of making them correctly.

state 1		state 2		state 3		state 4		'irregular' {state 5}
tenues	P	mediæ	B	aspirates	F		–	...
	C, K, Q(w)		G		H		–	...
	T		D		Th		–	...
	Ch		J		–		–	...
mediæ	B	aspirates	V		–	tenues	P	F
	G		–, W		–		C, K, Q(w)	Wh
	D		Dh		–		T	T
	M		V		–			F
Rare mutations								
F	V, H	forth > an vorth						
S	Z	saben > an zaben						
D	N	dor > an nor						
D	J	dyawl > an jawl; deth > an jeth						

---

57 {Jenner did not provide such a table but one is provided here.}

2.3. The article

2.3.1. The definite article.

The definite article 'the' is *an*, for all numbers and genders. When the noun that follows is feminine and singular, or masculine and plural, its initial, if mutable, is in the second state. If it is masculine and singular, or feminine and plural, the initial is in the first state.[58]

When the article *an* is preceded by a preposition or conjunction, and sometimes by other words, ending in a vowel, the article loses its vowel and is written *'n*. Thus:

> *Dên* 'man' masc. sing.; *an dên* 'the man'; *dhô'n dên* 'to the man'.
>
> *Benen* 'woman' fem. sing.; *an venen* 'the woman'; *dhô'n venen* 'to the woman'.
>
> *Tassow* 'fathers' masc. plur.; *an dassow* 'the fathers'; *dhô'n dassow* 'to the fathers'.
>
> *Benenes* 'women' fem. plur.; *an benenes* 'the women'; *dhô'n benenes* 'to the women'.

The apostrophe is not written for the elided *a* of *an* in the MSS, but the preposition and article appear as one word, *dhôn* 'to the', *dren* 'by the', *han* 'and the', etc. But it is better to write it, to avoid confusion, especially between *a'n* 'from the', and the simple article, *an*. There are certain cases of contraction which have been accepted as single words, and in these the apostrophe is not used. Thus *pandra* (= *pa an dra*, 'what (is) the thing?' i.e. 'what is it?') is used for the interrogative 'what?' but is never written **pa'n dra*.

---

58 See §2.4.1.2.

There are occasional further compounds of *pandra*, *e.g. pandrus* (or *pendrus*) = *pa an dra es*, or *pandryu* = *pa an dra yu*, both meaning 'what thing is?' *pandrama* = *pa an dra a wrama* 'what shall I do?' *pandrellen* = *pa an dra a wrellen*, 'what should I do?'

As in the other Celtic languages, when a noun is followed by another noun in the possessive appositional genitive, the first noun has no definite article. Thus *chŷ an dên* 'the house of the man', not **an chŷ an dên*. The same rule applies to a similar appositional genitive in Hebrew—a curious coincidence between two quite unconnected languages.

2.3.2. The indefinite article

As a rule a singular noun without any article expressed, except in the case of a noun followed by the appositional genitive, is considered to be in the indefinite state, and would be translated into English by a noun preceded by the indefinite article 'a' or 'an'. But partly as a corrupt following of English or French, and partly for emphasis, denoting 'a single one' (like *yr un* in Welsh), the word 'a' or 'an' is sometimes represented by *idn* (earlier *un*) 'one'. This is rare, especially in late Cornish. A similar indefinite article is common in Breton. Occasionally *idn* or *un* was used, as in Breton, with a verbal noun (or infinitive), to form what in English would be a present participle. *Yn un scolchye* 'skulking', lit. 'in a skulking' (*Passion*, 74, 2), *yn un garme* 'shouting, crying out', lit. 'in a shouting' (*Passion*, 168, i), *yn un fystyne* 'hastening', lit. 'in a hastening' (*Passion*, 178, i; 241, 4), but this construction is not found in late Cornish.

2.4. The noun

2.4.1. The formation of nouns.

Nouns are either primitive or derived. Primitive nouns have no special terminations to distinguish them from other words. Derived nouns, chiefly abstract, are formed from adjectives, verbs, or other nouns. There are also verbal nouns which have the form of the infinitive of verbs.

2.4.1.1. Nouns are derived from adjectives and occasionally from nouns and verbs, by adding *-der* or *-ter*. Thus:

dader 'goodness' from *da* 'good'.

gwîrder 'truth' from *gwîr* 'true'.

gwander 'weakness' from *gwan* or *gwadn* 'weak'.

golowder 'brightness' from *golow* 'light'.

tekter 'beauty' from *teg* 'beautiful'.

whekter 'sweetness' from *wheg* 'sweet'.

îthekter 'horror' from *îthek* 'horrible'.

melder 'sweetness' (to taste) from *mel* 'honey'.

yender 'coldness' from *yên* or *yein* 'cold'.

splander 'brightness, splendour' from *splan*, 'bright'.

tewlder 'darkness' from *tewal* 'dark'.

tewder 'thickness' from *tew* 'thick'.

tanowder 'thinness' from *tanow* 'thin'.

powsder 'heaviness' from *pows* 'heavy'.

scavder 'lightness' (of weight) from *scav* 'light'.

medhalder 'softness' from *medhal* 'soft'.

glanithder 'cleanness' from *glanith* 'clean'.

mŏgilder 'warmth' from *mŏgil* 'warm'.

tŏmder 'heat' from *tŏm* (or *tŭbm*) 'hot'.

downder 'depth' from *down* 'deep'.

sehter (or *zehar*) 'drought' from *segh* 'dry'.

ewhelder 'height' from *ewhel* 'high'.

crevder 'strength' from *crev* 'strong'.

Some adjectives ending in -*s* revert to an original -*t* in this formation. Thus:

calletter 'hardness' from *cales* 'hard'.

goscotter 'shelter' from *goskes* 'sheltering'.

ponvotter 'trouble' from *ponvos* 'trouble'.

It will be seen that this -*der* or -*ter* answers to the English termination -*ness*, and may be added to almost any adjective to form the corresponding abstract noun.

2.4.1.2. Abstract nouns are derived from other nouns or adjectives by the addition of -*eth* or -*neth*.

gwiryoneth 'truth' from *gwiryon* 'truthful'.

cosoleth 'rest, peace' from *cŏsel*, quiet'.

skîantoleth 'wisdom' from *skîantol* 'wise'.

folneth 'folly' from *fol* 'a fool'.

materneth 'royalty' from *matern* 'a king'.

gokeneth 'stupidity' from *goky* 'a fool'.

mescogneth[59] 'madness' from *mescok* 'a madman'.

gowegneth 'falsehood' from *gowek* 'a liar'.

roweth 'bounty' from *ro* 'a gift'.

This termination answers more or less to the Latin -*itas* or English -*ity*.

---

59 There is also a doubtful form *mescatter*, from *mescat*.

2.4.1.3. Abstract nouns are derived from verbs by the addition of *-ans*. Thus:

crejyans 'belief' from *cresy* (or *crejy*) 'to believe'.

givyans 'forgiveness' from *gava* 'to forgive'.

deskyans 'learning' from *desky* 'to learn'.

disqwedhyans 'discovery' from *disqwedhas* 'to discover'.

gordhyans (*gorryans*) 'glory' from *gordhya* (*gorrya*) 'to worship'.

bownans 'life' from *bewa* 'to live'.

marnans 'death' from *marwel* or *merwel* 'to die'.

selwans 'salvation' from *selwel* 'to save'.

tristyans 'sadness' from *trist* 'sad'.

tibyans 'thought' from *tibya* 'to think'.

This termination answers to the Latin *-antia* or *-entia*, and the English *-ance* or *-ence*. It is generally added to the root of the verb.

2.4.1.4. Nouns signifying agents or doers are derived from other nouns, adjectives, and verbs by the addition of *-or*, *-er*, *-ar*, or *-yas* (earlier *-iad* or *-iat*).

tŷor 'a tiler' from *tŷ* 'to cover'.

pestrior 'a wizard' from *pestry* 'magic'.

pescajor 'a fisherman' from *pescas* plur. of *pesk* 'fish'.[60]

cosŏlyer 'a counsellor' from *cŏsŏl* 'counsel'.

revader or *revajor* 'a rower' from *rev* 'an oar'.

trŏccyer 'a fuller'.

lyuyar 'a dyer' from *lyu* 'colour'.

gwîadar 'a weaver' from *gwîa* 'to weave'.

bŏnkyer 'a cooper' from *bŏnk* 'a blow'.

ŏmdowlar 'a wrestler' from *ŏmdowla* 'to wrestle'.

gŏnnador or *gonajor* 'a sower' from *gŏnas* 'to sow or plant'.[61]

mijar 'a reaper' from *mijy* 'to reap'.

---

60 {The form *pescajor* is unattested; the attested form has *-ador*, as *pùscador*.}

61 {The form *gonajor* is unattested; the attested form has *-ador*, as *gonador*.}

77

stênor 'a tinner' from *stên* 'tin'.

selwyas 'a saviour' from *selwel* 'to save'.

gwithyas (also *gwithyor*) 'a guardian' from *gwithya* 'to keep'.[62]

kernyas 'a trumpeter' from *corn* 'a horn'.

rennyas 'a carver' from *ranna* 'to divide'.

sewyas 'a tailor' from *sewy* 'to sew'.

pŭrkenyas 'an enchanter' from the intensive prefix *pur* (lit. 'very') and *cana* 'to sing'.

helhyas 'a pursuer' from *helhya* 'to hunt'.

scrivinyas 'a writer' from *scrîfa* 'to write'.

offeryas 'a priest' from *offeren* 'mass'.

hŏmbrŏnkyas 'a leader' from *hŏmbrŏnkya* 'to lead'.

Many words in *-yas* occur only in the Cottonian Vocabulary, and appear there as ending in *-iad* or *-iat*, but since all the Cottonian words in *-iad* and *-iat* which do appear in later MSS are made in the latter to end in *-yas* (or *-ias*), and since it may be taken as an invariable rule that all words ending in *-t* or *-d* in Welsh or Breton, if they occur at all in Cornish, end in *-s*, any Cottonian word in *-iat* or *-iad* may fairly be taken for purposes of modern Cornish to end in *-yas*.

2.4.2. The gender of nouns.

Nouns are of two genders, masculine and feminine. There is no neuter. There is no rule whereby to tell the gender of a word, except in the case of animate objects, where the gender simply follows the sex.

2.4.2.1. There are only three grammatical contexts in which gender matters at all.

2.4.2.1.1. When a noun or an adjective preceding a noun is preceded by the article *an* 'the'. If the noun or adjective is masculine singular or the noun feminine, or the adjective of either, plural, its initial remains in the first state. If the noun or adjective is

---

62 {The form *gwithyor* is unattested.}

feminine singular or the noun is masculine plural,[63] it is changed to the second state.

2.4.2.1.2. When a qualifying adjective follows a noun in the masculine or in the plural of either gender, the initial of the adjective remains in the first state. If the noun is feminine singular, the initial of the adjective changes to the second state.

2.4.2.1.3. The pronoun of the third person singular, used for a feminine noun, even when it signifies an inanimate object, is *hŷ* 'she', not *ev* 'he'. Examples:

tâs 'a father'; *an tâs* 'the father'.

tassow 'fathers'; *an dassow* 'the fathers'.

mergh 'a daughter'; *an vergh* 'the daughter'.

merhes 'daughters'; *an merhes* 'the daughters'.

tâs mas 'a good father'; *mergh vas* 'a good daughter'; *an vergh vas* 'the good daughter'.

tassow mas 'good fathers'; *merhes mas* 'good daughters'.

It will be evident, considering that a large number of nouns and adjectives do not begin with mutable letters, that the question of gender only applies to a limited number of nouns and adjectives, and therefore presents but little difficulty. Perhaps the best way to learn the genders of nouns with mutable initials is to get accustomed to their sound with the article prefixed.

2.4.2.2. The feminine equivalents of certain masculine nouns denoting animate objects are represented, as in other languages, in one of two ways, by the addition of a syllable or by different words.

2.4.2.2.1. By the addition of *-es*. This is the regular form.

arledh 'lord'; *arledhes* 'lady'.

pestrior 'a wizard'; *pestriores* 'a witch'.

coweth 'a companion', masc.; *cowethes* 'a companion', fem.

---

63 The change of initial of the masculine plural is by no means universal in the MSS, but it is not infrequent, and is the rule in Breton (with a few exceptions), so it seems fair to conjecture that it was the Cornish rule also.

mow 'a boy'; *mowes* 'a girl'.

sans 'a saint'; *sanses* 'a female saint'.

eneval 'an animal', masc.; *enevales* 'an animal', fem.

pehador or *pehajor* 'a sinner', masc.; *pehadores* 'a sinner', fem.[64]

Except in the case of the other class of feminines, of which a list is given below, it may be taken as a general rule that the corresponding feminine of any noun denoting a masculine animate object is formed in this way.

2.4.2.2.2. By a different word. These are mostly those which denote relationships and familiar animals, and there are in some cases, as in English, further words to denote the young of both sexes, or the neuter.

dên 'man'; *benen* 'woman'; *flogh* 'child'.

gour 'husband; *gwrêg* 'wife'.

mab 'son'; *mergh* 'daughter'.

ewiter 'uncle'; *modreb* 'aunt'.

tâs 'father'; *mam* 'mother'.

sîra 'father'; *dama* 'mother'.

sîra widn[65] 'grandfather'; *dama widn* 'grandmother'.

altrou 'godfather'; *altrewan* 'godmother'.

broder 'brother'; *hoer* 'sister'.

noy 'nephew'; *noys* 'niece'.

tarow 'bull'; *bewgh* 'cow'; *ŏjion* 'ox'; *lewgh* 'calf'; *lŏdn* 'bullock'; *lejek* 'heifer'.

hordh or *hŭr* 'ram'; *davas* 'sheep'; *mowls* 'wether'; *ôn* 'lamb'.

margh 'horse'; *caseg* 'mare'; *ebal* 'colt'.

bŏk 'he-goat'; *gavar* 'goat'; *min* 'kid'.

baedh 'boar'; *banew* 'sow'; *porhal*, 'little pig'; *gwîs* 'old sow'; *ragomogh* 'hog'; *mohen* 'pig' (plur. *mogh*); *torgh* 'hog'.

---

64 {The form *pehajor* is unattested.}

65 Note how a masculine ending in -*a* affects the initial of the adjective as if it were a feminine. {Lenition of *widn* in *sîra widn* has probably more to do with its use in an original genitive or vocative case.}

kŷ 'dog'; *gêst* 'bitch'.

gourgath 'tom-cat'; *cath* 'cat'.

carow 'stag'; *ewik* 'hind'; *lewgh-ewik* 'fawn'.

kŏtyorgh, 'roe buck'; *yorgh* 'roe doe'.

keliok 'cock'; *yar* 'hen'; *mabyer* 'chicken'.

keliokwôdh 'gander'; *gôdh* 'goose'.

keliokôs 'drake'; *hôs* 'duck'.

2.4.3. The cases of nouns.

All cases except the genitive and accusative are formed by prepositions, as in English. Of these prepositions some govern one state of the initial and some another, as will be seen in the chapter on prepositions, but when the article *an* 'the' comes between the preposition and the noun, the initial is not changed by the preposition, but only, if at all (in the case of a feminine singular or masculine plural), by the article.

2.4.3.1. The genitive, by which must here be understood (in its old-fashioned sense) all those conditions under which a noun would in English be preceded by *of*, or followed by *'s*, is formed in four ways, each of which has a different meaning.

2.4.3.1.1. The genitive of possession is the appositional genitive. This is formed by placing the noun that is in the genitive immediately after the noun which it qualifies, or, if the former has the definite article, or is qualified by a possessive pronoun or prefixed adjective, with only these intervening. No change of initial is made,[66] except the usual change of feminine singular or masculine

---

66 It sometimes happens (as Dr Stokes points out) that if the first noun is feminine, the noun in the genitive has its initial in the second state, in fact it is treated as an adjective qualifying the preceding noun, e.g. *bennath Varya* 'the blessing of Mary'; *carek Veryasek* 'the rock of Meriasek'; *fynten woys* 'a well of blood', but as this also happens at times when the first noun is masculine (e.g. *cledha dan*, Cr. 964), it probably

plural nouns after *an*, or the changes caused by possessive pronouns, etc. The first of the two nouns must have no article. Thus:

chŷ dên 'the house of a man' or 'a man's house'.

chŷ an dên 'the house of the man' or 'the man's house'.

chŷ benen 'the house of a woman'.

chŷ an venen 'the house of the woman'.

But not **an chŷ an dên* or **an chŷ an venen*.

If there is a succession of genitives, only the last noun can have an article. Thus:

darras chŷ gour an venen 'the door of the house of the husband of the woman'.

2.4.3.1.2. The inflected genitive. This, which only exists, and that doubtfully, in the case of a few words, is formed by the modification of the root vowel. It is one of the common genitives of the Gaelic dialects, and as such is important, for it is not recognized in Welsh or Breton. Lhuyd gives five instances of it—*margh* 'a horse', gen. *mergh*; *mergh* 'a daughter', gen. *myrgh*; *pen* 'a head', gen. *pyn* (used only in the quasi-preposition *erbyn* 'against'); *whêl* 'work', gen. *wheyl*; *crês* 'midst', gen. *creys*, but even these were very seldom used, and only probably in a few expressions. It would seem that the initial of the genitive word should in this case be in the second state. Thus:

rên vergh 'a horse's mane'.

2.4.3.1.3. The genitive of attribution, quality, origin, or quantity, denoted in English by the preposition *of*, but not expressible also by the possessive in *'s*, though in many cases an adjective might be substituted for it, is expressed in Cornish by the preposition *a*, which puts the initial in the second state. Thus:

2.4.3.1.3.1. Quality. *Arledh a 'ras* 'Lord of grace'; *an Matern a wordhyans* 'the King of glory'.

---

only means that mutations were rather loosely used. The last two are "genitives of material".

2.4.3.1.3.2. Origin. *an Tâs a'n Nev* 'the Father of Heaven' (cf. *Pater de cælis Deus*, translated in the English Prayer-book 'O God, the Father of Heaven'); *dên a Gernow* 'a man of Cornwall'.

2.4.3.1.3.3. Quantity. Words denoting number, quantity, etc., generally adjectives or numerals, may be followed by this form of genitive. Thus:

lên a 'ras 'full of grace'.

lower a ŷs 'plenty of corn'.

milyow a bensow 'thousands of pounds'.

2.4.3.1.4. The genitive of material is rather the use of a noun as an adjective. It differs from the appositional genitive in that the first noun may have the article before it, and the second does not, and that if the first noun be feminine singular, the initial of the second noun is in the second state. Thus:

tolyer predn 'a platter of wood'.

tre bredn 'a town of wood'.

2.4.3.2. The accusative or objective is usually the same as the nominative, but it is to be remembered that there are a certain number of verbs which in English are followed directly by an accusative, but in Cornish require the intervention of a preposition.

2.4.3.3. The vocative is preceded by *a*, which signifies 'O', or by a personal pronoun. The initial after *a* and sometimes after the pronoun changes to the second state. Thus:

mab 'son'; *a vab* 'O son'.

benen 'woman'; *a venen* 'O woman'; *tî venen* 'thou woman'.

why princis (*Resurrectio Domini*, iii. 124), 'ye princes'.

2.4.4. The plural of nouns.

There are seven ways of forming the plural of nouns.

2.4.4.1. In *-ow* or *-yow* (pronounced *o* or *yo* {[oʊ], [joʊ]}). This is the commonest form, and would naturally be used for most new words. It answers to the Welsh *-au* or *-iau*, and the Breton *-où* or *-ioù*.

alwedh 'a key', *alwedhow*.

dorn 'a hand', *dornow*.

arv 'a weapon', *arvow*.

bedh 'a grave', *bedhow*.

ro 'a gift', *roow*.

scovorn 'an ear', *scovornow*.

dêdh 'a day', *dêdhyow*.

Dew 'God', *dewow*.

enev 'soul', *enevow*.

cledh 'ditch', *cledhyow*,

gwredh 'root', *gwredhyow*.

menedh 'mountain', *menedhyow*.

trev, *tre* 'town', *trevow*.

tîr 'land', *tiryow*.

Some which follow this form have peculiarities of their own.

2.4.4.1.1. Some double the last consonant, which has the effect of shortening the sound of the preceding vowel, and if the last consonant is an *-s*, giving it the sound of *s* instead of *z*. Thus:

tâs 'father', *tassow*.

fôs 'wall', *fossow*.

lêr 'floor', *lerryow*.

gêr 'word', *gerryow*.

garget 'garter', *gargettow*.

2.4.4.1.2. Some, which end in *-er* or *-ar*, drop the last vowel. Thus:

levar 'book', *levrow*.

dagar 'tear', *dagrow*.

kenter 'nail', *kentrow*.

2.4.4.1.3. Some insert *-g* or *-k* after a final *-l*.

cŏsŏl 'counsel', *cŏsŏlgow*.

tewal 'dark', *tewlgow* or *tewalgow*.

del 'leaves' (collectively), *delkyow* (simple plural).

2.4.4.1.4. Some modify the root vowel. Thus:

mâl 'a joint', *melyow*.

2.4.4.2. In *-yon* or *-on*. This is also very common.

Cristiŏn 'a Christian', *Cristiŏnyon*.

sgwer 'esquire', *sgwerryon*.

caradow 'friend', *caradowyon*.

scŏlŏr 'scholar', *scŏlŏryon*.

deskibl 'disciple', *deskiblyon*.

Breth 'Briton', *Brethon*.

Sows 'Englishman', *Sowson*.

prev 'worm', *prevyon*.

When a word ends in *-k*, and has this form of the plural (as most words ending in *-k* have) the last letter becomes *-g*.

bohajak 'poor', *bohajagyon*.[67]

marrek 'knight', *marregyon*.

gowek 'liar', *gowegyon*.

Some modify the root vowel.

clav 'sick', *clevyon*.

mab 'son', *mebyon*.

gwas 'serving-man', *gwesyon*.

Yethow 'Jew', *Yethewon*.

Kernow 'Cornishman', *Kernewon*.[68]

kîf 'dear', *kefyon*.

gwîr 'true', *gweryon*.

Those ending in *-er* and *-ar*, after a mute, contract the last syllable of the root.

lader 'thief', *laddron*.

---

67 {Always *bohajogyon*.}

68 {The form should be *Kernowyon*.}

This termination is the only one used for the plural of adjectives. These are rarely inflected when in agreement with a plural noun, but when used as nouns they make their plural in this way. A large number of adjectives and also some nouns end in *-ek* or *-ak*. It is also the regular plural of words ending in or denoting an agent.

2.4.4.3. In *-y*. This termination is more common in Cornish than in Welsh or Breton, though it is not uncommon in those languages also. It is often written *i* in the MSS.

> *esel* 'limb', *esely*.
> *mowes* 'girl', *mowesy*.
> *Gwidhel* 'Irishman', *Gwidhely*.
> *castell* 'castle', *castelly*.
> *legast* 'lobster', *legesty* (with a change of vowel).
> *porhel* 'pig', *porhelly*.
> *bîgel* 'shepherd', *bîgely*.
> *profes* 'prophet', *profesy* or *profejy*.
> *servis* 'servant', *servisy* or *servijy*.[69]
> *gwithes* 'guardian', *gwithesy*.
> *arledh* 'lord', *arledhy*.
> *trahes* 'cutter', *trahesy* (e.g. *trahesy meyn* 'stone cutters').

This plural is mostly used for words ending in *-l* and *-s*, though not exclusively, and it occurs occasionally with other words. When a word ends in *-s* preceded by a thin vowel, that letter is sometimes written *-j-* in the plural.

2.4.4.4. In *-es* or *-edh*.[70] This is the equivalent of the Welsh *-edd*, *-ydd*, or *-oedd*, and the Breton *-ed*, though it is not

---

69 {The word *servis* means 'service', pl. *servisyow*; *servisy* ~ *servijy* are the plurals of *servyas* 'servant'; compare *servont*, pl. *servons*.}

70 {Unstressed *-edh* in plurals is probably better understood as *-eth*.}

necessarily used for the same words. Sometimes the vowel is modified. Thus:

mergh 'daughter', *merhes*.[71]

benen 'woman', *benenes.*

flogh 'child', *flehes*.[71]

côl 'coal', *côles.*

rôm 'room', *rômes.*

laha 'law', *lahes.*

best 'beast', *bestes.*

silly 'eel', *sillyes.*

abostol 'apostle', *abesteledh*.[72]

broder 'brother'; *brederedh* 'brethren'.[73]

el 'angel', *eledh*.[74]

gwrêg 'wife', *gwrêgedh*.[75]

A variant of this, written by Lhuyd *-az*, *-yz*, or *-oz*, the vowel being obscure {[ə]}, is best represented in this spelling by *-as*. It perhaps answers to the Welsh *-od*, and *-iaid*.

canker 'crab', *kencras.*

pesk 'fish', *pescas.*

bes 'finger', *besyas.*

bat 'staff', *battas.*

fow 'den', *fowas.*

cap 'cap', *cappas.*

---

71 Note that when a syllable is added to a word ending in *gh*, the *g* is omitted. {See §2.1.3.6.}

72 {The forms should be *abosteleth*, which is more frequently attested than *abesteleth*; the form *abestely* also occurs

73 {*Bredereth* may be an abstract masculine noun meaning 'brother-hood'.}

74 {The form should be *eleth.*}

75 {The attested forms are *gwrageth* and *gwregath.*}

2.4.4.5. By the modification of the vowel.

trôs 'foot', *treys*,

mên 'stone', *meyn*.

broder 'brother'; *breder* 'brothers'.

davas 'sheep', *deves*, but also *devejyow*.

margh 'horse', *mergh*.

tol 'hole', *tel*.

ascorn 'bone', *escarn*.

sans 'saint', *sens*, but also *sansow*.

dans 'tooth', *dens*.

yar 'hen', *yer*.

mab 'son', *mêb*, but also *mebyon*.[76]

manek 'glove', *menik*.

gavar 'goat', *gever*.[77]

2.4.4.6. By dropping the syllable *-en* or *-an* from the singular; or rather in this case the singular is formed from a plural, usually more or less collective, by adding the individualizing suffix *-an* or *-en*. The words to which this applies are mostly such as are more commonly used in the plural, and the *-en* becomes, as Norris calls it, "an individualizing particle". Thus:

dêl 'leaves, foliage'; *dêlen* 'a leaf'.

gwrîhon 'sparks'; *gwrîhonen* 'a spark'.

gwêdh 'trees'; *gwêdhen* 'a tree'.

gwêl 'rods, twigs'; *gwêlen* 'a rod, a twig'.

lûhas 'lightning'; *lûhesen* 'a flash of lightning'.

scow 'elder trees'; *scowen* 'an elder tree'.

eithin 'furze'; *eithinen* 'a furze bush'.

loggas 'mice'; *loggosan* or *loggojan* 'a mouse'.

low 'lice'; *lewen* 'a louse'.

---

76 {The form *mêb* is unattested.}

77 {Also *gyfras*.}

redan 'fern'; *redanen* 'a single fern'.

mor 'berries'; *moren* 'a berry'.

hern 'pilchards'; *hernen* 'a pilchard'.

mŭrryan 'ants'; *murryanen* 'an ant'.

on 'ash trees'; *onnen* 'an ash'.

enwedh 'ash trees'; *enwedhen* 'an ash' (from *on* 'ash', *gwêdh* 'trees').

glasten 'oaks'; *glastenen* 'an oak'.

gwern 'alders'; *gwernen* 'an alder'.

spern 'thorns'; *spernen* 'a thorn'.

bannol 'broom' (the plants collectively); *bannolen* 'a broom' (to sweep with).

And many others, chiefly names of plants and animals of a more or less gregarious nature. Some of these have other plurals, formed by adding one of the plural terminations to the collective plural. These would be used when the collective idea was not required. Thus:

dêl 'leaves' (collective); *delkyow* or *delgyow* 'leaves' (not collectively).

Some singulars in *-en* form their modern plurals from a lost collective plural, i.e. by dropping the *-en* and adding one of the ordinary plural terminations. Thus:

asen 'a rib'; *asow* 'ribs'.

gwillen 'a sea-gull'; *gwilles* 'gulls'.

2.4.4.7. In *-en*, with or without alteration of vowel and contraction. Thus:

kŷ 'dog'; *kîen*.

hanow 'name'; *henwen* (formerly *hynwyn*).

There is no general definite rule for the formation of plurals; they must be learnt by experience. Some words are found with two plurals, but this generally means a tendency in modern Cornish to consider *-yow* or *-ow* to be the normal termination, and to discard other endings in favour of it, just as the plural in -*s* in English has superseded all but a very few other forms. Thus:

escop (or *epscop*) 'bishop'; *escobyon* or *escobow*.

Dew 'God'; *dewon* or *dewow*.

flogh 'child'; *flehes* or *flehesow* (*flejow*).

delen 'leaf'; *dêlyow* or *delkyow*.

tîr 'land'; *terros* or *terryow*.

enes 'island'; *eneses* or *enesow*.

2.4.5. The so-called dual.

Parts of the body which are double (ears, eyes, hands, arms, shoulders, knees, etc.), when mentioned in reference to the two ears, eyes, etc. of the same person, are expressed by a compound with the numeral *deu* 'two' prefixed to the singular. The Welsh and Breton grammarians call this a dual. When eyes, ears, etc. are mentioned as belonging to more than one person, the plural is formed in one of the usual ways. Thus:

lâv 'hand'; dual *deulâv*.[78]

lagas 'eye'; dual *deulagas*; pl. *lagasow*.

scovorn 'ear'; dual *deuscovorn*; pl. *scovornow*.

glîn 'knee'; dual *deulin*.

elin 'elbow'; *deuelin*.

bregh 'arm'; *deuvregh*.

bron 'breast'; *deuvron*.

scoudh 'shoulder'; *deuscoudh*.

For 'hands' in general the plural is formed from *dorn* (which means more exactly 'fist'), *dornow*; there is, as in Welsh, no regular plural of *lâv*. A variant of *glîn* is *penglin* (lit. 'knee-end'), with a dual *pedndewlin*, cf. Welsh *penelin* 'elbow'.

Lastly, the plural of *dên* 'man' is almost always *tîs* (earlier *tus*) 'folk', though Lhuyd gives *dynion* as well {AB 243c; this Welsh plural is not otherwise attested in Cornish}.

---

78 {The form should be *dewla*.}

2.5. The adjective

Adjectives are primitive or derived. Primitive adjectives have no specially characteristic terminations. Derived adjectives are mostly formed by adding *-ek* to a noun or verb, which may be said to answer to *-ous*, *-ful*, etc., in English. Thus:

gallos 'power'; *gallosek* 'powerful'.

own 'fear'; *ownek* 'fearful'.

lowena 'joy'; *lowenek* 'joyful'.

marthes 'wonder'; *marthesek* 'marvellous'.

moreth 'grief'; *morethek* 'mournful'.

ponfos 'trouble'; *ponfôsek* 'troubled'.

anfês 'misfortune'; *anfêsek* 'unfortunate'.

whans 'desire'; *whansek* 'desirous'.

colon 'heart'; *colonnek* 'hearty'.

2.5.1. The feminine of an adjective is formed in two ways.

2.5.1.1. By changing the initial to the second state, if it is mutable. This only happens when the adjective *follows* a feminine singular noun. When the adjective *precedes* the noun, singular or plural, and when it follows a masculine singular noun or a plural of either gender, the initial of the adjective remains in its first state, unless by reason of other circumstances than agreement, e.g. preceding prepositions, pronouns, etc., or when the article *an* precedes an adjective qualifying a noun of feminine singular.

Unlike Breton, but like Welsh, an adjective qualifying and following a masculine plural does not change.

2.5.1.2. Rarely and irregularly, by the alteration of the root vowel as well as by the change of initial. This, however, though mentioned by Lhuyd and occasionally found in MSS, was practically obsolete long before his time.

2.5.2. The plural of adjectives is formed by the addition of *-yon* or *-on*. Rarely, chiefly in poetry, this plural is found in agreement with a plural noun, but usually qualifying adjectives are treated as indeclinable, but for the initial mutation, and the plural form is only used, as a general thing, when an adjective is used as a noun.

2.5.3. The normal position of the adjective is after the noun. Sometimes it precedes it, and in that case it changes the initial of the noun to the second state, unless the adjective is in the comparative or superlative degree, when the initial is unchanged. The adjectives that most commonly precede the noun are *drôg* 'evil'; *hen* 'old'; *lên* 'full'; *hager* 'ugly'; *fals* 'false'; *cam* 'crooked'. *Mêr* 'great' may come before or after.

2.5.4. The comparative degree is formed by adding *-ah* and the superlative by adding *-a* to the positive, but as in English they can also be formed by the use of *moy* 'more' and *moyha* 'most'. There are, of course, the usual irregular comparisons. The comparative or superlative adjective usually precedes the noun which it qualifies, though for the sake of verse or on account of emphasis it may follow it, sometimes with the definite article intervening. 'Than' after a comparative is *es* (older *ys* or *ages*) or *vel*.
Examples of the use of adjectives:
　Dên gallosek 'a powerful man'.
　Benen deg 'a fair woman'.

Mergh dewon or *mergh dew* 'black horses'.

Benenes teg 'fair women'.

An hen dhên 'the old man'. (The more usual expression is *an dên coth*.)

An hen venen 'the old woman'. (More usually *an venen goth*.)

An lowenegyon 'the joyful ones'.

Brassah gallos 'greater power'.

Gwîn a'n gwella, an gwella gwîn, gwîn gwella, 'the best wine'.

Whekkah es mel 'sweeter than honey'.

Bron Ewhella 'the highest hill' (now Brown Willy).

The irregular comparisons are:

Da (or *mas*) 'good'; *gwel* 'better'; *gwella* 'best'.

Drôg 'bad'; *gwêth* 'worse'; *gwêtha* 'worst'; but generally *lakkah*, comparative of *lak* ('loose, remiss, lax') is used to signify 'worse'.

Mêr 'great'; *moy* 'greater' or 'more'; *moyha* 'greatest' or 'most'; but also *bras*, comparative *brassah*, superlative *brassa*.

Bîan 'little'; *leh* 'less'; *lŷha* 'least'; but there is also a comparative *behadnah* and superlative *behadna* from an earlier form *behan*.

Ogas 'near'; *nes* 'nearer'; *nessa* 'nearest'.

2.6. The numerals

Cardinal		Ordinal	
1	*idn* or *ŏnen* (older *un, onan, onon*).[79]	1st	*kensa.*
2	*deu* (older *dyw, dew*).	2nd	*nessa* or *secund.*
3	*trŷ*, fem, *teir* (older *tyr*).	3rd	*trŷja* (older *tresse, trege*).
4	*pajer* (older, m. *peswar*, f. *peder*).	4th	*peswordha* (older *peswere, pyswere*).
5	*pemp* (older *pymp*).	5th	*pempes* (older *pympes*).
6	*wheh* (or *whe*).	6th	*whethes* (older *whefes*).
7	*seyth.*	7th	*seythes* (older *seythves*).
8	*eyth.*	8th	*eythes.*
9	*now* (pronounced as the English word *now*).	9th	*nowes.*
10	*deg* (older *dek*).	10th	*degves.*
11	*idnak.*	11th	*idn-dhegves.*
12	*dawdhak* (older *dewthak*).	12th	*dawdhegves.*
13	*tôrdhak.*	13th	*tôrdhegves.*
14	*peswôrdhak.*	14th	*peswôrdhegves.*
15	*pempthak.*	15th	*pempthegves.*
16	*whedhak.*	16th	*whedhegves.*
17	*seydhak.*	17th	*seydhegves.*
18	*eydhak.*	18th	*eydhegves.*
19	*nownjak* (*ow* as in *now*).	19th	*nownjakves.*

---

79 *Idn*, to qualify a noun; *ŏnen*, used by itself. Thus, *idn dên* one man, *Ŏnen hag Ol*, One and All. *Wŏnnen* is an alternative form of the latter.

94

Cardinal		Ordinal	
20	*igans.*	20th	*igansves.*
21	*ŏnen war igans.*	21st	*kensa war igans.*
22	*deu war igans,* etc.	22nd	*nessa war igans,* etc.
30	*deg war igans.*	30th	*degves war igans.*
31	*idnak war igans,* etc.	31st	*idn-dhegves war igans,* etc.
40	*deugans.*	40th	*deugansves.*
50	*deg war deugans* (or *hanter cans*).	50th	*degves war deugans.*
60	*trŷ igans.*	60th	*trŷ-igansves.*
70	*deg war trŷ igans* (or *trŷ igans ha deg*).	70th	*degves war trŷ-igans* (or *trŷ igans ha degves*).
80	*pajer igans.*	80th	*pajer-igansves.*
90	*deg war pajer igans* (or *pajer igans ha deg*).	90th	*degves war pajer-igansves* (or *pajer igans ha degves*).
100	*cans.*	100th	*cansves.*
200	*deu cans.*	200th	*deu cansves.*
300	*tryhans.*	300th	*tryhansves.*
1000	*mil.*	1000th	*milves.*
1,000,000	*milvil* or *milyon.*	1,000,000th	*milvilves.*

When compound numbers are used, the noun follows the first of them. Thus:

> *trŷ igans bledhan ha deg* '70 years' ('threescore years and ten'), or *deg bledhan war trŷ igans.*

Larger compounds are made somewhat as in English. Thus 'AD 1904' is *Bledhan agan Arledh nownjak cans ha pajer.*

The later lists of ordinal numbers usually have -*vas* for the termination, but the practice of the older MSS, the analogy of Welsh and Breton, and the very definite sound of the last syllable of *pempes* and *whethes* in the traditional fragments collected by the present writer in 1875, all point to -*e*- as the correct vowel.

2.6.1. Nouns which follow numerals are put in the singular number,[80] unless they are preceded by the preposition *a*, of. Thus:

wheh dên 'six men', not *wheh denyon or *wheh tîs.

trŷ mab 'three sons', not *trŷ mebyon.

pajer paw, not *pajer pawyow 'four feet' (a name still used in the English of Cornwall for a newt).

But sometimes, in a collective sense:

mil a bensow 'a thousand [of] pounds'.

wheh a vebyon ha wheh a verhes 'six sons and six daughters'.

The numerals, cardinal or ordinal, unlike certain of them in Welsh and Breton, do not change the initials of the nouns which follow them.

2.6.2. It may be well to add here certain applications of the numerals.

2.6.2.1. 'Once', 'twice', 'three times', etc. are represented by the cardinal numbers followed by *gweth* 'time' (in the above sense), with its initial in the second state, *idnweth*, *deuweth*, *trŷweth*, etc. Sometimes *plek* '-fold', is used, as *milblek* 'a thousand-fold'.

2.6.2.2. Proportional parts are: *qwartan* 'a quarter', *hanter* 'half', and for the rest the ordinal numeral followed by *radn* 'part', e.g. *trûja radn* 'the third part'.

---

80 It has been held that this apparent singular, which is used after numerals in Welsh and Breton also, is really a genitive plural. In the Gaelic languages, in which the case-inflections of nouns still exist, the genitive plural is usually (though not universally) the same as the nominative singular, except in Manx, where it is only distinguishable from the nominative plural by its article, but except in the cases of *dà* 'two', *fichead* 'twenty', *ceud* 'a hundred', and *mìle* 'a thousand', which precede nouns in the singular, the plural follows numerals in those languages. {This note of Jenner's is only partially correct.}

2.6.2.3. The divisions of time are: *secund* 'a second'; *minnis* 'a minute'; *êr* 'an hour'; *dêdh* 'a day'; *seithan* 'a week'; *mîs* 'a month'; *bledhan* 'a year'; *cansvledhan* 'a century'. 'O'clock' is expressed by *êr*; *trŷ êr* 'three o'clock'. 'Half-past three' is *hanter êr woja trŷ* = 'half-an-hour after three'. 'Midday' and 'midnight' are *hanter-dêdh* and *hanter-nos*. 'Half-past twelve' (noon) is *hanter êr woja hanter-dêdh*.

2.6.2.4. The names of coins are: *pevar* 'a farthing'; *demma* or *hanter-denar* 'a halfpenny'; *denar* 'a penny'; *whednar* [= *wheh denar*] 'sixpence'; *sôls* 'a shilling'; *hanter-corŭn* 'half-a-crown'; *corŭn* 'a crown'; *pens* 'a pound'.

2.6.2.5. Measurements of length are: *inch* 'inch'; *trôs* 'a foot'; *gwêlan* 'a yard'; *fadhom* 'fathom'; *mildir* 'a mile'.

2.6.2.6. Weights are: *ons* 'ounce'; *pens* 'pound'; *tŏn* 'ton'.

2.7. The pronouns

2.7.1. The personal pronouns.

There are four forms of the Personal pronouns. These forms are used under various circumstances, but they are mostly reducible to a single letter with or without its vowel for each person, the variations depending upon (*a*) the *state* of that letter, and (*b*) whether the vowel is placed before or after it. The vowel is elided in some cases, and coalesces with another vowel in others.

1. As the subject of a verb and preceding it.

2. As the subject or object of a verb and following it. This is for some pronouns the same as the first form, for others the first form with its initial in the second state.

3. As the object of a verb, but placed between a particle ending in a vowel and the verb. This form is used also for possessive pronouns of the first and second persons singular when they are preceded by the conjunction *ha* 'and', or by a preposition ending in a vowel, or by *en* 'in'.

4. In composition with a preposition, and for forming the persons of an inflected tense of a verb.

In the first and second the consonant is followed by a vowel. In the third and fourth the consonant ends the word.

2.7.1.1. *FIRST PERSON SINGULAR.* English 'I' or 'me'. Letter *M* (*V*).

1st form. *mî.*   *mî a vedn* 'I will'.

2nd form. *vî.*   *gwith vî* 'keep me'.

3rd form. *'m.*   *neb a'm gwrîg* 'he who made me'.

4th form. *-m* or *-v.*   *genev* 'with me'; *dhem* 'to me'; *carav* 'I love'.

The compounds of pronoun and preposition are written as one word, without an apostrophe, as the form of the preposition also is often affected by the composition. A list of these will be found later on, as they present some irregularities. {See §2.7.3.}

2.7.1.2. *SECOND PERSON SINGULAR.* English 'thou' or 'thee'. Letter *T* (*D*).

1st form, *tî* (pronounced nearly *chee*, and sometimes so written). *tî a vedn* 'thou wilt'.

2nd form, *dî* (often written *sy* or *gy* in the older MSS, and pronounced *jee*, nearly). *menjes dî* 'thou wouldst'.

3rd form, *'th* (often *'d* in the older MSS). This is followed by the second state of the initial, or in the case of *d-* by the fourth, *mî a'th bes* 'I pray thee', *re'th tynerchys* 'hath greeted thee' (Passion, 115, 2).

4th form. *-s. genes* 'with thee'.

2.7.1.3. *THIRD PERSON SINGULAR, MASCULINE.* English 'he' or 'him'. Letter *V* or *N*, or a vowel.

1st form, *ev* (with the *v* very lightly sounded, and often silent. The older form is *ef*). *ev a vedn* 'he will'.

2nd form, *ev* or *e.* *menja ev* 'he would'.

3rd form. *'n.*   *mî a'n pes* 'I pray him'. This form is commonly used in the earlier MSS. It represents an accusative *en* or *hen* which still exists in Breton {*hen*}. In more recent Cornish, with the frequent use of the auxiliary form of the verb, where the pronominal object precedes the infinitive in its possessive form, this construction became unusual.

99

4th form. *'o.*   *enno* 'in him', *ganso* 'with him'. In this form several words have an inserted *-dh-* between the preposition and the pronoun. *Ragdho* 'for him', *dhôdho* 'to him', not *rago, *dhôo. A similar euphonic *-dh-* occurs in the case of the third persons feminine and plural.

2.7.1.4. *THIRD PERSON SINGULAR, FEMININE.* English 'she', 'her'. Letter *H*, *S*, or a vowel.

    1st form. *hŷ.*   *hŷ a vedn* 'she will'.

    2nd form. *hŷ.*   *a medh hŷ* 'said she'.

    3rd form. *'s.*   *mî a's henow* 'I name her'. This form is rarely found in the later MSS. Either the possessive *î* or the form *hŷ* (the latter often put after the verb) was used, in the rare cases of this construction.

    4th form. *'î.*   *gensî* 'with her'; *dhedhî* 'to her'.

2.7.1.5. *FIRST PERSON PLURAL.* English 'we', 'us'. Letter *N*.

    1st form. *nŷ.*   *nŷ a vedn* 'we will'.

    2nd form. *nŷ.*   *na blamyough nŷ,* 'do not blame us'.

    3rd form. *'n.*   *ev a'n doro* 'he will bring us'. This form, perhaps owing to its being the same as the 3rd form of the third person singular, is rare even in the older MSS. The possessive *'gan* (for *agan*) is generally used instead of it, *ev a'gan doro*.

    4th form, *-n*, preceded by almost any vowel. *ragon* 'for us'; *genen* 'with us'; *dhen* 'to us'; *warnan* 'on us'.

2.7.1.6. *SECOND PERSON PLURAL.* English 'you'. Letter *Wh*, *Gh*, or *S*.

    1st form. *whŷ.*   *whŷ a vedn* 'you will'.

    2nd form. *whŷ.*   *nî wreugh whŷ* 'you do not'.

    3rd form. *'s.*   *ev a's doro* 'he will bring you'. This form is very rare even in the older MSS. The possessive *'gas* (for *agas*) is generally used instead.

    4th form. *-ugh.*   *genough* 'with you'; *dheugh* 'to you'.

2.7.1.7. *THIRD PERSON PLURAL*. English 'they', 'them'.

1st form. *ŷ, jŷ, an jŷ. ŷ a vedn, jŷ a vedn*, or *an jŷ a vedn* 'they will'. This last is the regular form in the latest Cornish. In the earlier MSS *y* only is used for 'they'; later *an gy* or *an dzhei* (as Lhuyd writes it) became usual. It is only found in the MSS of the end of the seventeenth and beginning of the eighteenth century, and probably originated in a wrong division of words. The third person plural of most inflected tenses of verbs ends in *-ons, -ans, -ens*. If the pronoun were added, this would take the form of *ons ŷ*, etc., as in *carons ŷ* (Latin *amant illi*) 'they love', and the usual pronunciation of *s* would soon bring this combination to *caronjy*, which is easily divided into *car onjy*. The compound preposition form in later Cornish often ended in *-ans*, followed or not followed by the 1st or 2nd form of the pronoun. Thus in Jordan's *Creation* (1611) we find *anodhans y* 'from them' for an older *anodhe*.[81] This would give an additional reason for the confusion.

2nd form. *ŷ*.   *medhons ŷ* (often written *medh an jŷ*) 'said they'.

3rd form, *'s*.   *mî a's agor* 'I will open them'.

4th form, *-ns, -e*.   *dhodhans* 'to them'; *gensans* or *genjans* 'with them'. The form in *-e* is older (*dhethe, ganse*, etc.), but became obsolete by the middle of the seventeenth century.

It will have been seen:

1. That the first and second persons singular are the only ones which possess the four separate forms complete.

2. That the second form of all but these two persons is usually the same as the first form.

3. That the third form is not much used in later Cornish except for the same two persons.

---

81 {The older form should be *anedhe, anedha*.}

It may also be noted that though the full and emphatic pronunciation of *hŷ, nŷ, whŷ*, and *jŷ*) is that of the English words *high, nigh,
why*, and the first part of *jibe*, when, as is often the case, there is no
emphasis of any sort on them, the same thing happens to them as
commonly happens in rapid speech in English to the word *my*, and
the *y* ceases to have the sound of *i* English, but has the sound of a
short (not obscure) *e* English. Thus in the common Cornish 'Thank
you', *mêr 'ras dhô whŷ*, which is sounded as one word, *merásdhawhy*,
the *y* has the short sound which the same letter usually has at the
end of a word. But it might happen otherwise. Thus the following
sentences are within the experience of most of us at the end of some
simple commercial transaction:

Customer (carelessly, having received the article and paid the
money): "Thank you."

Shopkeeper (in a half-reproving tone): "Thank *you*, sir."

In Cornish the customer would say "*Merásdhawhy*," in the
ordinary tone, but the shopkeeper might answer "*Merasdha whŷ,
sira*," and would sound the pronoun like the English word *why*,
unless, being a good Cornish speaker, he preferred to say "*Mêr 'ras
dhô'gas honan*" ('Thanks to yourself').

The same principle applies to *hŷ, nŷ*, and *an jŷ*, but less with the
last, which is generally treated as a dissyllable with the accent on
the last syllable.

2.7.2. The possessive pronouns.

2.7.2.1. *FIRST PERSON SINGULAR.* English 'my'.

ow, governing the third state.

When the initial of the noun has no third state, *ow* governs the
first state:

ow thâs 'my father'; *ow gwlas* 'my country'.

After a preposition ending in a vowel, after *en* 'in', changed to *e*,
or after the conjunction *ha* 'and', 'my' is generally represented by
'm, which governs the first state:

dhô'm tâs 'to my father'; *ha'm tâs* 'and my father'.

e'm corf 'in my body'.

Sometimes in these cases the preposition or conjunction is combined with *ow*. This is especially common in Jordan's play of *The Creation*. The initial, if possible, is then in the third state:

me haw mab 'I and my son'; *thow thas* 'to my father'.

2.7.2.2. *SECOND PERSON SINGULAR.* English 'thy'.

dha (older form *dhe, dhy*), governing the second state:

dha dâs 'thy father'.

After a preposition ending in a vowel, after *en*, or after *ha*, 'thy' is represented by *'th*, generally governing the second state, but sometimes, when the initial following it is *d-*, the fourth.

dhô'th dâs 'to thy father'; *ha'th dâs* 'and thy father'.

e'th gorf 'in thy body'; *a'th trôk* (RD 1730) 'from thy evil'.

Very often these mutations were not written in the Dramas. In later Cornish this form was not always used, but one often finds *dhô dha, ha dha, en dha*, etc. instead.

2.7.2.3. *THIRD PERSON SINGULAR, MASCULINE.* English 'his'.

e (older form *y*), governing the second state.

This, altered to *y*, coalesces with a preposition ending in a vowel, forming a diphthong, which is written with an apostrophe between the two vowels. It still governs the second state:

e dâs 'his father'; *dhô'y* (pronounced *dhoy*) *dâs* 'to his father'; *ha'y dâs* 'and his father'.

2.7.2.4. *THIRD PERSON SINGULAR, FEMININE.* English 'her'.

î, governing the third state, or when there is no third state, the first. It coalesces with prepositions ending in a vowel and with *ha* in the same way as the masculine:

î thâs 'her father'; *î gwlas* 'her country'; *ha'i thâs*, 'and her father'.

In the earlier MSS both these possessive pronouns were written *y*, the only distinction being in the initial mutation which followed. In the later MSS *î* is often written *e*.

2.7.2.5. *FIRST PERSON PLURAL.* English 'our'.

agan, governing the first state:

agan tâs 'our father'.

2.7.2.6. *SECOND PERSON PLURAL.* English 'your'.

agas, governing the first state:

agas tâs 'your father'.

2.7.2.7. *THIRD PERSON PLURAL.* English 'their'.

aga, governing the third, or failing that, the first state:

aga thâs 'their father'; *aga gwlas* 'their country'.

When preceded by a preposition ending in a vowel or by *ha*, the three plural possessive pronouns lose their initial *a-*:

dho'gas, ha'gan, etc.

The *a* of the last syllable of *agan, agas, aga* is obscure, and is often found represented by *e, o,* or *u* in the MSS. Even when not preceded by a vowel these words are often found as *gan, gas, ga* (*gun, gen, gon, gus, guz, ges, go*).

When a pronoun is the object of a verb in the infinitive or of a verb formed with the auxiliary verbs *gwîl* 'to do', *menny* 'to will', etc. and an infinitive, the pronoun-object is represented by the possessive pronoun preceding and governing (as to initial mutation) this infinitive:

ev a wrîg ow tholla 'he did deceive me'.

mî a vedn e grejy 'I will believe it'.

mî a wrîg agas danvon 'I did send you'.

The reason of this is that in Cornish, as in the other Celtic languages, the infinitive is counted as a verbal noun, signifying *the act of doing.* This conception of the infinitive explains many Celtic constructions. The literal force of the above examples would be 'he did (or made) the deceiving of me', 'I will the believing of it', 'I did the sending of you'. Similarly, when the object is a noun, it really follows the infinitive as an appositional genitive.

Frequently the second form of the corresponding personal pronoun follows a noun preceded by a possessive pronoun. This ought to be for emphasis, and, when it is so, the sound of the personal pronoun would be its full sound; but it is frequently merely redundant, and then it is enclitic, forming as it were an unaccented additional syllable tacked on to the noun:

> *agan Tâs ny* 'Our Father' (nearly *'gun Tázny*).
> *dhô'm brodar vî,* 'to my brother'.
> *agas levar why,* 'your book'.
> *herlya yu 'gan gwary ny,* 'hurling is our sport'.

The last sentence is a good example of possible pronunciations. If it is an independent statement, the phrase emphasis being on *hurling* and *sport,* it would be accented *hérlya yugan guáryny.* If, however, we wish to say that hurling is *our* sport but football is *yours* (*herlya yu 'gan gwary nŷ, mes pella-drôs yu 'gas gwary whŷ*), the second phrase-emphasis would be on *nŷ* and *whŷ,* and they would be sounded as the English words *nigh* and *why.* {[nɔɪ], [ʍɔɪ].}

Sometimes the personal pronoun as a genitive following the noun, with or without the preposition *a* 'of', was used instead of a possessive pronoun, but in this case it was probably not enclitic. Thus in a letter in verse by John Boson, in the Gwavas MS, dated 1710, we find:

> *Ma goz screfa compaz, den fir o* (for *a*) *vî* 'your writing is correct, my wise man', or, 'wise man of me'.

And in a song by John Tonkin of St Just in the same MS, the probable date of which is about 1700, we find:

An Prounter ni ez en Plew East 'our parson who is in the parish of
St Just'.

Or perhaps more correctly in a copy of one verse of this song in
the Borlase MS:

Prounter nei (ez) en pleu Est,

for the article *an* before a noun followed by an appositional genitive
seems incorrect, though one finds in the earliest known version of the
Lord's Prayer, given in John Davies's Welsh translation of Robert
Parsons' *Booke of Christian Exercise* (1632), *An Tas ni*, though this may
be a mistake for *agan*. In the song quoted above one finds also:

Dewe reffa sowia an eglez ni, Ha an prounterian da eze et an gy 'God
save our churches and the good parsons that are in them'.

And in Boson's version of the Commandments we find *gwitha gerrio
ve* for 'keep my commandments'.

2.7.3. Pronominal prepositions.

The prepositional form of the pronouns may be applied to
almost any preposition, but there are a certain number of common
cases in which the prepositions are modified by the composition,
vowels being altered or letters being inserted between the
preposition and this fragmentary pronoun, either for euphony or as
survivals of archaic forms of the preposition or pronoun. The most
usual of these modified forms occur in the composition of the
prepositions *a* 'of' or 'from', *dre* 'through', *gans* 'with', *dhŏrt* (earlier
dheworth and *adheworth*, Welsh *oddiwrth*) 'from', *orth* (or *worth*) 'at, to',
rag 'for', *dhô* 'to', *war* 'upon', *en* or *idn* 'in'.

ahanav 'from me'.	*dredhov* 'through me'.
ahanas 'from thee'.	*dredhos* 'through thee'.
anodho 'from him'.	*dredho* 'through him'.
anedhi 'from her'.	*dredhi* 'through her'.
ahanan 'from us'.	*dredhon* 'through us'.
ahanough 'from you'.	*dredhough* 'through you'.
anodhans 'from them'.	*dredhans* 'through them'.

Other instances are:

genev	*dhortam*	*orthev*	*ragov*	*dhem*	*warnav*[82]
genes	*dhortas*	*orthes*	*ragos*	*dhes*	*warnas*
ganso	*dhorto*	*orto*	*ragdho*[83]	*dhodho*	*warnodho*
gensi	*dhorti*	*orti*	*ragdhi*[83]	*dhedhi*	*warnedhi*
genen	*dhorten*	*orthen*	*ragon*	*dhen*	*warnan*
genough	*dhortough*	*orthough*	*ragough*	*dheugh*	*warnough*
gensans	*dhortans*	*ortans*	*ragdhans*[83]	*dhodhans*	*warnodhans*

and

ennov	or	*idnov*	or	*ettov*
ennos	or	*idnos*	or	*ettos*
enno	or	*idno*	or	*etto*
enni	or	*idni*	or	*etti*
ennon	or	*idnon*	or	*etton*
ennough	or	*idnough*	or	*ettough*
ennans	or	*idnans*	or	*ettans.*

There are many various spellings of these words in the manuscripts, and especially there is great uncertainty as to the vowel which precedes the pronominal suffix. As the accent is always on the preposition, the vowel of the pronoun is usually obscure, and there is not so very much difference of sound in the last syllables of *dredhov*, *genev*, and *warnav*, but still there is a slight difference, and there must have been even more in early days.

The older form of the third person plural ended in -*e* or -*a*, *anedha*, *dredha*, *ganse*, *orte*, *ragdha*, *dhedhe*, *warnedhe*, *ynna*; but this form became obsolete by the middle of the seventeenth century, and these pronominal prepositions were assimilated to the third person plural of verbs. In this the Cornish began by resembling Breton and ended by approaching more nearly to Welsh.

---

82 {The final segment of *ahanav*, *dredhov*, *genev*, *orthev*, *ragov*, *warnav*, and *ennov*, if it was pronounced at all, was most probably voiceless.}

83 {The forms should be *ragtho*, *ragthi*, *ragthans*.}

The pronominal preposition form of *dhô* has variants for the first and second persons singular and first person plural, *dhemmo* 'to me', *dheso, dheso dî* 'to thee', and *dhenny* 'to us'. These are formed by the addition of the personal pronoun in a fuller form. In the cases of the other prepositions it is not uncommon to add the personal pronouns at the end of the pronominal compound, forming thereby a single word with the accent on the last syllable. Thus:

genev vî 'with me', pronounced *genavî*.

genough whŷ 'with you', pronounced *genowhŷ*.

ragon nŷ 'for us', pronounced *ragonŷ*.

In later Cornish these pronominal prepositions compounds were often neglected, and the prepositions were often used with the second form of the personal pronoun, but this was only a corrupt following of English, not to be imitated.

2.7.4. The relative pronoun.

2.7.4.1. A simple relative, 'who' or 'which', whether in the nominative or accusative, is represented most frequently by the particle *a*, governing the second state of the verb. Thus:

An Tâs a wrîg Nev 'the Father who made heaven'.

An Nev a wrîg an Tâs e 'the Heaven which the Father made'.

If the verb following the relative begins with a vowel, *a* is often omitted. Thus:

Ow thîs es genev 'my people who are with me'.

If the relative sentence is negative, *nî* 'not' coalesces with *a*, producing *na*. Thus:

En le na vê dên bisqweth 'in a place in which man never was'.

When the relative is the object of the verb, or is preceded in English by a preposition, a redundant personal pronoun is added after the verb, with or without a combined preposition, but a preposition is never placed before the relative particle *a* itself. Thus:

An dên a dhanvonas Dew e 'the man whom God sent' (lit. 'whom God sent him').

An dên a vê an gêr cowses ganso 'the man by whom the word was spoken' (lit. 'whom the word was spoken by him').

2.7.4.2. *Neb* (earlier *nep*, and in late Cornish sometimes *leb*) is also used as a relative, with similar construction to that of *a* in the objective or prepositional condition. Properly it includes the antecedent, and should mean 'he who', 'those who', 'that which', 'those whom', etc., but it is commonly used as a simple relative, especially in late Cornish. Thus:

Agan Tâs ny neb es en Nêv 'Our Father who art in heaven', in one of the many extant versions of the Lord's Prayer. Another version is *Agan Tâs ny leb es en Nêv*.

Dhe [*tî*] *nep yu ioy ow holon* 'thou who art the joy of my heart' (RD 456).

An dên neb na'n gwrîg 'the man who did not do it'.

Neb yu moyha 'he who is greatest'.

An dên neb Dew a wrîg e dhanvon 'the man whom God did send'.

An dên neb an gêr a vê cowses ganso 'the man by whom the word was spoken'.

Neb mî e wrîg ragdho 'for whom I did it' (lit. 'whom I did it for him').

But, unlike *a*, *neb* can have a preposition before it on occasions, with or without the redundant pronoun. Thus:

Chŷ en neb na vê dên vîth (*enno*) 'a house in which no man was'.

2.7.5. The demonstrative pronoun.

2.7.5.1. Absolute. *Hem, hebma* (originally *hemma*) 'this' masculine; *hom, hobma* (*homma*) feminine.

Hen, hedna (originally *henna*) 'that' masculine; *hon, hodna* (*honna*) feminine.

An remma (= *an re-ma*) is used also for the plural 'these', *an renna* for 'those'.

2.7.5.2. In agreement. *An—ma* 'this', 'these', e.g. *an bês-ma* 'this world'.

An—na 'that', 'those', e.g. *an dên-na* 'that man'.

The noun is placed between *an* and *ma* or *na*, the latter being joined to it by a hyphen. In some cases when the noun ends in a vowel the *m* of *ma* is doubled, and the noun and demonstrative are written as one word:

> *an dremma* 'this town' (for *an dre-ma*); *an chymma* 'this house' (for *an chŷ-ma*); *alemma* 'hence' (for *a le-ma*) 'from this place'.

The same applies to the *n* of *na*. When the noun is preceded by a preposition, *an* is omitted: *war venedh-ma* 'on this mountain' not *war an menedh-ma. {No instance of this usage has been found.}

For emphasis, *keth* 'same' is added after *an*: *an keth den-ma* 'this very man', 'this same man'.

In very late Cornish, *hebma, hobma, hedna, hodna* were often corrupted into *hebba, hobba, hedda, hodda*.

In the *Life of St Meriasek*, *helma* and *holma* are used for 'this', and it is easy to imagine *helna* and *holna* for 'that'. The explanation suggested in Dr Whitley Stokes's note is "*helma = hen lemma*, this in this place". Cf. "this here" and "that there" of vulgar English.

2.7.6. The interrogative pronouns.

Pyu or *pyua* (written also *pu, piwa, pew*) 'who?' A contraction of *pe yu* 'who is?' or *pe yu a* 'who is it who?'

Pa 'what?'

Pandra (i.e. *pa an dra* 'what the thing') 'what?' e.g. *pandra vednough why gwîl* 'what will you do?'

Panin (i.e. *pa an in* 'which the one') 'whether of them?'

Penîl (i.e. *pa nîl* 'which of the two') 'which one?'

2.7.7. The indefinite pronouns.

Nep, neb, 'some or any'.

Neppeth 'somewhat' (*neb peth* 'some thing') 'anything'.

Nebin (*neb idn*) 'some one'.

Nebas 'somewhat', 'a little', 'a few'; also used to signify 'little', 'few', or 'hardly any'.

Pyupennak (sometimes *bennak*) 'whoever'.

Pa (or *pandra*) *pennak* 'whatever'.

Papennak ŏl 'whatsoever'.[84]

Ketep 'every'.

Kenifer 'each'; *kenifer ŏl* 'every one', 'as many as there are'. Lhuyd gives a very emphatic form, *peb kenifer ŏnen*, which would mean 'every single one'.

Pub or *peb* 'all', 'every'. Placed before the noun. *Pub dên* 'every man'.

Ŏl (or *ŭl*) 'all'. Placed before or after the noun. When placed before the noun the latter is preceded by *an*: *ŏl an dîs* 'all the people'.

Bîth or *vîth* 'any'; *travîth* 'anything'; *dên vîth* 'any man'. With negatives it signifies 'at all'; *ni wôr dên vîth* 'no man at all knoweth'; *nynsyw travîth* 'there is nothing at all'.

Mens (earlier *myns*) 'all', 'whatever'; *ŏl mens o* 'all that there was'; *cowsens dên mens a vedn* 'let a man say all that he will'. It is generally used as a relative combined with the antecedent 'all', but is also used without an expressed verb to follow it, though in such case probably the verb substantive is understood.

Kemmes, kebmes 'as many as', 'whosoever'; *kemmes a wrîg bodh ow Thâs* 'as many as have done the will of my Father'.

Nîl or *an nîl* and *e gîla* (formerly *nyl* and *y gyle*) signify 'the one' and 'the other'. *Nîl*, originally *an ail* 'the second', a word which, except in this case, has dropped out of Cornish in favour of *secund* and *nessa* (= 'the next'), though it remains in Welsh and Breton, signifies 'one of two'; *e gîla* (once *y gyle* or *y gele*) literally signifies 'his fellow', from *e* 'his' and *kila* (formerly *kyle*) 'fellow', 'companion'. Thus:

---

84 {Also *pennag ol dra*.}

Voz [*bes*] *an Frenkock feen parrez tho* [*dhô*] *cummeraz telhar wara niel* [*war an nîl*] *ha an sousenack nobla war e gilla* 'for the fine French seems to take place upon the one [i.e. on Breton] and the nobler English on the other [i.e. Cornish]' (from *Nebbaz Gerriau dro tho Camoack* by John Boson, ca. 1700).

The same expression occurs in the early Dramas, e.g. *an nyl a delle pymp cans, ha hanter cans y gyle* 'the one owed five hundred and half a hundred the other'.

Aral 'other', plural *erel*, is sometimes used for *e gila*. It is the usual word for 'other' or 'another': *dên aral* 'another man'.

Another form occasionally used in Cornish for either gender, though in Breton it is only used for the regular feminine of *e gila* (*e gile*) is *eben*, older form *yben*:

Heys Crist a gemeras a'n neyll lêf bys yn yben (*Poem of Passion* 178) 'the length of Christ they took from one hand to the other'.

Ken is also used for another:

Dhe ken pow 'to another country'; *yn ken lyu* 'in another colour'.

Nanîl 'neither one', 'neither of two'; it is *nîl* with the negative, and is sometimes written *noniel*. Boson uses it in a peculiar way:

Nanagu [*na nag yu*] *an pobel coth tho bose skoothez war noniel* 'nor are the old people to be depended upon neither'.

Panîl 'which of two' (see above) is compounded with *pa* 'which' and *nîl*.

Lîas 'many' is used, like a numeral, with a substantive in the singular: *lîas dôrn* 'many hands'.

Re 'some' (see §2.7.5), 'ones', 'things', is used also as a noun: *an re marow* 'the dead'; *an re bîan* 'the little ones'; *ma re a lavar* 'there are some who say'. Cf. Welsh *rhai*; Breton *re*.

Radn or *ran* 'part' is also used in the sense of 'some'.

Honan 'self' is used with possessive pronouns as in English: *ow honan* 'myself'; *dha honan* 'thyself', etc.

2.8. The verb in general

2.8.1. The nucleus of a Cornish verb is its root. This is used without any variation or addition for the third person singular of the present tense, and for the second person singular of the imperative. Other parts of the verb are formed on this root in three ways:

2.8.1.1. By the inflected form, that is to say by the addition of certain syllables indicating person, tense, etc., with or without a modification of the root vowel. In older Cornish the word thus formed indicated *person* as well as *tense* without the addition of a pronoun, though if emphasis on the subject was intended the pronoun was used before or after it. In later Cornish the pronoun was almost always added after the verb, and as the latter word often ended with the same consonant as the former began with, the final consonant of the verb was often, but incorrectly, omitted in writing, as it was in sound. Thus:

> Root *car* 'love'; first pers. sing, pres., *carav* 'I love', with pronoun *carav vî*, pronounced and often written *cara vî*; plural *caron* 'we love', *caron nŷ*, often written *caro nŷ*.

The inflected form is common in early Cornish, but in the later stages of the language it is hardly ever used, except *in negative, interrogative, and dependent sentences*, and in certain tenses of the verb *to be*. Even when it is used, it is more frequently the inflected form of an auxiliary verb with the infinitive or participle of the main verb.

2.8.1.2. By the impersonal form, as the Breton grammarians call it. This has inflections of tense but not of person, the latter being indicated by the personal pronouns, placed before the verb, which, being immediately preceded by the particle *a*, has its initial in the second state. This verb is the third person singular of the required tense. Thus:

Root *car*, third pers. sing, past, *caras*.

Impersonal form. *Mî a garas, tî a garas, ev a garas*, etc.

This form is frequently used in early and late Cornish for a direct affirmative sentence, beginning straight off with its nominative, or preceded only by 'and' or 'but', etc.; but not so frequently in late Cornish, as the impersonal form of an auxiliary verb, with the infinitive of the main verb.

2.8.1.3. By the auxiliary form, either inflected or impersonal, with the infinitive or a participle of the main verb. The auxiliaries are:

Gîl or *gwîl* (older forms *gruthil, guthil*, etc.) 'to do'.

Menny 'to wish', 'to will'.

Gally 'to be able'.

Gŏthvos 'to know'.

Bos 'to be'.

2.8.1.3.1. *Gwîl* is used to form several tenses, and is used (1) in its impersonal form in principal affirmative sentences, (2) in its inflected form in negative, interrogative, or dependent sentences, with the infinitive of the main verb, more frequently than any other form, for the present, preterite, conditional, and imperative. Its use is similar to that of 'do', in the Cornish manner of speaking English. Thus:

Mî a wra cara 'I love', lit. 'I do love'.

Tî a wrîg cara 'thou didst love'.

In these two sentences, *wra* and *wrîg* are proclitics, unaccented syllables joined in sound to the word which follows.

Mar qwressa an dên cara 'if the man would love'.

Gwra cara 'love thou' ('do thou love'); *gwreugh why cara* 'love ye'.

Gwrens e bos 'let him be'.

2.8.1.3.2. *Menny* is used as an auxiliary of the future and conditional. In principal affirmative sentences it is usually in its impersonal form, in negative, interrogative, or dependent sentences always in its inflected form. Thus:

Mî a vedn môs 'I will go'.

Mî a venja môs 'I would go'.

A vednough why môs? 'will you go?'

2.8.1.3.3. *Gally* is used, chiefly in the present and past, for 'can' and 'could', but also for 'may' and 'might'. {See §2.9.3.2.} Thus:

Mî a el môs 'I can go', 'I may go'.

Mî a alja môs 'I could go', 'I might go'.

2.8.1.3.4. *Gŏdhwos* in the present is sometimes used for 'can'. Thus:

Mî ôr môs 'I can go' (lit. 'I know [how] to go').

These follow the same rule as the others with regard to the use of their impersonal and inflected forms.

2.8.1.3.5. *Bos* 'to be' as an auxiliary, is used, much as in English, with the present or past participle, to form the continuous present, the continuous past, and the passive. It is generally used in the inflected form in its present and imperfect in any sort of sentence, but in principal affirmative sentences it is generally used in the impersonal form for other tenses. It can also be used with *gwîl* or *menny* and *gally* as an auxiliary to it, while it is itself an auxiliary to another verb, but this is only what is done in English with such expressions as 'can be', 'will be', 'shall be', etc.

The use of the various forms of the verb will be found more fully explained in the chapter on the construction of sentences.

When the auxiliaries *gwîl* and *gally* are used to form a passive, it is sometimes the auxiliary that takes the passive form. Thus:

> *Mar ny **wrer** y wythe* 'if he be not guarded' (RD 341), *mar **keller** y wythe* 'if he can be kept' (PC 3058).

But in modern Cornish this would be more likely to be formed with a double auxiliary:

> *Mar ni **wrello** bos gwithes.*
> *Mar **callo** bos gwithes.*

2.8.2. The tenses of the inflected verb.

The inflected verb is reducible to five tenses, with an imperative, two participles, and a verbal noun or infinitive. These are all formed on the root by the addition of terminations, and sometimes by a modification of the root vowel (indicated below by ~).

The tenses and their terminations are:

2.8.2.1. *PRESENT OR FUTURE.*

	Singular.	Plural.
1.	~av[85] or ~am.	~on [earlier ~en].
2.	~eth or ~es.	~ough.
3.	root alone.	~ons or ~ans.

2.8.2.2. *IMPERFECT OR SECONDARY PRESENT.*

	Singular.	Plural.
1.	~en.	~en.
2.	~es.	~eugh.
3.	~a.	~ens.

2.8.2.3. *PRETERITE.*

	Singular.	Plural.
1.	~ýs.	~son [earlier ~sen].
2.	~ses.	~sough.
3.	~as.	~sons or ~sans.

---

85 {When unstressed, ~av is probably ~af or ~a'.}

Re prefixed to this tense turned it into a preterperfect in middle Cornish, but in the later form *re* is only used for the optative.[86]

2.8.2.4. THE PLUPERFECT OR SECONDARY PERFECT. Largely used in late Cornish as a Conditional.

	Singular.	Plural.
1.	~*sen* (or ~*jen*).	~*sen* (or ~*jen*).
2.	~*ses* (or ~*jes*)	~*seugh* (or ~*jeugh*).
3.	~*sa* (or ~*ja*).	~*sens* (or ~*jens*).

2.8.2.5. THE SUBJUNCTIVE PRESENT.

	Singular.	Plural.
1.	~*ev*.	~*en*.
2.	~*y*.	~*eugh*
3.	~*o*.	~*ens* or ~*ons*.

2.8.2.6. THE SECOND FUTURE. An extra tense to some verbs. Found in the early MSS in the impersonal form as a simple future.

	Singular.	Plural.
1.	~*fym*, ~*vym*, ~*vyv*.	~*fon*, ~*von*.
2.	~*fyth*, ~*vyth*.	~*fough*, ~*vough*.
3.	~*iv*, ~*fyth*, ~*vyth*, ~*vo*.	~*fyns*, ~*vyns*, ~*vons*.

2.8.2.7. THE IMPERATIVE.

	Singular.	Plural.
1.	wanting.	~*en*.
2.	root alone.	~*eugh*.
3.	~*ens* or ~*es*.	~*ens*.

---

86 There is, however, some slight confusion in late Cornish MSS between this use of *re*, and the auxiliary form with *wrig*. The difference of sound in cases of verbs beginning with *g-* or *c-* would be very slight.

The Present Participle is formed by prefixing *ow* to the infinitive, the initial of which, if mutable in that manner, is changed to its fourth state. If a present participle governs a pronoun object, the latter in its possessive form immediately precedes (and governs as to initial) the infinitive, and is itself preceded by the preposition *worth*. In late Cornish *ow* was often written *a* or *o*.

Another participial form, common in Breton and occasionally found in Cornish, has been already mentioned in §2.3.2. This is made by placing the preposition *yn*, *en*, *in*, and the indefinite article *idn*, *un*, before the infinitive or verbal noun. Its use is chiefly adverbial. Thus, in the *Poem of the Passion* we find, *yn un scolchye* 'skulking'; *yn un garme* 'crying out'; *yn un fystyne* 'hurrying'.

The Infinitive or Verbal Noun is formed by adding *-a*, *-ya*, *-y*, *-as* or *-es*, *-al* or *-el*, to the root. In some verbs the root itself, without any addition, is the verbal noun.

The Past or Passive Participle is formed by adding *-es* to the root, with or without modification of the root vowel.

The Passive termination is *-er* for the present and *-es* for the preterite, but in Modern Cornish the Passive is almost always formed after the English model by the auxiliary verb *bos* 'to be' with the past participle.

The terminations *-ma* and *-ta* are often added to the first and second persons singular of various tenses in interrogative and subjunctive sentences, and in the case of the first person even in ordinary narration. Norris maintains that these are not forms of *mî* and *tî*, but only an *-a* suffixed to the verb termination, which in the first person reverts to a primary *-m* for *-v*, and in the second person reassumes a dropped *-t*. This theory is rather supported by our finding *-a* occasionally added to the third persons of tenses of the verb 'to be', but *-va* is also found. Whether this is the explanation or not, we find such forms as:

Pandra venta? 'what wilt thou?'	*Mar menta* 'if thou wilt'
A wresta? 'dost thou?'	*Pandra wrama?* 'what shall I do?'

There are some few differences between the inflected verb of the earlier MSS and that of modern Cornish, and among other changes the lighter termination *-en* or *-yn* of the first person plural, and *-ens* or *-yns* of the third person plural, in some cases had changed by Lhuyd's time to *-on* or *-an*, and *-ons* or *-ans*, but probably really the vowel is obscure {[ə]}. There was also considerable uncertainty about the modification of the vowel. Even in the early MSS the change of vowel is rather vague, but the general rule seems to have been that when the termination has a thin vowel (*e*, *i*, or *y*), a broad root vowel (*a*, *o*, *u*) is changed to a thin vowel, usually in late Cornish to *e* (cf. the Gaelic rule of *leathan le leathan agus caol le caol* 'broad with broad and thin with thin'). But this is by no means universal, and in some tenses, as in the imperfect and pluperfect, is not found at all.

There is some confusion in modern Cornish about the subjunctive or fifth tense. Norris considers that Lhuyd's subjunctive is really, except for the third person singular, the imperfect or second tense of the older MSS. But it seems to be more like a form of the present indicative, except in the third person singular, which is the old subjunctive. Lhuyd's change of the first person singular to *-am* instead of *-av* is not uncommon in certain verbs of late Cornish, when this tense is used in a subjunctive clause.

The inflected verb at the beginning of a sentence is often preceded in Middle Cornish by the verbal particle *y* (or before a vowel *yth*), which does not mean anything in particular. *Y* causes the third state in verbs whose radical is *p-*, *c-*, *t-*, and the fourth state in those whose radical is *d-*, and changes *gw-* to *wh-*.[87] In late Cornish it is rarely used except with the present of *môs* 'to go', and (in its apocopated form *th* or as *ăth*) with the present and imperfect of *bos* 'to be'.

---

87 {This is now called the Mixed Mutation.}

A reflexive verb may be formed from any transitive verb by prefixing *om-* (older forms *ym-*, as in Welsh, and *em-*, as in Breton), changing the initial to the second state.

cregy 'to hang'	*ŏmgregy* 'to hang oneself'.
brêsy 'to judge'	*ŏmvrêsy* 'to judge oneself'.
disqwedhas 'to show'	*ŏmdhisqwedhas* 'to show oneself'.
gweras 'to help'	*ŏmweras* 'to help oneself'.

Sometimes the prefix gives a mutual rather than a reflexive sense.

ŏmsewa 'to follow one another'.

ŏmladha 'to fight, contend' (cf. French *se battre*).

2.9. The auxiliary verbs

2.9.1. *Bos* 'to be'.

The verb 'to be' in Cornish, as in other Aryan languages, is made up of more than one verb. In Cornish it may be divided in two parts. The first of these consists of two tenses, a present and an imperfect, the second of the usual five tenses, the imperative and the infinitive.

The first division, by means of reduplications and additions, takes a variety of forms in the early literature, and there is a considerable uncertainty about the exact force of these forms. Some of them evidently mean little more than elongations and contractions for the sake of metre. The second division is formed with greater regularity on a root *b-*, changing under certain conditions to *v-* (often written *f-*) and *p-*.

2.9.1.1. *FIRST DIVISION.*

2.9.1.1.1. PRESENT TENSE. 'I am'.[88]

Sing. 1. *ov* (old form *of*), *ăthov, thov, oma, ăthoma, thoma.*

       2. *os, ăthos, thos, osta, ăthosta, thosta.*

       3. *yu, ăthyu, thyu, yua, ăthyua, thyua.*

Plur. 1. *on, ăthon, than.*

       2. *ough, ăthough, though.*

       3. *ens, ăthens, thens.*

---

88 {In the present there is a functional difference between *of, os, yu, yma,* etc. and *esof, esos, us, usy,* etc. Similarly in the imperfect there is a

There is little or no difference of meaning in these forms. The lengthened form *ăthov*, or its apocopated *thov*, is generally found at the beginning of an assertion. *Oma, osta, yua* and their lengthened forms are used interrogatively or after certain conjunctions. In the early literature the lengthened forms were written *ythof, assof, ossof, esof,* and even, with double lengthening, *ythesaf, ythesef, ythesof.* The first vowel is probably the obscure vowel (as *u* in *until*) {[ɔ]}, and the stress accent is on the syllable that follows the verbal prefix, so that even the consonant of the prefix is a little uncertain. Williams makes it *dh*, but *th* seems more probable. In late Cornish the vowel of the prefix was usually dropped. The personal pronouns are generally added after this tense, so that it practically becomes:

Thov vî, thos dî, yu ev (or *ev yu*), *thon ny, though why, thens y* (pronounced *thenjŷ*).

Occasionally the impersonal form of this verb is used: *mî yu, tî yu, ev yu, nŷ yu, whŷ yu, ŷ yu.* The negative is formed by adding *nyns* to the short form, *nynsov* or *nynsoma, nynsos* or *nynsosta, nynsyu,* etc. Similarly this tense may be compounded with *mar* 'if', *ken* 'though', *may* 'that', into *marsov, kensov, maythov.* The *-s-*, which is sometimes altered to *-th-*, is probably the *th* of the verbal prefix.

2.9.1.1.1.1. There are two other forms of the third person present, *ema* (or *ma*), plural *emons* (or *mons*), and *es* (older *us*), or *esy* or *ejy* (older *usy, ugy*).

2.9.1.1.1.1.1. *ema, ma, emons, mons* must, according to Lhuyd, always be used narratively, never negatively, interrogatively (except after *ple* 'where'), or with relatives. They must always precede their subject. Thus:

Ema'n levar en ow chŷ 'the book is in my house'.

Ema levar en ow chŷ 'there is a book in my house'.

---

functional difference between *en, es, o,* etc. and *esen, eses, esa,* etc. (§2.9.1.1.2). In Late Cornish the difference was not always observed.}

Nynsyw levar en ow chŷ 'there is not a book in my house'.
Ple yu'n levar? Ple ma'n levar? 'where is the book?'
'Yu'n levar ŭbma? 'is the book here?'

2.9.1.1.1.1.2. *emons* is only used when the pronoun 'they' is the subject. When a noun is the subject, whether singular or plural, a singular verb is used.

Emons ŷ en ow chŷ 'they are in my house'.
Ema'n levrow en ow chŷ 'the books are in my house'.

2.9.1.1.1.1.3. *es, esy, ejy* are chiefly used with relatives or interrogatively in the sense of 'is there', 'is there not'.

An levar es en ow chŷ 'the book which is in my house' (in this case *es = a es* 'which is').

'Es levar en ow chŷ? 'Is there a book in my house?'

Nag es levar en ow chŷ? 'Is there not a book in my house?'

In the first of these two interrogations the interrogative particle *a* coalesces with *es*, in the second *nag = ni ag*, *ag* being the same interrogative particle, with a -*g* added before a vowel.

The ordinary interrogative of this tense is merely the form *'oma, 'osta, 'yua, 'on nŷ, 'ough whŷ, 'ens ŷ* (pronounced *enjŷ*), which should be preceded by an apostrophe to show that the interrogative particle *a* is elided. The negative interrogative is the same preceded by *nag*.

The difference between the use of *ema, yu,* and *es* is not quite so distinct in Cornish as between the corresponding *y mae, yw,* and *oes* in Welsh, but if there is any difference in meaning between *ema* and *yu*, it is that *ema* has more often the sense of 'there is', 'it is', and *yu* more commonly that of 'is' only; also *yu* can be used interrogatively and negatively, while *ema*, except after *ple* 'where' should not be used interrogatively, and is never used negatively at all. Its negative and interrogative equivalent is *es*.

2.9.1.1.2. IMPERFECT TENSE. 'I was'.

Old form: Singular.	Plural.
1. *esen, ythesen, en.*	1. *esen, ythesen.*
2. *eses, ytheses, es.*	2. *eseugh, ytheseugh.*
3. *esa, ytheses.*	3. *esens, ythesens.*

Late form: Singular.	Plural.
1. *erav, eram, erama, therav, theram.*	1. *eron, theron.*
2. *eras, erasta, theras.*	2. *erough, therough.*
3. *era, thera.*	3. *erons, therons.*

The change from *s* to *r* in this tense, and the assimilation of the inflections to the present, does not occur in the written language until the middle of the seventeenth century. The personal pronouns were always used with this tense in its late form, and the final consonants of the personal inflections generally coalesced with the pronouns, and so were omitted in writing, thus *therav vî, theron nŷ, therough whŷ*, were written, though incorrectly, *thera vî, thera nŷ, thero whŷ*.

An alternative third person singular is *o*. It is used with relatives as an equivalent of *a o* 'who was', and with negatives as *nynso* 'there was not'. It is in fact the past equivalent of *es*, but it is often used in a simple assertion also. The simple interrogative is *'erama* 'was I?', the negative interrogative is *nag erama* 'was I not?', and the simple negative *nynseram* 'I was not'.

2.9.1.2. *SECOND DIVISION.*

INFINITIVE. *bos* 'to be'; an older form, used chiefly when an extra syllable was required for a verse, *bones*.

2.9.1.2.1. FUTURE TENSE. 'I shall be'.

Singular.	Plural.
1. *bedhav* (older *bydhaf*).	1. *bedhon.*
2. *bedheth* (*bydhith*).	2. *bedhough.*
3. *bedh* (*bydh*).	3. *bedhons* (*bedhens*).

This tense is used more commonly in the impersonal form, *mî a vedh, tî a vedh*, etc. Another common future is *mî a vedn bos*, formed with *menny* 'to will'.

2.9.1.2.2. IMPERFECT OR SECONDARY PRESENT. 'I was being'.

Singular.	Plural.
1. *bedhen, ben.*	1. *bedhen, ben.*
2. *bedhes, bes, besta.*	2. *bedheugh, beugh.*
3. *bedha, be, beva.*	3. *bedhens, bens.*

This tense is used rather as a conditional, 'I should be', or a subjunctive after *pan* 'when', *mar* 'if', etc.

2.9.1.2.3. PRETERITE. 'I was', 'I have been'.

Singular.	Plural.
1. *bêv* (older *buf, buef*).	1. *bên* (older *buen*).
2. *bês* (older *bus, bues*) *besta.*	2. *beugh.*
3. *bê* (older *bue*).	3. *bons.*

This tense is more frequently used in the impersonal, *mî a vê, tî a vê*, etc.

2.9.1.2.4. PLUPERFECT. 'I had been'.

Singular.	Plural.
1. *bîen* (older written *byen*).	1. *bîen* (*byen*).
2. *bîes* (*byes*).	2. *bîeugh* (*byeugh*).
3. *bîa* (*bye*).	3. *bîens* (*byens*).

Lhuyd gives a pluperfect *beazen, beazes*, etc. corresponding with the Welsh *buaswn*, but it does not appear to be used.

2.9.1.2.5. SUBJUNCTIVE. 'I may be'.

Singular.	Plural.
1. *bev* (older *byf, beyf*).	1. *ben.*
2. *by.*	2. *beugh.*
3. *bo.*	3. *bons.*

This and the second {imperfect} tense are not very clearly distinguished.

2.9.1.2.6. IMPERATIVE.

Singular.	Plural.
1. wanting.	1. *bedhon* 'let us be'.
2. *bedh* 'be thou'.	2. *bedhough* 'be ye'.
3. *bedhens* (*bedhes, boes, bes*)	3. *bedhens* 'let them be'.
'let him be'.	

A common variant of the imperative is formed with the auxiliary *gwîl* 'to do'.

Singular.	Plural.
1. wanting.	1. *gwren ny bos.*
2. *gwra bos.*	2. *gwreugh bos.*
3. *gwrens e bos.*	3. *gwrens y bos.*

2.9.2. *Gwîl* (older forms *gruthil, guthil, gul*) 'to do'.

2.9.2.1. PRESENT OR FUTURE TENSE. 'I do', or 'I shall do'.

2.9.2.1.1. INFLECTED.

Singular.	Plural.
1. *gwrav, gwrama.*	1. *gwren, gwron.*
2. *gwreth, gwrês, gwresta.*	2. *gwreugh, gwrough.*
3. *gwra.*	3. *gwrons.*

Gwrama, gwresta, in the second mutation *wrama, wresta*, are used in interrogative and negative sentences, and after *mar* 'if', in the fourth mutation *qwrama, qwresta*. The older form of *gwresta* was *gwreta*. Occasionally in late Cornish a form of this present is found exactly like the imperfect of *bos; therama, thera*, etc. This is probably *wrama, wra*, with the verbal particle *ăth* (*yth*) prefixed. It occurs in cases where it cannot possibly be the imperfect of *bos*. Lhuyd (pp. 246, 253) was rather puzzled by it, but with his usual clearness of sight was able to find out the real facts.

2.9.2.1.2. IMPERSONAL.

Mî a wra, tî a wra, ev a wra, etc.

2.9.2.2. *THE IMPERFECT TENSE.* 'I was doing'.
2.9.2.2.1. INFLECTED.

Singular.	Plural.
1. *gwrellen, gwren.*	1. *gwrellen, gwren.*
2. *gwrelles, gwres.*	2. *gwrelleugh.*
3. *gwrella, gwre.*	3. *gwrellens.*

2.9.2.2.2. IMPERSONAL.

Mî a wrella, tî a wrella, etc.

This tense is seldom used as an auxiliary, and is often confused with the subjunctive.

2.9.2.3. *THE PERFECT TENSE.* 'I did'.
2.9.2.3.1. INFLECTED.

Old form: Singular. Plural.

1. *gwrugaf, gwruge.*	1. *gwrussyn.*
2. *gwrussys.*	2. *gwrussough.*
3. *gwruk.*	3. *gwrussons.*

Later form of old form: Singular. Plural.

1. *gwrîgaf, gwrîga.*	1. *gwressen, gwreithen.*
2. *gwresses.*	2. *gwressough, gwreithough.*
3. *gwrîg.*	3. *gwressons, gwreithons.*

Modern form: Singular. Plural.

1. *gwrîgav vî.*	1. *gwrîgon ny.*
2. *gwrîs, gwrîsta, gwrîges dî.*	2. *gwrîgough why.*
3. *gwrîg, gwrîga, gwrês.*	3. *gwrîgans y.*

The last form seems to have completely superseded the other in late Cornish. It seems to be formed by taking the irregular third person singular as a root, and forming the rest of the persons from it on the analogy of the present tense. Where it is found—and the first person occurs as early as Jordan's Drama of *The Creation* (e.g. *ny wrugaf*, CW 1662)—it is generally written without the final consonants of the verb, which, as in the imperfect tense of the verb 'to be', seem to coalesce with the initials of the pronouns. One finds the forms *rig a vee, rigga vee, rigon ny, rigo why, rig an jy*, these being preceded by adverbs, conjunctions, etc., such as *na, pan*, etc., which put the initial in the second state, and the *w* being almost silent is omitted. The form *wruge* (= *wríga*), occurs in OM 2250, and PC 930, for the first person singular, preceded by *pan* 'when'. The same word occurs for the third person in OM 423, and in the form *wrega* in CW 2216. This is *wríg* with the added *a* (see §2.8.2.7). A form of the third person singular of this tense, *ros* (for *wros*, second state of *gwros*), may possibly be found in the *Ordinalia* and in *St Meriasek*, in the expression, *re Thu am ros* 'by God who made me'. But it is more probably the preterite of *ry* 'to give', as it occurs also in the phrase *re'n arluth dhen beys am ros* 'by the Lord who gave me to the world'. *Wraze* (= *wrês*, cf. Breton *greas*) occurs in Genesis 3:7.

2.9.2.3.2. IMPERSONAL.
  Mî a wríg, tî a wríg, etc.

2.9.2.4. *THE PLUPERFECT OR CONDITIONAL TENSE.* 'I had or would have done'.
  2.9.2.4.1. INFLECTED.

Singular.	Plural.
1. *gwressen* (older *gwrussen*).	1. *gwressen*.
2. *gwresses*.	2. *gwresseugh*.
3. *gwressa*.	3. *gwressens*.

2.9.2.4.2. IMPERSONAL.
  Mî a wressa, tî a wressa, etc.

2.9.2.5. *THE SUBJUNCTIVE.* 'I may do'.

2.9.2.5.1. INFLECTED.

	Singular.		Plural.
1. *gwrellev* (older *gwryllyf*).		1. *gwrellon, gwrellen.*	
2. *gwrelly, gwrelles.*		2. *gwrellough, gwrelleugh.*	
3. *gwrello, gwreffa.*		3. *gwrellens, gwrons.*	

There is rather a confusion of the subjunctive and imperfect, and the two are used rather indiscriminately. The third person plural, *gwrons*, is borrowed from the imperative.

2.9.2.5.2. THE IMPERSONAL.

Mî a wrello, tî a wrello, etc.

Mî a wreffa, tî a wreffa, etc.

2.9.2.6. THE IMPERATIVE.

	Singular.		Plural.
1. wanting.		1. *gwren* 'let us do'.	
2. *gwra* 'do thou'.		2. *gwreugh* 'do ye'.	
3. *gwrens* 'let him do'.		3. *gwrens, gwrons* 'let them do'.	

2.9.2.7. *INFINITIVE. gîl, gwîl* 'to do'.

2.9.2.8. *PARTICIPLE. PRESENT OR ACTIVE, ow kîl* 'doing'; Past or Passive, *gwrês* 'done'.

When this verb is used otherwise than as an auxiliary, the future is *mî a vedn gwîl* 'I will do', etc. It means, as a principal verb, 'to do' or 'to make', and tenses may be formed with its own tenses as auxiliaries to its infinitive. Thus:

Mî a wra gwîl 'I do' or 'I make'.

Tî a wrîg gwîl 'thou hast made'.

Mar qwressa'n dên e wîl 'if the man would make it'.

2.9.3. *Gally* 'to be able'.[89]

2.9.3.1. *PRESENT OR FUTURE.* 'I can' or 'I may'.

2.9.3.1.1. INFLECTED.

Singular.	Plural.
1. *gellam, gallam, gellav.*	1. *gellen.*
2. *gallos, gelleth.*	2. *gellough, gallough.*
3. *gel.*	3. *gellons.*

2.9.3.1.2. IMPERSONAL.

Mî a el or *mî el*, etc.

2.9.3.2. *PAST (MIXED PRETERITE AND PLUPERFECT).* 'I could' or 'I might'.

2.9.3.2.1. INFLECTED.

Singular.	Plural.
1. *galjen, gelles.*	1. *galjen, gelsen.*
2. *galjes.*	2. *galjeugh, gelseugh.*
3. *galja, gallas.*	3. *galjens, gellens.*

2.9.3.2.2. IMPERSONAL.

Mî alja, etc.

2.9.3.3. *SUBJUNCTIVE.* 'I may be able'.

2.9.3.3.1. INFLECTED.

Singular.	Plural.
1. *gellev, gallen.*	1. *gellen.*
2. *gelly.*	2. *gelleugh, gallough.*
3. *gallo, gelly.*	3. *gallons.*

This verb is chiefly used (as has been said) as an auxiliary in the present and past tenses, in the sense of 'can', 'could', or 'may', 'might'. In direct sentences the impersonal form is most usual, in negative, interrogative, and dependent sentences the inflected form in the

---

89 {More often *gallos, gallus.*}

second state of the initial, which is influenced by the particle *a*, generally, however, not expressed, or by *na* 'not'. When the inflected form has been used in the question, the inflected form is often used also, preceded by the personal pronoun, in affirmative answers. Thus:

> *'Ellough why clappya Kernûak?* 'Can you speak Cornish?'
> *Mî ellam* (not *mî a el*). 'I can'.
> *'Aljesta scrifa Sowsnak?* 'Couldst thou write English?'
> *Mî aljen.* 'I could'.
> *'Allosta môs dhô'n chŷ?* 'Canst thou go to the house?'
> *Mî ellam.* 'I can'.
> *Na orama dr'el an Kembrîan gwîl rag dhô witha'ga thavas.*[84] 'I know not what the Welsh may do to preserve their language'. (Boson's *Nebbaz Gerriau.*)
> *Radn alja bos parres dhô lavarel.*[90] 'Some might be prepared to say'. (Boson's *Nebbaz Gerriau.*)

Sometimes the verb *gŏthvos* 'to know' (for which see §2.11), is used to express 'can', especially when mental capability is more or less intended. *Mî ôr* (or *mî wôr*) *cowsa Sowsnak* 'I can speak English'. Compare a similar use of *savoir* in French.

2.9.4. *Menny* 'to will', 'to wish'.[91]
2.9.4.1. *PRESENT.* 'I will'.
2.9.4.1.1. INFLECTED.

Singular.	Plural.
1. *mennav, mednav, mednama.*	1. *mennon, mednon.*
2. *menneth, medneth, menta.*	2. *mennough, mednough.*
3. *medn.*	3. *mennons, mednons.*

---

90 Spelling assimilated to that of this grammar.
91 {More often *mynnes, mednas.*}

2.9.4.1.2. IMPERSONAL.
Mî a vedn, tî a vedn, etc.

2.9.4.2. *PAST*. 'I would'. This is really the pluperfect.
2.9.4.2.1. INFLECTED.

Singular.	Plural.
1. *menjon, menjam* (older *mensen*)	1. *menjon* (*mensen*).
2. *menjes* (*menses*).	2. *menjough* (*menseugh*).
3. *menja* (*mensa*).	3. *menjons* (*mensens*).

2.9.4.2.2. IMPERSONAL.
Mî a venja, tî a venja, etc.

These are the only two tenses in common use as auxiliaries. Lhuyd gives another of mixed imperfect and preterite:

Singular.	Plural.
1. *mennen*	1. *mennen*
2. *mennyz*	2. *menneh*
3. *mennaz*	3. *mennenz.*

2.10. Paradigm of a regular verb

The following is a complete paradigm of a regular verb, showing the various forms. Most tenses have at least two forms, the simple verb, whether in the inflected or impersonal conjugation, and the compound, or verb with auxiliaries. In late Cornish the compound is by far the more usual in almost every tense. The general principal on which the different forms are used is:

Affirmative Sentences. Simple Impersonal or Auxiliary Impersonal, generally the latter.

Negative, Interrogative, or Dependent Sentences. Inflected Simple or Inflected Auxiliary, generally the latter, but the Simple Inflected is more common in these than the Simple Impersonal is in affirmative sentences.

2.10.1. Root. *Car* 'to love'.

2.10.1.1. *VERBAL NOUN OR INFINITIVE. Cara* 'the act of loving', 'to love'.

2.10.1.2. *PRESENT PARTICIPLE. Ow cara* 'loving'.

2.10.1.3. *PAST OR PASSIVE PARTICIPLE. Keres* 'loved'.

2.10.1.4. *PRESENT.* Originally used also as future.

2.10.1.4.1. INFLECTED FORM.

	Singular.	Plural.

1. *carav* (*vî*)[92] 'I love'.   1. *caron* (*nŷ*), older *keryn* 'we love'.

2. *keres* or *kereth* (*dî*) 'thou lovest'. 2. *carough* (*whŷ*) 'you love'.

3. *car* (*ev*) 'he loves'.   3. *carons* (*ŷ*), or *carans* 'they love'.

As this form, except occasionally in verse, is only used in negative, interrogative, or dependent sentences, the initial is generally changed to the second state by some preceding particle, such as *a*, *ni*, *pan*, etc.

2.10.1.4.2. IMPERSONAL FORM.

Mî, tî, ev, nŷ, whŷ, ŷ (late form often *anjŷ* or *jŷ*) *a gar*.

2.10.1.4.3. INFLECTED AUXILIARY.

Gwrav vî cara.

For the rest of the tense see the present of *gwîl* 'to do'.

2.10.1.4.4. IMPERSONAL AUXILIARY.

Mî, tî, ev, nŷ, whŷ, ŷ (or *anjŷ* or *jŷ*) *a wra cara*.

The forms *wrama*, *wresta* are generally used for the inflected auxiliary first and second persons singular in interrogative and dependent sentences, *a wrama cara?* 'do I love?' *pan wresta cara* 'when thou dost love'. The particle *a* of the impersonal form is not infrequently omitted, especially when the pronouns ending in vowels immediately precede it.[93]

2.10.1.4.5. The Continuous or Habitual Present.

Thov vi ow cara 'I am loving'.

---

92 It will not be necessary to add the pronouns to every tense. {In all verbs, what Jenner writes as unstressed *-av* of the first person singular is probably more correctly *-af* or *-a'*.}

93 The remarks on the use of the different forms of this tense apply *mutatis mutandis* to the other tenses. See also §2.14.1.

The rest as in the present tense of *bos* 'to be', followed by the present participle. The negative form of this is:

Nynsoma or *nynsov ow cara*, etc.

2.10.1.4.6. THE PASSIVE PRESENT.

Dhov vî keres 'I am loved'. {Recte: *Thov vî keres* per §2.9.1.1.1.}

The rest as the present of *bos*, followed by the past participle.

Or the older passive:

Mî, tî, ev, nŷ, whŷ, ŷ (or *anjŷ* or *jŷ*) *a gerer.*

Or the auxiliary form of the older passive:

Mî, tî, etc., *a wrer cara.*

In this case *wrer* is for *gwrer*, the passive of *gwîl* 'to do'.

2.10.1.5. *THE IMPERFECT.* Used also more or less as a Subjunctive.

2.10.1.5.1. INFLECTED.

Singular.	Plural.
1. *caren* 'I was loving'.	1. *caren* 'we were loving'.
2. *cares* 'thou wert loving'.	2. *careugh* 'you were loving'.
3. *cara* 'he was loving'.	3. *carens* 'they were loving'.

2.10.1.5.2. IMPERSONAL.

Mî, tî, etc., *a gara.*

2.10.1.5.3. AUXILIARY.

Therav vi ow cara.

The rest as the imperfect of *bos* 'to be' with the present participle.

The negative form of this tense is either:

nî garen, etc., or

nynseram ow cara, etc.

The interrogative is either:

a garen? etc., or

'erama, etc., *ow cara?*

2.10.1.6. *The Preterite or Past Tense.*

2.10.1.6.1. INFLECTED.

Singular.	Plural.
1. *kerŷs* 'I loved'.	1. *carson* or *kersen* 'we loved'.
2. *kerses* 'thou lovedst'.	2. *carsough* 'you loved'.
3. *caras* 'he loved'.	3. *carsons* or *carsans* 'they loved'.

2.10.1.6.2. IMPERSONAL.

Mî, tî, etc., *a garas.*

2.10.1.6.3. INFLECTED AUXILIARY.

Gwrîgav vî cara.

The rest as the past tense of *gwîl* 'to do' followed by the infinitive.

2.10.1.6.4. IMPERSONAL AUXILIARY.

Mî, tî, etc., *a wrîg cara.*

Sometimes *re* is prefixed to this tense, as: *mî re garas, mî re wrîg cara.* This turns it into a preterperfect, 'I have loved', but in late Cornish there is usually no distinction between preterite and perfect, except that the latter is seldom expressed by anything except the auxiliary form, while either may be used for the former.

The passive of this tense is either:

> *mî, tî*, etc., *a gares,*   or   *mî, tî*, etc., *a vê keres.*

The latter is the more usual.

2.10.1.7. *The Pluperfect, Secondary Perfect, or Conditional.*[94]

2.10.1.7.1. INFLECTED.

Singular.	Plural.
1. *carsen* 'I had loved', or 'I would love'.	1. *carsen* 'we had loved'.
2. *carses* 'thou hadst loved'.	2. *carseugh* 'you had loved'.
3. *carsa* 'he had loved'.	3. *carsens* 'they had loved'.

---

94 {As pluperfect rather than conditional this tense in any verb is confined to the *Mount Calvary* or PA.}

Pronounced and sometimes written *carjen* (or *cargen* with soft *g* in MSS), etc.

2.10.1.7.2. IMPERSONAL.
Mî, tî, etc., *a garsa.*

2.10.1.7.3. INFLECTED AUXILIARY.
Gwressen cara, etc., or *menjam cara,* etc.
The rest as the pluperfect of *gwîl,* or of *menny* 'to will', with the infinitive.

2.10.1.7.5. IMPERSONAL AUXILIARY.
Mî, tî, etc., *a wressa cara,* or *a venja cara.*
The passive of this tense is formed by the pluperfect of *bos* 'to be', followed by the past participle.

2.10.1.7. *THE SUBJUNCTIVE.*
2.10.1.7.1. INFLECTED.

Singular.	Plural.
1. *kerev* or *carev* 'I may love'	1. *keren* or *caren* 'we may love'.
2. *kery* or *cary* 'thou mayest love'.	2. *kereugh* or *careugh* 'you may love'.
3. *caro* 'he may love'.	3. *carens* or *carons* 'they may love'.

2.10.1.7.2. IMPERSONAL.
Mî, tî, etc., *a garo.*

2.10.1.7.3. INFLECTED AUXILIARY.
Gwrellev vî (or *gwrellen*) *cara.*
And the rest as the subjunctive or imperfect of *gwîl* with the infinitive.

2.10.1.7.4. IMPERSONAL AUXILIARY.
Mî, tî, etc., *a wrello* (or *wreffa*) *cara.*

The passive of this tense is formed by the present tense of *gally* 'to be able', followed by the infinitive *bos* 'to be', and the past participle of the main verb:

Mî, tî, etc., *a el bos keres*, 'I, thou', etc., 'may be loved'.

This tense is not necessarily used after conjunctions which in other languages (Latin, for example) govern a subjunctive, but rather when uncertainty, expectation, or contingency is signified, in fact, when in English one would use 'may' as an auxiliary. There is a good deal of confusion between this tense and the imperfect.

Re prefixed to the inflected or inflected auxiliary form of this tense makes it an optative:

Re wrellen cara 'would that I might love', etc.

2.10.1.8. *THE FUTURE.*

In older Cornish the present, whether in its inflected, impersonal, or auxiliary form, was commonly used to express a future, and sometimes the subjunctive was used as a future. Some verbs have an extra tense which is a specially inflected future, resembling one form of the Breton conditional, as follows:

Singular.	Plural.
1. *carvym, carvyv.*	1. *carvon.*
2. *carvyth.*	2. *carvough.*
3. *carvyth, carvo.*	3. *carvons.*

This is more commonly found in the impersonal form, *mî, tî*, etc., *a garvyth*. It is formed, as may be clearly seen, by suffixing the future or subjunctive of *bos* 'to be' (perhaps in its sense of 'to have'[95]), to the root of the verb. (Cf. the suffixing of the present of *avoir* to an infinitive to form a future in French, *je parler-ai*, and its unamalgamated prototype, the future form, *resurgere habent*, in the very low Latin of the antepenultimate verse of the Athanasian Creed.) But

95 See §2.14.

in late Cornish the regular future was formed by the auxiliary verb *menny* 'to will':

Mednav vî cara, etc.

Mî, tî, etc., *a vedn cara*, etc.

The forms *mednama, menta*, usually in the second state of the initial, are used for interrogative and dependent sentences:

A vednama cara? 'shall I love?'

Mar menta cara 'if thou wilt love'.

The negative is either *nî vednav vî cara* or *mî nî vednav cara*.

The latter form, with the *-v* of the termination omitted as being nearly inaudible, is used in Carew's phrase, *meea navidua cowzasawz-neck* 'I will speak no English', for *mî na vednav cowsa Sowsnak*.

The passive is formed by the present of *menny*, the infinitive of *bos*, and the past participle:

Mî, tî, etc., *a vedn bos keres*.

2.10.1.9. *The Imperative.*
2.10.1.9.1. Inflected.

Singular.	Plural.
1. wanting.	1. *caren* 'let us love'.
2. *car* 'love thou'.	2. *careugh* 'love ye'.
3. *cares* (or *carens*) 'let him love'.	3. *carens* 'let them love'.

2.10.1.9.2. Auxiliary.

Singular.	Plural.
1. wanting.	1. *gwren cara*.
2. *gwra cara*.	2. *gwreugh cara*.
3. *gwrens cara* or *gwrens e cara*.	3. *gwrens ŷ cara*.

2.11. The irregular verbs

The irregular verbs are:

môs (earlier *mones*) 'to go'.

dôs (earlier *dones*) 'to come'.

dôn 'to bear', 'to carry'.

drŷ 'to bring'.

rŷ 'to give'.

gŏdhvos 'to know'.

Of these, *môs* and *dôn* are each made up of two different verbs. The irregularities of *dôs*, *drŷ*, and *rŷ* are due to contractions, and those of *gŏdhvas* chiefly to its being compounded with *bos* 'to be'.

There are irregularities also in the auxiliary verbs *gwîl* 'to do', and *gally* 'to be able', but these have been already given in §2.9.2.2 and §2.9.2.3.

In earlier Cornish the inflected forms of the irregular verbs were freely used, but later these are comparatively rare, and the impersonal and auxiliary forms became so much commoner that the full inflected form can only be gathered from the early writings and from the rather imperfect paradigms given by Lhuyd.

It is not necessary to give anything more than the inflected verbs here, for the impersonal and auxiliary tenses can easily be worked out from these on the model of the regular verb. These are given without pronouns, though of course pronouns are used, as with other verbs.

In the latest Cornish the infinitives of *môs*, *dôs*, *drŷ*, *rŷ*, were often used colloquially to express the imperative, without much discrimination between singular and plural. These verbs, especially *môs* and *dôs*, are generally found in late Cornish in the auxiliary form with *gwîl* and *menny*, but rarely in the simple inflected.

2.11.1. *Môs* 'to go'.

2.11.1.1. *PRESENT OR FUTURE.*

Singular.	Plural.
1. *av* or *ăthov* (older *af*).	1. *en* or *ăthen*.
2. *eth* or *ătheth*.	2. *eugh* or *ătheugh*.
3. *a* or *ătha*.	3. *ans* or *ăthans*.

2.11.1.2. *IMPERFECT OR SECONDARY PRESENT.*

Singular.	Plural.
1. *ellen*.	1. *ellen*.
2. *elles*.	2. *elleugh*.
3. *ella*.	3. *ellens*.

2.11.1.3. *PRETERITE.*

Singular.	Plural.
1. *êthen*.	1. *êthen*.
2. *êthes*.	2. *êtheugh*.
3. *êth, ellas*.	3. *êthons*.

2.11.1.4. *PLUPERFECT OR CONDITIONAL* (probable, but not found).

Singular.	Plural.
1. *elsen*.	1. *elsen*.
2. *elses*.	2. *elseugh*.
3. *elsa*.	3. *elsens*.

2.11.1.5. *SUBJUNCTIVE.*

Singular.	Plural.
1. *ellev.*	1. *ellen.*
2. *elly.*	2. *elleugh.*
3. *ello.*	3. *ellons.*

2.11.1.6. *IMPERATIVE.*

Singular.	Plural.
1. wanting.	1. *en.*
2. *kê, kejy, kehejy.*[96]	2. *eugh.*
3. *ens.*	3. *ens.*

Infinitive, *môs.*

Present Participle, *ow môs.*

Past Participle, *gilles* (supplied from *gylly* or *gelly* 'to go').

In the impersonal form of the preterite, the verbal particle *a* often takes an *s* or *j* at the end of it, *mî aj êth* 'I went', but generally in this form *a* is omitted, *mî â* 'I go'; *mî êth* 'I went'; *mî ello* 'I may go', etc. In the *Ordinalia* and other Dramas the forms *reseth* and *regeth* (*rejeth*) are found for the perfect. This is the preterite *êth* with the particle *re* and *s* (*j*), for *th*, prefixed.

2.11.2. *Dôs* (earlier *devonos, donos, devos*) 'to come'.

2.11.2.1. *PRESENT.*

Singular.	Plural.
1. *dov* (older *duf*).	1. *down* (*duen, dun*).
2. *dêth* (*dueth*).	2. *dough, deugh.*
3. *dê* (*due*).	3. *dons, desons.*

---

96 *Kegy, kehegy* (in BM), are *ke, kehe*, with *jy* or *gy* (= *dî*), the personal pronoun added.

2.11.2.2. *IMPERFECT.*

Singular.	Plural.
1. *deffen.*	1. *deffen.*
2. *deffes.*	2. *deffeugh.*
3. *deffa.*	3. *deffens.*

2.11.2.3. *PRETERITE.*

Singular.	Plural.
1. *dêtha, dêth* (older *duth, dueyth*).	*dêthon* (*duthon*).
2. *dêthes, dês* (older *duthys, dues*).	*dêtheugh* (*dutheugh*).
3. *dêth* (older *dueth, duth*).	*dêthons, desons* (*duthens*).

2.11.2.4. *PLUPERFECT.* Not found, except third person singular, *dothye* or *dethye*, and third pl. *dothyans.*

Singular.	Plural.
1. *dothyen, dethyen.*	1. *dothyen, dethyen.*
2. *dothyes, dethyes.*	2. *dothyeugh, dethyeugh.*
3. *dothya, dethya.*	3. *dothyens, dethyens.*

2.11.2.5. *SUBJUNCTIVE.*

Singular.	Plural.
1. *deffev.*	1. *deffen.*
2. *deffy.*	2. *deffeugh.*
3. *deffo.*	3. *deffens.*

2.11.2.6. *IMPERATIVE.*

Singular.	Plural.
1. wanting.	1. *dewn* (*dun, duen*).
2. *dês* (*dues, dus*).	2. *deugh* (*dugh*).
3. *dêns.*	3. *dêns.*

2.11.2.7. *INFINITIVE. dôs.*

2.11.2.8. *PARTICIPLES.* PRESENT, *ow tôs*; PAST, *devedhes.*
'I am come' is *devedhes ov.*

The root vowels of this verb vary a good deal in the MSS. The *ue* is evidently a single syllable according to the rhythm, and so is the *ye* or *ya.*

2.11.3. *Dôn* 'to bear', 'to carry' (earlier also *doen, doyn*).

2.11.3.1. *PRESENT.*

Singular.	Plural.
1. *degav.*	1. *degon.*
2. *deges.*	2. *degough.*
3. *deg, dog.*	3. *degons.*

2.11.3.2. *IMPERFECT.* Not found.

2.11.3.3. *PRETERITE.*

Singular.	Plural.
1. *dîges* (older *duges*).	1. *dîgon.*
2. *dîges* (*duges*).	2. *dîgough.*
3. *dîg* (*dug, duk*).	3. *dîgons.*

2.11.3.4. *PLUPERFECT.* Not found.

2.11.3.5. *SUBJUNCTIVE.*

Singular.	Plural.
1. *dogev.*	1. *dogen.*
2. *dogy.*	2. *dogeugh.*
3. *dogo, doga.*	3. *dogens.*

2.11.3.6. *IMPERATIVE.*

Singular.	Plural.
1. wanting.	1. *degen.*
2. *dog, doga.*	2. *degeugh.*
3. *degens.*	3. *degens.*

2.11.3.7. *INFINITIVE*, *dôn, doga*, or *degy*.

2.11.3.8. *PARTICIPLES.* PRESENT, *ow tôn* or *ow tegy*; PAST, *deges*.

2.11.4. *Rŷ* 'to give'.

2.11.4.1. *PRESENT.*

Singular.	Plural.
1. *rov.*	1. *ren.*
2. *reth.*	2. *reugh.*
3. *re.*	3. *rens.*

2.11.4.2. *IMPERFECT.*

Singular.	Plural.
1. *ren.*	1. *ren.*
2. *res.*	2. *reugh.*
3. *re.*	3. *rens.*

2.11.4.3. *PRETERITE.*

Singular.	Plural.
1. *rês.*	1. *resen.*
2. *resses.*	2. *rosough.*
3. *ros.*	3. *rosons.*

2.11.4.4. *PLUPERFECT.*

Singular.	Plural.
1. *rosen.*	1. *rosen.*
2. *roses.*	2. *roseugh.*
3. *rosa.*	3. *rosens.*

2.11.4.5. *SUBJUNCTIVE.*

Singular.	Plural.
1. *rollen.*	1. *rollen.*
2. *rolly.*	2. *rolleugh.*
3. *rollo.*	3. *rollens, rollons.*

2.11.4.6. *IMPERATIVE.*

Singular.	Plural.
1. wanting.	1. *ren.*
2. *ro.*	2. *reugh.*
3. *roy.*	3. *rens.*

2.11.4.7. *INFINITIVE, rŷ.*

2.11.4.8. *PARTICIPLES.* PRESENT, *ow rŷ*; PAST, *reys.*

2.11.5. *Drŷ* 'to bring'.

Except that the present is:

Singular.	Plural.
1. *dorov* or *drov.*	1. *doren* or *dren.*
2. *doreth* or *dreth.*	2. *dorough* or *dreugh.*
3. *dore* or *dre.*	3. *dorens* or *drens,*

the second person singular of the imperative is *doro* or *dro*, and the preterite third person singular is *dres* or *dros*, this verb is *rŷ* with a *d*-prefixed. The present participle is *ow trŷ*.

2.11.6. *Gŏdhvos,* or *gŏdhvas* 'to know'. Compounded of *godh* or *gŭdh* 'knowledge' and *bos* 'to be'.

2.11.6.1. *PRESENT.*

Singular.	Plural.
1. *gôn* or *goram.*	1. *gŏdhon.*
2. *gŏdhas.*	2. *gŏdhough.*
3. *gôr* (2nd state *wôr* or *'ôr*).	3. *gŏdhons.*

2.11.6.2. *IMPERFECT.* Used also as Perfect.

Singular.	Plural.
1. *gŏdhen, gŏdhyen.*	1. *gŏdhen, gŏdhyen.*
2. *gŏdhes, gŏdhyes.*	2. *gŏdheugh, gŏdhyeugh.*
3. *gŏdha, gŏdhya.*	3. *gŏdhens, gŏdhyens.*

2.11.6.3. *PRETERITE.* The second form, given by Lhuyd, is a rather improbable tense, and is not found elsewhere.

Singular.	Plural.
1. *gŏdhvên, gwedhun.*	1. *gŏdhvên, gwedhyn.*
2. *gŏdhvês, gwedhys.*	2. *gŏdhveugh, gwedheugh.*
3. *gŏdhvê, gwedhewys.*	3. *gŏdhvons, gwedhans, gweians.*

2.11.6.4. *PLUPERFECT OR CONDITIONAL.*

Singular.	Plural.
1. *gŏdhvîen.*	1. *gŏdhvîen.*
2. *gŏdhvîes.*	2. *gŏdhvîeugh.*
3. *gŏdhvîa.*	3. *gŏdhvîens.*

2.11.6.5. *SUBJUNCTIVE.*

Singular.	Plural.
1. *gŏdhevav, gŏdhav.*	1. *gŏdhven.*
2. *gŏdhvy, gŏdhy.*	2. *gŏdhveugh.*
3. *gŏdhvo.*	3. *gŏdhvens* or *gŏdhans.*

2.11.6.6. *FUTURE.*

Singular.	Plural.
1. *gŏdhvedhav, gŏffedhav.*	1. *gŏdhvedhen, gŏffedhen.*
2. *gŏdhvedhes, gŏffedhes.*	2. *gŏdhvedheugh, gŏffedheugh.*
3. *gŏdhvedh, gŏffedh.*	3. *gŏdhvedhens, gŏffedhens.*

2.11.6.7. *OPTATIVE.*

Singular.	Plural.
1. *re wŏffen.*	1. *re wŏffen.*
2. *re wŏffas.*	2. *re wŏffeugh.*
3. *re wŏffa.*	3. *re wŏffens.*

2.11.6.8. *IMPERATIVE.*

Singular.	Plural.
1. wanting.	1. *gŏdhvedhen.*
2. *gŏdhvedh.*	2. *gŏdhvedheugh.*
3. *gŏdhvedhens.*	3. *gŏdhvedhens.*

2.11.6.9. *INFINITIVE, gŏdhvos, gŏdhvas, gŏvos.*

2.11.6.10. *PARTICIPLES.* PRESENT, *ow cŏdhvos*; PAST, *gŏdhvedhes.*

2.11.6.11. *INFLECTED PASSIVE, gŏdher.*

In the impersonal form and elsewhere, when this verb has its initial in the second state, *w* is substituted for *g*. The Optative *re wŏffen*, etc. seems to be formed on the imperfect mixed up with the subjunctive.

2.12. Prepositions, conjunctions, adverbs

Prepositions are of two kinds, simple and compound. Simple prepositions govern various states of the initial. Compound prepositions, when, as is generally the case, they are made up of a simple preposition and a noun, govern the first state, for the noun which follows is really in the appositional genitive. If a compound preposition govern a personal pronoun, the latter is often placed, in its possessive form, between the two component parts of the preposition, governing the initial of the noun-half of it. Sometimes, however, the second part of a compound preposition is a simple preposition, and in that case the government is that of the last preposition of the compound.

2.12.1. Simple prepositions.

a 'of, from', governs second state.

avel, vel 'like, as'.

bis 'up to, as far as' (Lat. *usque ad*).

dadn or *en dadn* 'under'.

der, dre 'by, through', governs second state.

dres 'over, beyond, above'.

dhô 'to', governs second state.

en, edn, et 'in'.[96]

er see *war*.

gan, gans 'with, by'.

heb 'without', governs second state.

kens 'before' (of time).

---

96 Older *yn*. When this is followed by a possessive pronoun of the first or second person the *n* is dropped, and the possessive pronoun takes the form which follows a preposition ending in a vowel, *e'm, e'th*. When the definite article would follow the two coalesce and *en* = *en an*.

lebmen, lemmen 'except, but'.

ŏja, wŏja 'after' (older form *wose*).

rag 'for, because of'.

re 'by' (in swearing), governs
  second state.

reb 'by, near, beside'.

saw 'save, except, but'.

treba, tereba 'until'.

troha 'towards'.

tewa (tewaha, tyha, tîgh) 'towards'.

war 'on, upon' (also *er*), governs
  second state.

worth, orth 'at, to, against'.

2.12.2. Compound prepositions.

adres 'across, beyond'.

adro dho, drodho 'about, concern-
  ing', govern second state.

abarth, abarh 'beside, on the side
  of'.

aberth, aberh 'within, inside of'.

adheller dhô, dheller dhô (originally
  a dhellergh) 'behind', governs
  second state.

a dhirag, dhirag 'before, in the
  presence of'.

adheworth, dheworth, dhŏrt 'from'.

ajŷ, 'jŷ 'within' (*a* + *chŷ* 'house'),
  generally followed by *dhô*,
  governing the second state.

a eugh 'above, over'.

a mes, a ves, mes, en mes 'out of'.

a mesk, mesk, en mesk 'among'.

a wos 'because of, for the sake
  of'.

entrê 'among'.

erbidn or *erbyn, warbidn* 'against'.

herwedh 'according to'.

mamas 'except, but'.

rag carenja 'for the sake of'.

warlergh 'after'.

ogastî dhô near to (*ogastî = ogas*
  'near', *tî = tew* 'side').

Of these *abarth, a mesk* or *en mesk, erbidn, rag carenja,* and *warlergh,* are
  separable when they govern pronouns. Thus:

a'gan parth 'beside us'.

en agas mesk 'among you'.

er ow fyn 'against me'.

rag dha garenja 'for thy sake'.

war e lergh 'after him'.

2.12.3. Conjunctions.

ha 'and'. Before a vowel, *hag*, except when followed by the article *an*, or by a pronoun beginning with a vowel, in which case the vowel of the second word is elided.

bes, mes 'but'.

saw 'but, except'.

ma, may 'that, in order that'.

dre, dro 'that'.

erna 'until'.

bis pan 'until'.

treba, tereba 'until'.

ken 'though, although'.

awos 'although, notwithstanding'.

pan, pa, pur or *per* (= *pa-er*), 'when', govern second state.

hedre 'whilst'.

spas 'whilst'.

perag, prag, fraga 'why, wherefore'.

po 'or'. *po—po—* 'either—or—'.

mar, mara, a 'if', govern fourth state.

marnas (*mar + na + es*) 'unless'.

ponî, ponag 'unless'.

aban 'since, because'.

dreven 'since, because'.

rag 'for'.

rag own 'lest, for fear'.

vel 'than'.

ages, es 'than'.

na 'nor'.

maga 'so, as much as'.

2.12.4. Adverbs.

Adverbs may be formed from adjectives by prefixing *en*, which generally changes the initial to the second state. Thus *glan* 'pure', *en 'lan* 'purely'. There are some exceptions to this change; *b* and *m* sometimes change to *f*, not *v*: *bras* 'great', *en fras* 'greatly'; *mas* 'good', *en fas* 'well'; *d* sometimes changes to the fourth state: *da* 'good', *en ta* 'well'; and *t* sometimes remains unchanged: *tin* 'sharp', *en tin* 'sharply'. But we find also *en dhiugel* 'certainly', from *diugel* 'secure'. {The mutation is now called the Mixed Mutation.}

2.12.4.1. Adverbs of Time.

en êrma 'now' ('in this hour').

lemman, lebman 'now'.

en tor-ma 'now' ('in this turn').

nam, nana, nanna, nans 'now'.

agensow 'just now'.

hedhew 'today'.

avorow 'tomorrow'.

trenzha 'the day after tomorrow'.

151

jedreva = *dedreja* = *dedh trúja* 'the third day hence'.

an journa-ma war seithan 'this day week'.

de 'yesterday'.

genzhete (*kens de dedh*) 'the day before yesterday'.

ternos 'the next day'.

en kenzhoha 'in the morning'.

boregweth 'in the morning'.

dohajedh 'in the afternoon'.

gorthewer 'in the evening'.

zîlgweth 'on Sundays'.

fast 'presently'.

prest, scon, dewháns, eskes, defry, dhesempes 'soon, quickly, immediately'.

whath 'still, yet'.

kens 'before' (of time).

kensemman 'ere now'.

kensenna 'ere that'.

ŏja, wŏja, ŏj' henna, wŏja hedna 'afterwards'.

nenna, nana, en êrna 'then'.

ŏj' hemma, wŏja hebma 'henceforth'.

warlergh 'afterwards'.

esos 'already'.

avar 'early'.

dewedhes 'late'.

arta 'again'.

kettoth, kettoth ha 'as soon as'.

nevra 'ever'.

rag nevra 'for ever'.

benary 'for ever'.

biken 'ever'; *bis viken* 'for ever'.

besca, besqweth 'ever'.

benethy, dho venethy 'for ever'.

bepprês 'always'.

hedre, spas 'whilst'.

pols 'a while'.

2.12.4.2. Adverbs of Place.

ple 'where' (either interrogative or not).

a pele, a ble 'whence' (either interrogative or not).

ŭbma, ŭmma 'here, hither'.

enna 'there'.

lemma, lebma 'here' (in this place).

alemma, alebma 'hence'.

alenna, en mes alenna 'thence'.

aban, avan 'up, above, on high'.

aman 'up, upwards'.

awartha 'above, over'.

awollas, warwollas 'below'.

warban 'on high, up above'.

warnans 'down below'.

en hans, en nans 'down'.

lêr, lôr (*luer*) 'down'.

aberth, aberh 'within'.

ajŷ, jŷ 'within'.

aves, ames 'outside'.

tre 'at home'.

adre 'homewards'.

ales 'abroad' (*scattya ales* 'to "scat" abroad).

dhô ves 'away'.

kerh (formerly *kerdh*) 'away' (*môs kerh* 'to go away').

pel 'far'.

enogas, ogas 'near'; *ogastî*, 'nearby'.

a rag 'in front'.

en rag 'forward'.

dirag 'forth, before' (of place).

dheller (*dellergh*), 'behind'.

war dheller 'backwards'.

adro 'around'.

adres 'athwart'.

a hes 'along'.

2.12.4.3. Adverbs of Quantity.

mêr 'much'.

îthek 'hugely'.

îthek tra 'ever so much'.

vîth mar 'ever so'.

nepeth, nebas 'a little'.

lour, lŭk lour, lŭk 'enough'.

re 'too much'.

kemmes, kebmes 'as much'.

vîth 'at all'.

hanter 'half'.

2.12.4.4. Adverbs of Comparison.

mar 'so, as'.

ky…mal, ky…vel as…as (*ky gwerdh vel gwels* 'as green as grass').

del 'as'.

della, en della, en delna 'so, in such manner'.

cara, pocara, kepara, kepar del 'like as, even as, likewise'.

maga (governing fourth state), 'as'; *maga ta* 'as well, likewise'.

keffres, kekeffres 'likewise, also'.

hagŏl, hagensŏl 'also'.

a wedh, enwedh 'also'.

gwell 'better'.

lakkah 'worse'.

moy 'more'.

leh 'less'.

kens vel 'rather than'.

2.12.4.5. Miscellaneous Adverbs.

cowal, cowl 'quite'.

namna 'almost'.

ken 'else'.

martesan 'perhaps'.

betegens 'nevertheless'.

moghya 'mostly'.

ketel, ketella 'so'.

pŭr (governing second state), 'very'.

brâs, fest (placed after an adjective) 'very'.

ogastî 'nearly, almost'.

warbarth, warbarh 'together'.

ni, nyns, nig, na, nag 'not'.[97]

hepmar 'doubtless'.

perag, prag, fraga 'why'.

patla, fatel, fatla 'how'.

pelta 'much'; *pelta gwel* 'much better'.

otta, welta 'behold'.

nahen 'otherwise'.

---

97 *na = ni + a* (*nag* before a vowel), ought only to be used with interrogatives, but the later writers of Cornish did not always do as they ought.

2.13. Swear-words and expletives

Cornish is a disappointing language in respect of swearwords, for it is by no means rich in those "ornaments to conversation". Except for a few very distressing expressions, now better forgotten, which are put into the mouths of the evil characters in the Dramas, the swears are mostly quite harmless, and even pious. It is not at all difficult or morally dangerous to learn to swear in Cornish.

Surprise is generally expressed by *Re Varía!* 'By Mary!' 'By Our Lady!' shortened at times to *Aría!* and *Ría!* This is used as an Englishman might say 'By Jove!' or 'By George!' or a Frenchman 'Dame!'

If there is an element of annoyance mingled with the surprise, *An Jowl!* 'The Devil!', may be mentioned with effect, perhaps by those to whom *Re Varía!* savours too much of Popery; but *Re Varía!* is in better taste. *An Jowl* may be used, as in English, after words signifying 'where', 'what', 'why', 'when', to strengthen a question.

An assertion is strengthened by the use of the name of a saint, preferably the patron of one's own parish (though any Cornishman may swear by St Michael[98]), with or without the particle *re*, which

---

98 In CW 599, "*Myhall sera thewgh gramercy*," though Keigwin and Dr Stokes both read *my hall* = 'I may', one is inclined to find this form of swear, and to translate it 'Michael! Sir, grammercy to you!' Compare the English use of "Marry!" (for 'Mary!') or "Gad!" (for 'God!') without *by* before them. It is written all in one word and spelt the same as the name of St Michael in the same play. It is no more of an anachronism to make Eve swear by St Michael than (in RD 1387) to make St Thomas swear by St Mary.

puts the initial in the second state, prefixed. The title 'saint' is usually omitted. Thus:

Re *Yêst!* 'By St Just!' *Re Gŏlom!* 'By St Columb!' *Re Îa!* 'By St Ia' [Ives]. *Re Vîhal!* or *Mîhal!* 'By St Michael!'

A little stronger, for those whose principles will allow them to mention it, is *Re'n Offeren!* 'By the Mass!' and some bold, bad persons have been known under great pressure to say *Re Dhew!* In the Dramas, *Re thu am ros* (*Re Dhew a'm ros*) 'By God who made me!' (or 'who gave me') is a more elaborate form of this swear. One also finds *Abarth Dew* 'On God's part' = 'In God's name', and in the mouths of pagans, *Abarth Malan* (a Celtic goddess) and even *Abarth Satnas*.

Ill-temper is generally expressed by variations on *mollath* 'curse', pl. *mollathow*. A moderate amount of anger may be indicated by *Mollath!* or *Mollathow!* alone, or *Mollathow dheugh!* 'Curses to you!' or *Mollath warnough!* 'A curse upon you!' A little more is expressed by specifying the number, generally large, of these curses, *Mil mollath warnough!* or even *Cans mil mollath warnough!*

Some, moved by very great indignation, have been known to say *Mollath Dew warnas!* 'God's curse upon thee!' and Carew in his Survey of Cornwall of 1602 gives a by no means nice phrase (which he spells all anyhow and translates wrong), *Mollath Dew en dha 'las!* 'The curse of God in thy belly!' Another serio-comic but rather cryptic expletive, peculiar to Camborne, or at any rate to the Drama of *St Meriasek*, is *Mollath Dew en gegin!* 'God's curse in the kitchen!' It does not seem to mean anything in particular, except perhaps that one's food may not agree with one, though it makes quite as much sense as the "universal adjective" of English swearing, and is a good deal less offensive. *Venjens*, a borrowed English word, may be substituted for *Mollath*.[99] One finds *Mil*

---

99 *Vengeans y'th glas!* is used by the wife of the smith who makes the nails for the Cross in the Drama of *The Passion* (PC 2716).

venjens warnas! and even *Venjens en dha 'las!* But all these last expressions represent unusually violent states of mind, and cannot be recommended for general use; for if one were to use up such expletives as these on matters of little moment, there would be nothing left for state occasions.

The expressions *Malbe, Malbew, Malbew dam, Malbe dam,* found in *The Creation* and in *St Meriasek,* are considered by Professor Loth to be maledictions referring to the French expression *Mal beau* or *Beau mal,* a euphonism for epilepsy, so that *Malbe dam* has no connection with the similar sound of part of it in English, but only means 'Epilepsy to me!'

The seventeenth and eighteenth century speakers of Cornish sometimes wished to express contempt or dislike by abusive terms. These often take the form of epithets added to the word *pedn* 'head'. Thus, *Pedn brâs,* literally 'great head', is equivalent to the impolite English "fat-head"; *Pedn Jowl* 'devil's head'; *Pedn mousak* 'stinking head'; these three are given as common terms of abuse by Carew. When the late Mrs Dolly Pentreath was at all put out, she is reported to have used the term *Cronak an hagar deu* ('The ugly black toad'), and there are several equally uncomplimentary epithets scattered up and down among the Dramas. But these words do not accord with the polite manners of those who belong to the most gentlemanlike race, except the Scottish Highlanders, in all Christendom, and those Cornishmen who require that their conversation should be a little more forcible than 'yea' and 'nay' (for which, by the way, there is no real Cornish) are recommended not to go beyond *Re Varîa, Re'n Offeren,* and an invocation of St Michael of the Mount, or of the patron saints of their own parishes.[100] What would happen if one were to swear by the patron of some other parish does not appear, but probably, if a St Ives man were to

---

100 {Scottish Highlanders notwithstanding, 'yea' is *ea* or *yâ* in Cornish, and 'nay' is *nâ.*}

strengthen his assertion by an appeal to St Meriasek of Camborne, instead of his own St Ia, he might be suspected of a wilful economy of truth. The more forcible expressions may be left to the "Anglo-Saxon", for Cornishmen and Celts generally, even of the lowest position, are not, and never have been, foul-mouthed.

The usual interjections, 'Oh!' 'Ah!' 'Alas!' are borrowed from English. 'Woe!' is expressed by *Trew!* 'Woe is me!' is *Govî!* 'Woe to him!' *Goev!* compounds of *gew* 'woe' with pronouns.

'Lo', 'Behold' (the *voilà, voici* of French) is expressed by *otta* (older forms *awatta, awatte, wette, otte* = perhaps *a wel dî?* 'dost thou see?'). This combines with pronouns, e.g.:

Singular.	Plural.
ottavî 'me voici'	*ottany*
ottadî	*ottawhy*
ottavê or *ottensa*	*ottanjy.*

These compounds are often followed by a participle, e.g. *ottavî pares* 'behold me prepared'. The distinction of *voilà* and *voici* is expressed by *ottama* and *ottana.*

2.14. The construction of sentences, idioms, etc.

2.14.1. General remarks.

In later Cornish there was a strong tendency to assimilate the order of words and the construction of sentences to those of English, but nevertheless certain idioms persisted throughout.

In English the normal order of words in a simple sentence is:

Subject—Verb—Complement of Predicate (Object, etc.).

This order is used in Cornish also when the impersonal form of the main verb or of the auxiliary is used, and the object is not a personal pronoun. Thus:

Dew a gar an bês 'God loveth the world'.

Dew a wra cara an bês 'God doth love the world'.

One of these two forms is the most usual in a direct affirmative principal sentence when the object is not a pronoun.

If the object is a pronoun, the order is:

Subject—Particle—Object—Verb.

Thus:

Dew a'th gar 'God loveth thee'.

Or:

Subject—Particle—Auxiliary—Pronoun in the Possessive Form—Infinitive of Main Verb. Thus:

Dew a wra dha gara 'God doth love thee'.

If the auxiliary verb is *bos* 'to be', it often happens that the inflected form of it is used in an affirmative sentence when the tense is the continuous present or imperfect. In these cases the order is:

Auxiliary—Verb—Subject—Participle of Main Verb—Complement.

Thus:

Thov vî ow môs dhô Loundres 'I am going to London'.

Therough why ow tôs adre 'you were coming home'.

But with the preterite tense the simple impersonal form is more usual. Thus:

Mî a vê gennes en Kernow 'I was born in Cornwall'.

The same applies to the present and imperfect of *bos* when it is not an auxiliary. Thus:

Thov vî lowen dhô'gas gwelas 'I am glad to see you'.

The inflected form of the verb is rare in simple direct affirmative sentences, except when it is used as a Celtic substitute for 'yes'. It may be used in verse, but it is rather affected in prose. In negative, interrogative, and dependent sentences it is the only form to use, but even then it is the inflected auxiliaries, parts of *gwîl* 'to do', *menny* 'to will', *gally* 'to be able', etc., with the infinitive of the main verb that are more commonly used, rather than the inflected form of the main verb itself. In the third person singular it is of course only distinguishable from the impersonal form by the position of the subject, which in the inflected form would follow the verb. The inflectional form of the third person plural is only used when the pronoun 'they' is the subject. When the subject is a plural noun the verb is always in the singular. The inflected form, either of the auxiliary *gwîl* with the infinitive of the main verb, or of the main verb itself, is always used for the imperative. In late Cornish, except in the case of answers for 'yes' and 'no', and of the peculiar forms of the first, second, and third persons singular in *ma*, *ta*, and *va*, the subject personal pronoun is almost always expressed, except, of course, when the subject is a noun.

2.14.2. Negative and interrogative sentences.

For a negative sentence it is never correct to use the impersonal, but always the inflected form of the verb or of the auxiliary, preceded by the negative particle *ni* (older *ny*) or *nyns*. The order is:

1. Negative Particle—Verb—Subject—Complement of Predicate. Or:

2. Negative Particle—Auxiliary (inflected)—Subject—Infinitive of Main Verb—Complement

If the object is a pronoun, in the first case it follows the negative particle in its third form, in the second case it precedes the infinitive in the possessive form. Thus:

1. *Ni welav vî an dên* 'I do not see the man'.

   Ni wôr dên vîth an êr 'no man knoweth the hour'.

2. *Ni wrîgav vî gwelas an dên* 'I did not see the man'.

1. *Ni'th welav vî* 'I do not see thee'.

2. *Ni wrîgav vî dha welas* 'I did not see thee'.

In the case of the present and imperfect of *bos* 'to be', the particle *nyns* is often used, and it is sometimes found with other words beginning with vowels, but its use is rare in late Cornish, and *ni*, or less correctly *na* (or *nag* before a vowel) is more usual.

It is allowable to use the inflected form with the subject-pronoun preceding the negative particle, but it should only be used for emphasis on the subject, and is better avoided.

Interrogative sentences are formed with the interrogative particle *a*, or by the use of some interrogative pronoun or adverb. In all cases the inflected form of the main verb or auxiliary (usually the latter) follows the particle, pronoun, or adverb, and usually with its initial in the second state. Thus:

A wrîgough why besca gwelas? 'Did you ever see?'

A wreugh why agan gwelas? 'Do you see us?'

Fatla wreugh why crŷa hedna? 'How do you call that?'

Fraga wreugh why gwîl hebma? 'Why do you do this?'

A vednough why môs genev vî? 'Will you go with me?'

161

The particle *a* is often omitted colloquially, but its effect is perceptible in the change of the initial of the verb. If the verb begins with a vowel, *a* is always omitted.

With interrogative sentences should come the answers to them. It must be understood that by nature no Celt can ever say a plain 'yes' or 'no'. There are "dictionary words" for 'yes' and 'no' in Welsh and Cornish, and they are used a very little in translations from other languages; but they do not "belong" to be used in speaking or writing Welsh or Cornish. In Gaelic there are not even "dictionary words" for them.[101] In Breton *ya* and *nann* are used freely for 'yes' and 'no', as in French, but that is probably quite modern French influence. The Celtic practice is to repeat the inflected verb of the question, affirmatively or negatively, in the necessary person. Thus:

'Ellough why cowsa Kernûak? 'Can you speak Cornish?'

Gellam or *mî ellam.* 'I can' ('Yes'). *Ni ellam*, or (less correctly) *nag ellam* 'I cannot' ('No').

A vednough why dôs genev vî? 'Will you come with me?'

Mednav. 'I will' ('Yes'). *Ni vednav* 'I will not' ('No').

A wrîg ev môs dhô Benzans? 'Did he go to Penzance?'

Gwrîg. 'He did'. *Ni wrîg.* 'He did not'.

'Esta ajŷ? 'Art thou at home?'

Thoma. 'I am'. *Nynsov*, or *nynsoma*, or (less correctly), *nag ov.* 'I am not'.

In the case of a negative interrogative sentence the verb is immediately preceded by *na* = *nî* + *a*, whether it begins the sentence or is itself preceded by an interrogative conjunction. Thus:

Na wrîsta gwelas? 'Didst thou not see?'

Fraga na wrîsta crejŷ? 'Why didst thou not believe?'

---

101 {'Yea' is *ea* or *yâ* in Cornish, and 'nay' is *nâ*. In Welsh, *ie* and *nage* are now often used as phatic expressions for 'yes' and 'no'. *Is ea* (*sea*) and *ní hea* are used similarly in Irish, though in general grammar restricts their usage and they are not entirely equivalent to 'yes' and 'no'.}

2.14.3. Dependent sentences or subordinate clauses.

These are of three kinds:

1. Those introduced by conjunctions, such as 'if', 'that', 'as', etc., or by a relative pronoun.

2. Those analogous to the "accusative with the infinitive" of Latin.[102]

3. The absolute clause.

2.14.3.1. The ordinary dependent clause introduced by a conjunction has its verb in the indicative, unless the so-called subjunctive is required to express uncertainty or contingency, without reference to any preceding conjunction. The verb is always in the simple inflected or inflected auxiliary form. The verb which follows the conjunction *mar* or *mara* 'if', has its initial in the fourth state, and *tre*, *tro*, or *dro* 'that', governs the second state.

A dependent sentence may sometimes precede its principal sentence, as in English. A very good instance of two sorts of dependent clauses may be seen in the following sentence from Boson's *Nebbaz Gerriau*. The English is:

"If that learned wise man [John Keigwin] should see this [i.e. this essay], he would find reason to correct it in orthography, etc."

Boson's Cornish, the spelling and division of words assimilated to that of the present grammar, is:

Mar qwressa   an dên deskes   fîr-na gwelas hemma,
'If   should [do] that man learned wise   see   this,

ev a venja   cavos fraga e   ewna   en scrîfa-composter.
'he   would find why it to amend in writing correctness'.

In this sentence *qwressa* is for *gwressa* (third person singular of the conditional or pluperfect of the auxiliary *gwîl* 'to do'), with the

---

102 {An example of the accusative with the infinitive is *dixit **eas** in urbem **ire*** 'he said they are going to town', where the first verb *dixit* is conjugated, the second verb *ire* is an infinitive, and its subject *eas* is in the accusative (literally 'he-said them to town to-go').}

initial in its fourth state after *mar*. Boson writes it *markressa*, all in one word. *Fraga e ewna* is an example of a variant of the second form of dependent sentence. The principal verb *ev a venja cavos* is in the impersonal auxiliary form, and of the two dependent clause verbs, one, *qwressa an dên deskes fir-na gwelas*, is in the inflected auxiliary form, and the other, *ewna*, is infinitive.

In a relative sentence, if the relative pronoun is the subject, the verb appears to be in the impersonal form. That is to say, it is always in the form of the third person singular, and does not show any agreement with its antecedent, whatever person or number that may be in. The other peculiarities of relative sentences are given in §2.7.4.

2.14.3.2. "Instead of using the conjunction 'that' with another verb in the indicative mood, as in most European languages, it is usual to put the second verb in the infinitive preceded by the personal pronoun, as is common in Latin." Thus says Norris, speaking in a manner perhaps rather less clear than usual, of an idiom found in the Dramas. This idiom, analogous to the "accusative with the infinitive" of Latin, is found down to the latest period of Cornish literature, though not to the complete exclusion of a finite clause beginning with 'that'. The instances given by Norris are:

> *Ha cous ef dhe dhasserhy* 'and say that he is risen'.
>
> *Marth a'm bues ty dhe leverel folneth* 'I have wonder that thou shouldst speak folly'.
>
> *Nyns a y'm colon why dhe gewsel* 'it goes not into my heart' (i.e. I do not believe) 'that you have spoken'.
>
> *Del won dhe bos* {error for *del won ty dhe vos*} 'as I know thee to be'.

Here are some later instances:

> *Ny a wel an tîs younk dho e clappya leh ha leh*[103] 'we see that the young people speak it less and less' (*Nebbaz Gerriau*).

---

103 The spelling and mutations corrected.

Dre wrama crejy hedna dho bos gwîr yu scrîfes enna[104] 'that I do believe that that is true that is written therein' (*Nebbaz Gerriau*).

Nevertheless, one finds in the same piece:

Ev a lavarras drova gever ŏl[104] 'he said that it was Goats All'.

Bes mî a or hemma, dhort e hoer an Kernuak, drova talves bes nebbas[104] 'but I know this, by her sister the Cornish, that it is worth but little'.

And in Keigwin's translation of Genesis 1:

Ha Dew a wellas trova da[104] 'And God saw that it was good'.

A somewhat similar construction is sometimes used after *dreven* 'because', and *treba* 'until':

Dreven tî dhô wîl hemma[104] 'because thou hast done this' (Kerew's Genesis 3:14).

Dreven tî dhô wolsowas dhô dalla dha wrêg[104] 'because thou didst listen to the voice of thy wife' (Genesis 3:17).

Treba tî dhô draylya dhô'n nôr[104] 'until thou turn again to the earth' (Genesis 3:19).

Yet even there one finds

Dreven o hy dama a ŏl bewa[104] 'because she was the mother of all living' (Genesis 3:20).

Lhuyd mentions a similar construction after *rag own* 'for fear', 'lest':

Rag own whŷ dho gôdha po an rew dho derry ha whŷ dho vos bidhes[104] 'lest you fall or the ice break and you be drowned' (literally, 'for fear you to fall or the ice to break and you to be drowned').

With *fraga* 'why' one finds a similar form:

Ev a venja cavos fraga e ewna 'he would find why to amend it'.

But when *fraga* introduces an interrogative sentence, an ordinary finite verb is used:

Fraga (or *rag fraga* 'for why') *na grejeth dhô'm lavarow?* 'Why dost thou not believe my words?'

---

104 The spelling and mutations corrected.

When 'that' signifies 'in order that', the ordinary finite verb is used after it.

There is a peculiar construction, found chiefly in Jordan's *Creation* but also in the *Ordinalia* (e.g. PC 1120), for expressing 'that I am'. It consists of the infinitive *bos* 'to be', preceded by a possessive pronoun and followed by a pronominal suffix:

> *Me a vyn may fo gwellys* **ow bosaf** *Dew heb parow* 'I will that it may be seen, that I am God without equals'.

And a still more confused one of the second person with the verbal particle *y* before *bos*, the pronominal suffix *-ta* and the pronoun *ge = dî*:

> *Me ny allaf convethas,* **y bosta ge** *ow hendas* 'I cannot understand that thou art my ancestor'.

The first is analogous to the Welsh "infinitive construction", as Rowland calls it, e.g. *gŵyr* **fy mod i** *yn dyfod* 'he knows that I am coming' (lit. 'he knows my being in coming'), only the Cornish form uses the pronominal suffix instead of the redundant personal pronoun.

2.14.3.3. The Absolute Clause. This construction, which answers more or less to the ablative absolute of Latin, and the genitive absolute of Greek, is common to all the Celtic languages.[105] It is translated into English by a sentence introduced by 'when', 'while', 'whilst', or 'though', with a verb generally in the continuous form of the present or past tense, or by a participle. In the Celtic languages the absolute clause has two forms.

2.14.3.3.1. The affirmative, generally consisting of the conjunction 'and', a subject, noun or pronoun, and generally a participle. Rowland calls the conjunction, *a, ac,* of the Welsh form "the absolute particle," and Professor Anwyl identifies it with *a, ag*

---

106 {While "answering" to the Latin and Greek absolutes, the Cornish formulation really has nothing to do with them, so the editor will not describe them here.}

'with', in an archaic form. But in Cornish *ha* or *hag* is used, and in Gaelic *agus* 'and', in exactly the same way. The following are examples in Cornish, Welsh, and Gaelic:

Cornish. *An jy a ve gwarnes gan Dew, ha'n jy ow cusca*[107] 'they were warned by God, and they sleeping' or 'while they slept' (Kerew's translation of Matthew 2:12, Gwav. MS).

El a'n leverys dethy haneth, ha hy yn gwely pur thyfun 'an angel said it to her this night, and she in her bed quite awake' (PC 2202–4).

Welsh. *Pa ham, a mi yn disgwyl iddi dwyn grawnwin, y dug hi rawn gwylltlon?* 'Wherefore, and I looking to it to bring forth grapes [Auth. Vers., when I looked that it should bring forth grapes], brought it forth wild grapes?' (Isaiah 5:4).

Gaelic. *Do chonnaic Seaghán an duine, agus é ag teacht a-bhaile* 'John saw the man, and he coming home', i.e. 'when he was coming home'.

2.14.3.3.2. The negative, in which 'not' is expressed in Welsh and Cornish by *heb*, and in Gaelic by *gan*, both meaning 'without', followed by an infinitive:

An delna ema stel ow tegy warnodha, heb wara dhodha teller vîth[107] 'so it is still closing in upon it without leaving it any place' (Boson's *Nebbaz Gerriau*).

In many such cases this negative clause can be translated literally into English, and it is the usual form of negation with an infinitive or present participle.

A somewhat similar absolute clause of a descriptive character occurs occasionally:

An golom, glas hy lagas, yn mes gura hy delyfre 'the dove, blue her eyes, do set her free' (OM 1105–6).

Un flogh yonk, gwyn y dhyllas 'a young child, white his raiment' (PA 254, 3).

---

107 The spelling and mutations corrected.

In a similar construction in Welsh the adjective here agrees with the first noun, and the translation would be rather 'The dove blue [as to] her eyes', but in Cornish this is not so, for in this sentence *golom* (second state of *colom*) is feminine, so that the adjective would be *las*, not *glas*, if it agreed with it.

2.14.4. The infinitive or verbal noun.

The infinitive of a verb is treated almost exactly like a noun. If its object is a pronoun, this precedes the infinitive in the possessive form and governs its initial as it would that of a noun. If the object is not a pronoun, it follows the infinitive without change of initial, after the manner of an appositional genitive.

Very often the infinitive is governed by *dhô* 'to', as in English, and under much the same circumstances, except that it is not so governed when it comes as the subject of another verb, and of course *dhô* is not used after auxiliary verbs. It is especially used after verbs implying motion.

Mî a vedn môs dhô'gas gwelas 'I will go to see you'.

Mî eth dhô vetya an trên 'I went to meet the train'.

Lowen on ny dhô'gas gwelas why 'we are glad to see you'.

When the sense of 'to' is 'in order to', or the preceding verb implies an intention, the infinitive is generally preceded by *rag* or *rag dhô* 'for to', or by *a dhô* 'of to'.

2.14.5. Some idioms and expressions.

2.14.5.1. 'To have' is expressed in three ways.

2.14.5.1.1. By the verb *bos* 'to be', with the thing possessed as subject and the possessor in the dative form, i.e. preceded by *dhô* 'to'; cf. *est mihi* {'it is to me'} in Latin.

Affirmative.　　　*Ema levar dhem* 'there is a book to me'.

Negative.　*Nynsyu levar dhem* 'there is not a book to me'.

Interrogative.　　*'Es levar dhem?* 'Is there a book to me?'

This is the common form in late Cornish.

2.14.5.1.2. By the verb *cafos* or *cavos* 'to find', 'to obtain', used as an ordinary transitive verb with the possessor as subject and the thing possessed as object. This is not used for the present tense. Lhuyd gives a past tense, *mî a gavaz* or *mî 'rig gavaz* 'I had', and a future, *mî ven gavaz* 'I will have', but he, Norris, and Williams are all inclined to confuse this with the third form.

2.14.5.1.3. By a peculiar idiom compounded of a form of the verb *bos* 'to be', and the third form of the personal (or else the possessive) pronouns. The explanation, as far as it goes, of this verb is to be found in Breton. Even there it has been confused a good deal, though its use is plain enough. Legonidec calls it "le verbe *kaout* [= Cornish *cavos*] 'avoir'", which he distinguishes from *kavout* or *kaout* 'trouver'; Maunoir, whose Breton, according to a picture in Quimper Cathedral, was received miraculously from an angel, wisely does not commit himself, but calls the verb, Latin fashion, after the first person singular of the present. Professor Loth rightly speaks of it as "*le verbe dit avoir*" {'the so-called verb *to have*'}, and Mr Ernault calls it "*Verbe **beza** ['to be'] au sens de 'avoir'*" {'Verb *bezañ* in the sense of *to have*'}, and he explains it to be the verb 'to be', combined with the "pronoms régimes" {'object pronouns'}, which is just what it is. In Breton it is not only used as the ordinary verb 'to have' = 'to possess', but also as an auxiliary verb in the same manner as *avoir*, *have*, *haben*, are used in French, English, and German. This verb came to be used in Breton with or without the nominative pronoun being expressed. In Cornish the expressed nominative pronoun is less usual, except in the second person singular, where it is the rule. That it should be used at all in either language is a sign that in practice the original formation of the verb has been forgotten. Occasionally in Cornish this oblivion has resulted even in the application of pronominal inflections to the verb.

This form is found frequently in the *Ordinalia* and in the *Poem of the Passion*; it is fairly common in the *Life of St Meriasek*, it is rarer in the *Creation*, and is not found at all in Cornish of the latest period (except in a doubtful and muddled form in Keigwin's version of the Commandments), though Lhuyd gives a fragment of it in his Grammar, evidently taken from the earlier Dramas and not from oral tradition, for he takes the *g* of *geffi* and *gefyth* to be a hard *g*, whereas it is plainly a soft *g* for a *d*, as the analogy of *tevyth*, and of the Breton *deveus*, *devez*, etc., shows. Moreover, it is sometimes written *ieves*, which is intended to represent *jeves*.

It will be well, by way of making this form clearer, to give not only the Cornish but also the corresponding Breton.[108]

The tenses that are found are as follows:

2.14.5.1.3.1. The Present.

Singular.

Cornish.	Breton.
1. [*mî*] *am bes* [*bus, bues, bues*].	[*me*] *am eus.*
2. [*tî*] *ath ĕs* (*thues*).	[*te*] *ac'h eus.*
3. m. [*ev*] *an jeves* (for *deves*).	[*eñ*] *en deus* or *devez*.[109]
3. f. [*hy*] *as teves.*	[*hi*] *he deus.*

Plural.

1. [*ny*] *an bes.*	[*ni*] *hon eus.*
2. [*why*] *as bes.*	[*c'hwi*] *hoc'h eus.*
3. [*y*] *as teves.*	[*i*] *o deus* or *devez*.[109]

This tense is formed on *us, eus, es* (Breton *eus*), one of the forms of the third person singular of the verb substantive. To this is prefixed the verbal particle *a*, with the letter which is the third form of the personal pronoun, '*m*, '*th*, '*n*, '*s*, '*n*, '*s*, '*s*, with the peculiar addition of *jev* and *tev* to the third persons and *b* to the others. The '*th* of the second person singular is found written in this but not always in the other tenses, for it was probably often silent before *f* by a sort of assimilation. Its effect is observable in the initial mutation. Of this tense the first, second, and third persons singular and the second

---

108 { The Breton citations are given here in modern spelling.}

109 {Breton *devez* is a present habitual form.}

person plural are found. But for the existence of the form *as bes* [*bues*] for the last, one might suppose, with Williams, that the *b* of *am bes* was only the addition of a cognate letter to the *m*. But cf. the addition of *b* to *oa* and *oe* of the same verb in Breton.

2.14.5.1.3.2. The Future.

Singular.

Cornish.	Breton
1. [*mî*] *am bedh* (*byth, beth*).	[*me*] *em* (or *am*) *bez*.[110]
2. *tî a*[*th*] *fedh* (*fyth*).	[*te*] *ez* (or *az*) *pez*.
3. m.[*ev*] *an jevedh* (for *devedh*).	[*eñ*] *en devez*.
3. f. [*hy*] *as tevedh*.	[*hi*] *he devez*.

Plural.

1. [*ny*] *an* (or *agan*) *bedh*.	[*ni*] *hor bez*.
2. [*why*] *as* (or *agas*) *bedh*.	[*c'hei*] *ho pez*.
3. [*y*] *as tevedh*.	[*i*] *o devez*.

It will be seen here and in the other tenses that the pronouns in Breton do not produce exactly the same mutations as in Cornish. The *dh* of Cornish is always written *z* in Breton, though that is pronounced *dh* in some dialects. The whole of this tense is found in the MSS.

2.14.5.1.3.3. The Preterite.

Singular.

Cornish.	Breton.
1. [*mî*] *am bê* [*bue*].	[*me*] *em* (or *am*) *boe*.
2. *tî ath fê*.	[*te*] *ez* (or *az*) *poe*.
3. m.[*ev*] *an jeve*.	[*eñ*] *en doe, devoe*.
3. f. [*hy*] *as teve*.	[*hi*] *he doe, devoe*.

---

110 {The Cornish future was originally the present habitual; the Breton retains the present habitual sense.}

Plural.

1.	[*ny*] *an* (or *agan*) *bê*.	[*ni*] *hor boe*.
2.	[*why*] *as* (or *agas*) *bê*.	[*c'hwi*] *ho poe*.
3.	[*y*] *as teve*.	[*i*] *o doe, devoe*.

Only part of this tense is found in the MSS, but the rest is easily formed by analogy.

2.14.5.1.3.4. The Subjunctive (or Optative).

Singular.

	Cornish.	Breton.
1.	[*mî*] *am bo*.	*r'am bezo, bo*.[111]
2.	*tî ath fo, fetho*.	*r'az pezo, po*.
3. m.	[*ev*] *an jevo* (for *devo*, written *gefo* or *geffo*).	*r'en devezo, devo*.
3. f.	[*hy*] *as tevo*.	*r'he devezo, devo*.

Plural.

1.	[*ny*] *an* (or *agan*) *bo*.	*r'hor bezo, bo*.
2.	[*why*] *as* (or *agas*) bo.	*r'ho pezo, po*.
3.	[*y*] *as tevo* (written *teffo, tefo*).	*r'o devezo, devo*.

In this tense the Breton does not use the nominative personal pronoun, except when it is a form of the future, but prefixes *r'* (*ra*). In Cornish *re* is used to make the optative and perfect, and in this case the *'th* of the second person singular is not omitted, for *re'th fo* and *re'th fê* are the forms found.

A rather doubtful second tense (secondary present or imperfect), equivalent to the Breton *am boa*, may be conjectured in *am beua* (BM 47, 1686), *am bethe* may be the equivalent of the Breton imperfect subjunctive, *am bize, bije, befe*, and the third person singular of this may be the *an geffa* of BM 20, 159. Dr Whitley Stokes gives both

---

111 {The Breton future was originally the subjunctive; the Cornish retains the subjunctive sense. The optative particle *ra* restores the subjunctive sense in Breton.}

these forms as secondary presents.[112] There is also a possible pluperfect *te ny vea*, and *nyn gyfye*, found in the second and third persons singular.

One finds such forms as *am buef, as bethough, may'stefons*, etc., as instances of pronominal inflections added to this verb, showing how completely its derivation was forgotten, and it is further confused by being perhaps mixed up with the verb *pewa* (Welsh *piau*, Breton *piaouañ*) 'to possess', a verb which in all three languages requires rather more disentangling than it has as yet received.

There are very full examples of this verb in Zeuss' *Grammatica Celtica* (ed. 1871, p. 565).

2.14.5.2. Besides 'to have', certain other verbs are expressed with *bos* and the preposition *dhô*. Thus:

Ma cov dhem [pronounced *ma códhem*] 'I remember', lit. 'there is remembrance to me'.

Ma whans dhem 'I want', lit. 'there is want to me'.

Ma whêr dhem 'I am sorry', lit. 'there is grief to me'.

Ma own dhem 'I fear', lit. 'there is fear to me'.

Ma dout dhem 'I doubt', lit. 'there is doubt to me'.

Ma reys dhem, or *reys yw dhem* 'I must', lit. there is need to me'.

Another expression for 'to remember' is *perthy cov* 'to bear memory'. The imperative was sometimes written *perco* in one word. *Perthy* is used similarly with other nouns: *na berth medh* 'be not ashamed', *na berth own* 'be not afraid', *na berth whêr* 'be not sorry', *an vuscogyon orto a borthas avy* 'the fools hated him' (*Passion* 26, 3), *na berth dout* 'do not doubt'. The literal meaning is 'to bear shame, fear, sorrow, envy, doubt', etc.

Similarly nouns and adjectives are used with *gan* 'with', as in Welsh, to represent states of mind. Thus:

---

112 {Analogical reshaping of the subjunctive tenses of this verb in both Cornish and Breton mean that not all forms in one language have exact counterparts in the other.}

Da yu genev 'I like', lit. 'it is good with me'.

Drôg yu genev 'I am sorry', lit. 'it is bad with me'.

Gwell yu genev 'I prefer', lit. 'it is better with me'.

Marth yu genev 'I am astonished', lit. 'wonder is with me'.

Cas yu genev 'I hate', lit. 'hate is with me'.

The verbs *dal* and *goth*, signifying 'ought', 'it behoves', are used either impersonally or, though this is a late corruption, as ordinary verbs.

Ni dal dhen ny, or *Ni goth dhen ny* 'we ought not'. Or:

Mî a dal, or *Mî a godh* 'I ought'.

2.14.5.3. *Gwyn an bês*. This poetical expression is common to Cornish, Welsh, and Breton. It signifies, 'fair the world', i.e. 'happy', and is used with possessive pronouns and appositional genitives.

Gwyn ow bês 'fair my world', 'happy I'.

Gwyn dha vês 'happy thou'.

Gwyn e vês 'happy he'.

Gwyn bês an dên na wrîg cerdhes en cŏsŏl an gamhinsegyon 'blessed is the man who hath not walked in the counsel of the ungodly'.

In Welsh, when the possessor of this 'fair world' is expressed by a noun, there is a redundant possessive pronoun before *byd* (*bês*). Thus Psalm 1 begins *Gwyn ei fyd y gŵr* 'fair his world of the man'. But this is not the Cornish form, which uses the simple appositional genitive in such cases. There is a contrary expression, *drôg pês*, found in the *Ordinalia* (PC 3089), *drok pys of* 'unhappy am I'. In this case *drôg* seems to put the initial of *bês* in its fourth state.

2.14.5.4. The following phrases are in common use, and are generally run into one or two words in pronunciation.

Mêr 'ras dhô Dhew (pronounced *merásthadew*) 'Great thanks be to God'.

Mêr 'ras dheugh why (pron. *merásdhawhy*). 'Great thanks to you'.

Dew re dala dheugh why (pron. *Durdáladhawhy*). 'God repay to you'.

Dew re sona dheugh why (pron. *Dursónadhawhy*). 'God sain you'.

Bennath Dew genough why (pronounced *Bénatew génawhy*). 'The blessing of God be with you'.

Dew genough why (pronounced *Dew génawhy*). 'God be with you'.

Pandráma? (i.e. *pa'n dra wrama*). 'What shall I do?'

Pandréllen? (i.e. *pa'n dra wrellen*). 'What should I do?'

Pándres? (i.e. *pa'n dra es*). 'What is there?'

Pandryu? (i.e. *pa'n dra yu*). 'What is?'

Pandresses? (i.e. *pa'n dra wresses*). 'What shouldst thou do?'

Fatla genough why? (pronounced *fatla génawhy*). 'How are you?'

Trova (i.e. *tre o-va*) 'that he was'.

2.14.6. Rules for initial mutations.

2.14.6.1. THE SECOND STATE.

2.14.6.1.1. A *feminine singular* or *masculine plural* noun (or adjective used as a noun) preceded by the definite article *an* 'the' or the numeral *idn* 'one' has its initial in the second state.

2.14.6.1.2. An adjective which follows and qualifies a *feminine singular* noun, has its initial in the second state.

2.14.6.1.3. A noun preceded by an adjective qualifying it, of whatever gender or number, has its initial in the second state.

2.14.6.1.4. If the adjective preceding and qualifying a *feminine singular* noun follows the article *an* 'the', the initial of the adjective is also in the second state.

2.14.6.1.5. A noun in the vocative preceded by the particle *a* 'O' (expressed or omitted for the sake of verse), has its initial in the second state.

2.14.6.1.6. The possessive pronouns *dha* 'thy' and *e* 'his' are followed by words, whether nouns, adjectives, or verbal nouns (infinitives) in the second state. The form *'th* 'thee' or 'thy' generally puts the word which follows in the second state, but sometimes in the fourth, or changes *b* to *f*, not *v*.

2.14.6.1.7. The verbal prefix *ă* (older *y*, *yth*) is generally followed by a verb in the second state.

2.14.6.1.8. The verbal particles *a* and *re* and the interrogative particle *a* are followed by a verb in the second state.

2.14.6.1.9. The prepositions *a*, *der* or *dre*, *dhô*, *heb*, *re*, and *war*, and compound prepositions ending in any of them, are followed by words in the second state.

2.14.6.1.10. The conjunctions *tre*, *tro* 'that', *pan* 'when', *erna* 'until', *hedre* 'whilst' are followed by the second state.

2.14.6.1.11. The adverbial particle *en* is followed generally by an adjective in the second state.

2.14.6.1.12. The adverbs *pŭr* 'very', *ni*, *na* 'not', *fraga* 'why', *fatla* 'how' are followed by initials in the second state.

2.14.6.2. THE THIRD STATE.

2.14.6.2.1. The possessive pronouns *ow* 'my', *î* 'her', and *aga* 'their' are followed by words in the third state.

2.14.6.2.2. *Ma, may* 'that' are sometimes followed by verbs in the third state, and sometimes by a variant, *g* becoming *h*, and *gw* becoming *wh*.

2.14.6.3. THE FOURTH STATE.

2.14.6.3.1. The particle *ow*, which forms the present participle, is followed by a verbal noun (or infinitive) in the fourth state.

2.14.6.3.2. The conjunctions *a*, *mar*, *mara* 'if' are followed by verbs in the fourth state.

2.14.6.3.2. The adverb *maga* 'as' (in 'as well', etc.) is followed by an adjective in the fourth state.

2.14.6.3.3. Sometimes an adjective beginning with *d*, when preceded by the adverbial particle *en*, has its initial in the fourth state, and rarely a noun beginning with *d*, when it follows in the appositional genitive a word ending in *th*.

2.14.6.3.4. The verbal prefix ă (*y*), when followed by verbs whose radical initial is *d*, often changes that initial to the fourth state, and in the case of those beginning with *gw* to *wh*. The conjunction *ken* 'though' does the same.

2.14.6.3.5. The third form of the second personal pronoun singular *'th* not infrequently changes the initial of a verb beginning with *d* to the fourth state, and that of one beginning with *g* or *gw* to *wh*. It also sometimes changes *b* to *f*.

The exact usage of the mutations is not very clear, for even the older writers used them rather wildly, but the above rules are the general principles of them. There are valuable notes on their phonetic principles in Dr Whitley Stokes's notes to *St Meriasek*, and in a paper of additional notes which he published later. In the latest Cornish there was a tendency to use the second state after nearly anything, especially prepositions, except the few words which govern the other two mutations.

2.15. Prosody

2.15.1. The prosody of the Celtic languages is often very elaborate, but the more modern tendency has generally been in the direction of assimilating it to the prosody of English, or, in the case of Breton, to that of French. In Welsh two systems exist at the present day, and the rules of them are known respectively as *y Rheolau Caethion* and *y Rheolau Rhyddion*, the bond or strict rules and the free rules. The former are founded on elaborate rules of *Cynghanedd* or consonance, which term includes alliteration and rhyme, and every imaginable correspondence of consonant and vowel sounds, reduced to a system which Welsh-speaking Welshmen profess to be able to appreciate, and no doubt really can, though it is not easily understood by the rest of the world. The rules of *Cynghanedd* are applied in various ways to the four-and-twenty metres of the Venedotian (Gwynedd or North Wales) school, and to the metres of the Dimetian (Dyfed or South-West Wales) and the Glamorgan schools. Modern Welsh bards, however, though they often use the strict rules as *tours-de-force* for Eisteddfod purposes, as often compose poetry according to the free rules, which are mostly the ordinary go-as-you-please metres of the Saxon. The Bretons follow the ordinary French rules as to the strict number of syllables, the caesura, and the rhyming, taking very little account of the stress accent either of words or sentences.

The prosody of the older Cornish literature has little in common with the strict system of Welsh. Though one does find alliterations and "internal" rhyming and correspondence of consonants, they do not seem to be at all systematic, but are only either introduced as casual ornaments or purely accidentally. The rules of the older Cornish prosody have more in common with those of Breton, except that, but for one case in the Dramas of a five-syllabled couplet, and the rather irregular Add. Charter fragment in the British Museum, there are only two lengths of lines, seven or four syllables, and the caesura is not very definite.

The seven-syllabled lines are the more common. The whole of the *Poem of the Passion* is in stanzas of eight seven-syllabled lines, rhyming alternately, but written as fourteen-syllabled lines; and the greater part of the Dramas is in lines of the same length, though with varying arrangements of rhymes. Sometimes whole passages of four-syllabled lines occur, and frequently four-syllabled lines occur in the same stanza with those of seven syllables. The rhythmic accent seems to be trochaic, and the heptasyllabic line to consist of three trochees and a long syllable, but as the stress accent of words is absolutely disregarded, and the strong beats of the rhythm sometimes fall on monosyllables which out of poetry would probably be enclitic or proclitic, or at any rate very slightly accented, one can only be sure of the fact that the poet of the *Ordinalia* was careful to count his syllables exactly, and to make the last syllable of every line rhyme with the last syllable of some other line. The author of the *Poem of the Passion* was not quite so careful, and Jordan was still less so. Diphthongs, as in Breton, are occasionally counted as two syllables, a *y* followed by another vowel is sometimes a vowel and sometimes a consonant, and there are occasional elisions and perhaps contractions, understood but not expressed,[113] but with these few exceptions the number of syllables

---

113 Probably the apparent eight syllables in line 6 of the *Poem of the Passion* may be accounted for in this way, and one should read *levarow* as *larow*; cf. in the Breton of Treguier, *laret* for *lavarout*, and the late Cornish *lawle* for *lavarel*.

to a line is strictly accurate, and in the *Ordinalia* is never varied by the unaccented and uncounted syllables that often occur in English verse. The rhymes are quite strict to the eye, but that is no doubt because in the days when one could spell as one pleased, the writer might arrange his spelling to suit, but there appear to be cases where the *dh* and *th* {[ð], [θ]}, both written *th*, as final consonants are made to rhyme together, and the three sounds of *u* (*oo* and the French *u* and *eu* {[u], [y], [ø]}) are sometimes confused. Though the rhymes are always "masculine" (i.e. of one syllable), there are occasionally cases where, unless one counts the rhymes as "feminine" (i.e. of two syllables), they would not be rhymes at all, and yet feminine rhymes would throw out the rhythm.[114]

The metres of late Cornish were usually rather more assimilated to English, but apparently some memory of Celtic prosody lingered on. Lhuyd quotes a proverb, of which he gives two versions, in the old three-lined metre known in Welsh as the *Triban Milwr*, or 'Warrior's Triplets', which is found as early as Llywarch Hen's Laments for Geraint ap Erbyn and for the Death of Cynddylan, in the sixth century. Lhuyd himself wrote a Cornish Lament for William of Orange in what he claimed as the same metre, a singularly inappropriate subject for the language of a nation of loyal Jacobites, as the Cornish certainly were as late as 1715. Boson (Gwavas MS, f. 7) wrote a short elegy on James Jenkins of Alverton, also in rhyming triplets. The curious little song, which is all that remains of Jenkins's poetry, seems to show indications of a feeling

---

114 It may be that the Cornish ear for rhymes was like the French, and that the explanation is to be sought in a theory like that of the *rimes riches* and the *consonne d'appui* of modern French. In French *chercher*— *rocher* is a better rhyme than *aimer*—*rocher* (in each case with the accent on the last syllable). In English the first would be no rhyme. {This last comment is obscure to me; to my ear [ʃɛʁ'ʃe] and [ʁo'ʃe] and [ɛ'me] all rhyme. But then I was raised on Dr Seuss, who approved of *rimes pauvres* more than Jenner evidently did.}

for internal rhymes and something like a rudimentary *Cynghanedd*, but there is not enough of it to reduce to any definite rules. Even in Boson's verses and in those of Gwavas and Tonkin of St Just (not the historian), in the Gwavas MS, the old system of counting syllables and taking very little account of the stress accents of words, is occasionally found, but generally in the later verse the extra unaccented syllables freely introduced show that a sense of accent and beats of rhythm had come in.

2.15.2. Specimens of Cornish verse.

2.15.2.1. Five- (or four-) syllabled lines, with occasional six-syllabled, rhyming AABCCB. From the fragment on the back of Additional Charter 19,491 in the British Museum, late fourteenth century.

Golsow ty cowedh, (5)	Hearken, thou comrade,
Byth na borth medh, (4)	Never be ashamed,
Dyyskyn ha powes (6)	Alight and rest
Ha dhymo dus nes. (5)	And to me come near.
Mar codhes dhe les; (5)	If thou knowest thy advantage;
Ha dhys y rof mowes, (6)	And to thee I will give a girl,
Ha fest unan dek (5)	And truly a fair one
Genes war a plek. (5)	To thee if she is pleasing.
Ha tanha y; (4)	Go take her now;
Kemmerr y dhoth wrek, (5)	Take her to thy wife,
Sconye dhys ny vek (5)	Refuse thee she will not
Ha ty a vydh hy. (5)[115]	And thou shalt have her.

It is probable that this metre is intended to be five-syllabled throughout, except that a "feminine" or double rhyme is occasionally allowable (e.g. *powes—mowes*), and that the light first syllable of

---

115 The numerals denote the number of syllables to each line. In the original a long *z* {that is, a yogh, ȝ} is used for *dh* and *th*.

a line may be omitted. This accounts for the two six-syllabled and two four-syllabled lines respectively. In the rest of the poem there are lines of four, five, seven, eight, and even nine syllables. The whole fragment of forty-one lines, though not much earlier than the *Ordinalia*, is much less regular in rhythm, and is much less syllabic.

2.15.2.2. One of the commonest metres of the Dramas, and indeed of much medieval verse in other languages, consists of seven-syllabled lines rhyming A A B C C B, or A A B A A B.

From *Passio Christi*, the second of the *Ordinalia*, fifteenth century. (Our Lord's speech to the *Pueri Hebræorum*.) {PC 265–270.}

Ow benneth ol ragas bo	My blessing be all upon you
Ow tos yn onor thymmo	Coming in honour to me
Cans branchis flowrys kefrys.	With branches and flowers likewise.
Un deyth a thue yredy	A day shall soon come
Ma'n talvethaf ol thywhy	When I shall repay it all to you
Kemmys enor thym yu gwrys.	As much honour as is done to me.

This is the metre of the well-known Whitsunday Sequence, *Veni Sancte Spiritus* ('Come, thou Holy Spirit, come').

Note that *gwrys* (*gwres* in Modern Cornish) is a monosyllable, and that the *ue* of *dhue* is a single vowel = *eu* {[ø]}. This metre is varied by being made into eight-lined stanzas, rhyming A A A B C C C B.

2.15.2.3. Another very common metre in the Dramas consists of stanzas of eight lines of seven syllables, rhyming alternately. Usually the stanza only contains two rhymes, but sometimes, especially if four lines of the eight are given to one character and four to another, the rhymes of the two quatrains are independent of one another.

From the *Ordinale de Origine Mundi*, fifteenth century. (Eve's speech to Adam after gathering the apple.) {OM 213–220.}

My pan esen ou quandre	I when I was wandering
Clewys a'n nyl tenewen	Heard on the one side
Un el ou talleth cane	An angel beginning to sing
A ughaf war an wethen.	Above me on the tree.
Ef a wruk ow husullye	He did counsel me
Frut annethy may torren	Fruit from it that I should break;
Moy es Deu ny a vye	More than God we should be
Bys venytha na sorren.	Nor be troubled for ever.

Note the apparent "feminine" rhymes, *torren—sorren*, which are really *rimes riches* in the French style.

The whole *Poem of the Passion* is in this metre, but is written in lines of fourteen syllables.

2.15.2.4. Four-syllabled lines, often written as eight-syllabled, rhyming alternately. Thus (PC 35–38):

A mester whek · gorthys re by	O sweet master, glorified be thou,
Pan wreth mar tek · agan dysky.	When thou dost so sweetly teach us.
Asson whansek · ol the pysy,	How we desire all to pray,
Lettrys na lek · war Thu mercy!	Learned and lay, to God for mercy!

The same two rhymes run through a stanza of eight (written as four) lines.

2.15.2.5. Four-syllabled lines in six-lined stanzas, rhyming AABAAB (PC 169–172).

Gorthyans ha gras	Glory and thanks
The Dew ow thas	To God my Father,
Luen a verci,	Full of mercy,
Pan danvonas	When he sent
Yn onor bras	In great honour
Thym servysi.	Servants to me.

2.15.2.6. Sometimes a mixture of the last two forms of stanza is found extended to ten lines. Thus (OM 1271–1276):

Dyvythys of	Come am I
The'th volungeth,	To thy will.
Arluth porth cof	Lord remember
Yn deyth dyweth	In the last day
A'm enef vy.	My soul.
Lavar thymmo	Tell me
Pandra wrama;	What I shall do;
Y'n gwraf ytho	I will do it now
Scon yn tor-ma	Soon in this turn
Yn pur deffry.	Very seriously.

2.15.2.7. Mixed seven and four syllabled lines. Sometimes these are only the metre of §2.15.2.2, with the third and sixth lines four-syllabled instead of seven-syllabled.

Thus in *Origo Mundi* {OM 911–916}, we find:

Ou banneth theughwhy pub prys,	My blessing to you always,
Mar tha y wreugh ou nygys	So well you do my business
Prest yn pub le.	Quickly everywhere.
Gorreugh an fals nygethys	Put the false flier
Gans Abel a desempys	With Abel immediately
The yssethe.	To sit.

2.15.2.8. Sometimes alternations of stanzas of four and seven-syllabled lines are found. A very remarkable and effective set opens the Drama of *The Passion*. It is in stanzas of thirteen lines, eight lines of four syllables (written as four of eight syllables), rhyming ABABABAB, one line of seven syllables with rhyme C, three lines of seven syllables with rhyme D, and a seven-syllabled line with rhyme C. {PA 1–9}

Thyugh lavara · Ow dyskyblyon,	To you I say, my disciples,
Pyseygh toythda · Ol kescolon	Pray quickly, all of one heart
Deu dreys pup tra · Eus a huhon	God above everything, who is on high
Theygh yn bys-ma · Y grath danvon	To you in this world His grace to send
Yn dyweth may feugh sylwys.	In the end that ye may be saved.
Gans an eleth yu golow,	With the angels there is light,
Yn nef agas enefow	In heaven your souls
Neffre a tryg hep ponow	Ever shall dwell without pains
Yn joy na vyth dywythys.	In joy that shall not be ended.

2.15.2.9. In the Drama of *St Meriasek* there are no less than ten classes of stanza, counting by the number of lines to the stanza, and these may be considerably multiplied by alternating or mixing seven-syllabled with four-syllabled lines in various orders, and by varying the number of sets of rhymes to a stanza and the order of those rhymes. Perhaps one of the most elaborated {BM 168–180} will serve as a specimen. It is a thirteen-lined stanza of twelve seven-syllabled lines, and one (the ninth) four-syllabled line, with four sets of rhymes, rhyming A B A B A B A B C [four syllables] D D D C.

Gelwys ydhof Conany,	Called am I Conan,
Mytern yn Bryton Vyan;	King in Little Britain;
Han gulascor pur yredy	And the kingdom very readily
Me a beu olyn tyan.	I own all entirely.
Der avys ou arlydhy	Through the advice of my lords
Mones y fannaf lemman	I will go now
The Duk pen a chevalry,	To the Duke the chief of knighthood.
Nesse dhymmo yn certan	Second to me certainly
Par del yu ef	Like as he is.
Yma maryag galosek	There is a mighty marriage
Cowsys dhyn rag Meryasek	Spoken to us for Meriasek

Mergh dhe vyghtern gallosek,   Of the daughter to a mighty king,
Nynses brassa yn dan nef.   There is not a greater under heaven.

It is evident that by varying the number of lines and rhymes to a stanza, varying the distribution of the rhymes, and mixing lines of different length, an almost infinite variety may be obtained, even with only two forms of line.

2.15.2.10. The metres of Jordan's Drama of *The Creation* (1611) do not differ materially in intention from those of the *Ordinalia*, on which they are evidently modelled. But in this play one begins to find signs of a tendency to a less accurate ear for exact syllabic rhythm. About eighty lines out of the 2548 of which the play consists have eight syllables, about twenty have only six, and in each case these ought to be seven-syllabled. Also there are two cases of three and six of five syllables in what ought to be four-syllabled lines, and there are several cases of nine syllables in a line, and one case of ten. No doubt some of these discrepancies may be accounted for by elisions and contractions not expressed in writing (as is often the case in Latin), and some of the short lines contain diphthongs which may be meant to count as two syllables, but by no means all are explainable by anything but the influence of English, or, as is less probable, a reversion to some such archaic idea of rhythm as that of the Add. Charter Fragment.

After this we come to the verses of late Cornish. These are few, poor, corrupt, and illiterate, and for the most part without value for metrical purposes.[116] The strictly syllabic metres of the older Cornish have nearly disappeared, and though the tonic accent is still disregarded when convenient, extra unaccented syllables, as

---

116 {In the spirit of *tota Cornicitas* we no longer disdain any remnant of Traditional Cornish left to us. It may however be true that Late Cornish verse offers us little insight into Celtic metres, because it is influenced by English metrics.}

often in inferior, and sometimes in good English verse, are freely introduced by way of anacrusis, etc., in a manner that shows that accent was considered in a sort of way, and that the accents of a line rather than the syllables were counted. John Boson wrote a few lines in three-lined stanzas somewhat after the fashion of the Welsh *Triban Milwr*, and Lhuyd's artificial elegy on William of Orange is another instance of the same. The only poem remaining of James Jenkins of Alverton (printed by Pryce and Davies Gilbert) is a sort of irregular ode, which refuses to be satisfactorily analysed. The lines are all sorts of lengths, they may begin with an accent or they may have one or two light syllables before the first strong beat, the rhymes may be single or double. The principle of the first part seems to be little lines of two beats, varying from three to seven syllables rhyming in couplets. Thus:

Ma léeaz gwréag	There are many wives
Lácka vel zéag,	Worse than grains [brewers' refuse],
Gwéll gerrés (or *gwéll gérres*)	Better left
Vel kómmerés (or *vél komméres*),	Than taken,
Ha ma léeaz bénnen	And there are many women
Pókar an gwénen	Like the bees,
Ey vedn gwérraz de go tées	They will help their men
Dendle péath an béaz.	To earn the goods of the world.
Fléhaz heb skéeanz	Children without knowledge
Vedn guíl go séeanz;	Will do [according to] their sense;
Buz mar crówngy predéry	But if they do consider
Pan dél go gwáry	What their play is like,
Ha mádra tá	And consider well
Pandrig séera ha dámma,	What did father and mother,
Na ra hens [*wrans?*] *móaz*	They will not go to
dan cóoz	the wood
Do kúntle go bóoz.[117]	To gather their food.

117 The spelling of one of the original MSS has been preserved here,

The latter part has lines of four beats, with a very variable number of unaccented syllables, which in reading were probably hurried over rather vaguely. This rhythm may be compared with the "new principle" (as the author calls it in his preface) of Coleridge's *Christabel*.[118]

Boson's triplets are mostly of ten-syllabled lines, Lhuyd's are generally of eight syllables, but sometimes of nine or even ten and eleven.

Tonkin of St Just, a tailor, wrote two songs, which are in the Gwavas MS. They are in four-lined stanzas generally of seven-syllabled lines, though as often as not having an extra light syllable to begin with. Thus:

Pa wrîg ev gŏrra trôz war tîr	When he [William of Orange] did put foot on land
Ev vê welcombes me ôr gwîr.	He was welcomed I know well.
Ha devethes dhô Caresk	And having come [came] to Exeter
Maga saw besca vê pesk.[119]	As sate as ever was fish.

The epigrams printed by Pryce and Davies Gilbert were mostly composed by Boson and Gwavas. Eight-syllabled lines are frequent among them, but they are of little or no value, and are altogether on English models, and not very good models at that.

Should any one wish to attempt verse-writing in Cornish, it would be best either to use one of the seven or four syllabled (or mixed) metres of the Dramas, using their purely syllabic methods, which undoubtedly work all right in modern Breton, or to extend

---

except that, in order to avoid confusion as to the number of syllables, the final mute *e* is omitted. In this *ee* = *î*, *ea* = *ê*, *oo* = *ô*.

118 "I have only to add that the metre of *Christabel* is not properly speaking irregular, though it may seem so through its being founded on a new principle, namely, that of counting in each line the accents, not the syllables." (Preface to 1816 edition of *Christabel*.)

119 Spelling adapted to that of this grammar.

the same principles, as the Bretons do, to lines of other lengths. The triplets of old Welsh and perhaps of very old Cornish are effective metres, but are not so easy as they look, for it is not enough merely to write rhyming triplets. Lhuyd in his one attempt has produced a peculiar though allowable metre, with lines of all sorts of lengths, and the old specimens, Llywarch Hen's *Marwnad Geraint ap Erbin*, and the Englynion called *Eiry Mynydd*, are largely in lines of seven syllables, and some of them, such as the Song of the Death of Cynddylan, and the curious ninth-century poem in the Cambridge *Juvencus*, seem to have also the *gair cyrch*, that strange little tag to the first line of the triplet, outside of the rhyme but not outside of the assonance or alliteration, which is so marked a characteristic of the four-lined Englyn, while in most of them there are alliterations, vowel correspondences, and internal rhymes, which are not so haphazard as they look. It is well not to attempt to force a Celtic language into a Teutonic mould. Some of the most beautiful metres that the world has ever known are to be found among the works of English poets, but they are no more suitable to Cornish than hexameters, sapphics, and alcaics on strict quantity lines would be to English. It is possible, however, to write ten-syllabled blank verse in Cornish, provided a fair amount of alliteration is used.

One word about inversions of the order of words in poetry. This should be done very sparingly, and it is not easy to lay down very definite rules as to what is allowable and what not. It is best not to deviate from the usual order of words unless one can find a precedent in one of the Dramas. Some inversions, however, are quite allowable. Thus one may put the complement of a predicate, e.g. an infinitive, an accusative, or a participle, at the beginning of a phrase:

> *bewa ythesaf pub eare* (CW 1667), 'living I am always'.
> *banna ny allaf gwelas* (CW 1622), 'a drop I cannot see'.
> *defalebys os ha cabm* (CW 1603), 'deformed thou art, and crooked'.

yn bushes ow crowetha (CW 1606), 'in bushes lying'.

gans dean pen vo convethys (CW 1618), 'by man when it is discovered'.

worthaf ve sertan ny dale (CW 1619), 'with me, certainly, ought not'.

determys ove dha un dra (CW 236), 'determined I am of one thing'.

mos then menythe me a vyn (CW 1082), 'go to the mountain I will'.

These are all taken from Jordan's *Creation*, and mostly at random from the same page. Still, the less one inverts the normal order of words the better.

2.16. Note on the interpretation of Cornish names

2.16.1. One of the practical interests in the study of Cornish is in the interpretation of place-names. As quite ninety per cent of the place-names of Cornwall are Celtic, and as a very large proportion of these are descriptive names, usually in a fairly uncorrupted state, this gives much opportunity of research. There are, however, certain considerations, grammatical and topographical, which should be kept carefully in mind in attempting to discover the meanings of these names, and it is a disregard of these considerations that has made most of the published works on the subject so singularly valueless.

The great majority of Cornish names are composed of epithets suffixed to certain nouns, such as *tre*, *trev* 'town'; *pol* 'pool'; *pen* or *pedn* 'head' or 'top';[120] *rôs*, often written *rose* 'heath';[121] *car* 'fort' or 'camp'; *lan* 'enclosure' or 'church'; *eglos* 'church'; *bal* 'mine'; *whêl* or *wheal* 'a work' (i.e. 'a mine'); *chy*, *ty* 'house'; *park* 'field'; *porth* 'creek' or 'harbour'; *nans* 'valley'; *carn* 'cairn' or 'heap of rocks'; *hal* 'moor'; *gûn*, *goon* 'a down'; *gwêl*, *gweal* 'field'; *bod*, *bos*, *bo* 'dwelling'; *les* 'court', 'palace'; *carrack* 'rock'; *creeg* 'tumulus'; *crows* 'cross'; *din*, *dun* 'hill-fort'; *fenton* or *venton* 'a spring'; *kelly*, *killy* 'grove'; *cos*, *coose* 'a wood'; *mên* 'stone'; *tol* 'hole'; *triga*, *trigva* 'dwelling-place'; *melan*, *mellan*, *vellan* 'mill';

---

120 {*Pen*, *pedn* is better translated as 'settlement'.}

121 {*Rôs*, *rose* does not translate as 'heath', but as 'promontory, hillspur, coastal slope, roughland', depending upon the site.}

zawn, zawns 'cove'; *bron, bryn* 'hill';[122] *bar, bor, bur* 'summit'; *tor* 'hill'.[123] These are the commonest of the nouns. The epithets may be:

1. Adjectives, signifying size, colour, position, etc., e.g. *mêr, mear, vear* 'great'; *bîan, bean, vean* 'little'; *glas* 'blue'; *dew* 'black'; *gwin, gwidn, widn* 'white'; *gwartha, wartha, gwarra* 'upper';[124] *gollas, gullas, wallas* 'lower', etc., in agreement with the noun.

2. Other nouns in the appositional genitive.

3. Proper names.

4. Adjectives or nouns preceded by the article *an* 'the', or by a preposition such as *war* 'on'.

2.16.2. The following points should be considered:

2.16.2.1. The gender of the noun. Of the nouns mentioned above, *tre, ros, car, lan, whêl, hal, goon, carrack, crows, fenton, kelly, trigva, mellan, bron, tor*, are feminine, so that the initial of the adjective epithet is changed to the second state. This may often, more or less, determine whether the epithet is an adjective or a noun in the genitive. Thus, in the name *Tremaine*, we may be sure that the second syllable is not an adjective or it would be **Trevaine*, so the meaning is not, as one would think, 'the stone house', not a very distinguishing epithet in Cornwall, but probably the 'house of the stones', i.e. of some stone circle or other prehistoric remains.[125] Sometimes, however, the initial of an appositional genitive, and

---

122 {*Zawn, zawns* (the latter is not known) is a vertically sided blind chasm in a coastal cliff.}

123 {*Tor*, literally 'belly', means a hump, bulge, or other eminence in the landscape.}

124 {*Gwarra* should be deleted from the given variants of *gwartha* (see note 53 above).}

125 {Mutation is notoriously irregular in place-names and, therefore Jenner's observations regarding the names *Tremaine, Trevaine* can be discounted.}

sometimes that of an epithet of a masculine noun is irregularly changed in composition.

2.16.2.2. The stress accent of the compound. This is of great importance, especially in determining whether an article or preposition intervenes between the noun and its epithet, and also, in the rare cases in which it occurs, in deciding whether the epithet may not precede the noun. *The stress accent is almost invariably on the epithet*, and it is astonishing to see how even in East Cornwall, where the language has been dead for three centuries, this accentuation is still preserved. If the epithet suffix is a monosyllable, the accent of the compounded word is on the last syllable; if not, the accent is usually on the last but one, but the intervening article or preposition is always a proclitic, and is disregarded as to accent. The same sort of thing happens in English. Thus, even if it were the custom to write *Stratfordonavon* all in one word, we should know by the accent that it meant *Stratford-on-Avon*; but one, say some German philologist, who had never heard it pronounced, and knew nothing of British topography and the distribution of surnames, might conjecture that it was *Stratfor Dónavon*, might compare it with *Lydiard Tregoze, Stoke Dabernon, Sutton Valence*, or *Compton Wyniates*, and might build thereon a beautiful theory of an Irish settlement in Warwickshire. Things every whit as absurd as this have been done with Cornish names.

2.16.2.3. The position and general features of the place. Thus when we find that a rather important town is situated at the innermost point of a bay called in Cornish (cf. Boson's Pilchard Song) *Zanz Garrak Loos en Kûz*, we may doubt whether its name signifies 'the holy head or headland', and not 'the head of the bay'.[126] In this case there is a slight complication, because there is actually something of a headland about the Battery Rocks, and the town

---

126 {The meaning of 'bay' given to the word *Zanz* 'holy', is a mistake on the part of John Boson.}

arms are St John Baptist's head in a charger; but when we find that *Tremaine* is some ten miles, as the crow flies, from the nearest point of the coast, we may be quite justified in doubting whether Pryce is right in calling it "the town on shore or sea coast".

2.16.3. The following specimens of names about whose meaning there can be no doubt, will serve as examples of the construction of Cornish place-names:

2.16.3.1. Epithet following noun.

2.16.3.1.1. Masculine. *Porthmear* (in Zennor), 'the great porth or creek'. (Murray's Handbook says that it means the 'sea-port', but Murray's interpretations are intricately and ingeniously wrong-headed).

2.16.3.1.2. Feminine. *Trevean* 'the little town'. *Tre* signifies 'town' in the modern Cornish and old English sense, a farmhouse with its out-buildings. It is the commonest of these generic prefixes. In Brittany, though it is occasionally found, its place is usually taken by *Kêr* (Cornish *Car*, Welsh *Caer*), probably the Latin *castrum*, 'a fortified town or camp', a difference which has its historical significance.

2.16.3.2. Epithet preceding noun.

Hendrea, the old town (in Sancreed). Note that this is *Héndrea*, not *Hendréa*. Note also the change of initial in *tre*.[127]

2.16.3.3. Intervening particles.

2.16.3.3.1. The definite article. *Crows-an-wra* 'the witch's cross'. (Murray says that it means "the wayside cross," but *gwragh, gwrah,*

---

127 {Compounds, such as *Hendra* (Jenner's *Hendrea*), are now a recognized feature of Cornish toponymy. In these, the usual word order is reversed, the preceding adjective then causing lenition to the noun.}

gwra, Breton *gwrac'h*, certainly means 'a hag' or 'a witch', and the change of initial after the article shows that the noun is feminine.) *Chy-an-dowr* 'the house of the water'.

2.16.3.3.2. Preposition. *Tywardreath* 'the house on the sands'; *Tywarnhaile* (= *Ty war an hayle*) 'the house on the tidal river'. Note that the syllable *war* in these words is unaccented. In *Trewartha* 'the upper house', the accent is on *war*, so that even if we were not accustomed to the epithet *wartha* we should know that *war* is here not a preposition.

2.16.3.4. Appositional genitive without article. *Chytan* 'the house of fire';[128] *Chypons* 'the bridge house'; *Pentreath* 'the head of the sands'; *Portreath* (= *Porth-treath*) 'creek of the sands'. *Nancemelling* (= *Nans-mellan*) 'the valley of the mill'.

2.16.3.5. Proper names as appositional genitives. *Trejago* 'the house of Jago' (or 'James'). *Chykembra* 'the Welshman's house'. *Gûn-an-Guidal* (or *Anguidal Downs*) 'the down of the Irishman'.[129]

2.16.4. In West Cornwall, especially in Penwith, where the spoken language lingered latest, there is a greater tendency to the use of the article *an* than in the more eastern part of the Duchy. Sometimes the article is prefixed to the noun itself. Thus, *Andrewartha* (= *an dre wartha*) 'the upper town', in Gwithian, now called Upton, but inhabited by a family of the older name; *Angarrack* 'the rock', between Hayle and Gwinear Road; *Angove* 'the smith', and *Angwin* 'the white', family names; *Angrouse* 'the cross', in

---

128 {*Chytan* (*Chytane* on the current maps) is, in fact, a contaction of *Chywarton*, 'house on pastureland'.}

130 {*Gûn-an-Guidal* does not have the derivation given by Jenner. It was *Goone agga Idniall* 1670, becoming *Agnidal downs* 1769 and finally *Nangidnall Croft* (TA). The true derivation is: *goon ajy idnyal* 'downs of a desloate pass or gap'.}

Mullion; *Angear* 'the castle'; *Annear* or *Ennor* 'the earth'; *Angilley* or *Anguilly* 'the grove'.[130]

Generally when the article comes between the generic noun and some other word the latter is a noun also, an appositional genitive, but occasionally it is an adjective, as in *Ponsanooth* (in Perran Arworthal and Gluvias), which is probably *Pons-an-nowedh*, the new bridge.[131] The generic prefix *Pleu* or *Plou* 'parish', so common in Brittany, is altogether unknown in Cornish place-names of to-day, unless, as some hold, *Bleu Bridge* in Madron means 'the parish bridge', and is a partial translation of *Pons-an-bleu*, but the word is common enough in Cornish, and the names of parishes called after saints frequently began in Cornish writings with *Pleu* (*plu*, *plui*)— *Pleu East* 'St Just'; *Pleu Paul* 'St Paul'; *Pleu Vudhick* 'St Budock'. Though the word occurs in the expression *tîz pleu* 'people of [his] parish', in the tale of *John of Chy-an-Hur*, the three parishes mentioned there, St Levan, St Hillary, and Buryan, are called by their ordinary English names. The prefix *lan*, originally 'an enclosure' (cf. the English 'lawn'), but later used to signify a church with its churchyard, is still frequently found, with occasional variants of *la*, *lam*, and *land*, but it is nothing like so frequent as the Welsh equivalent *llan*. In earlier days it was more common in Cornwall than it is now, and a number of parishes which now have the prefix "Saint" appear in the Domesday Survey with *Lan*.

2.16.5. The family names of Cornwall, omitting those of the few great Norman houses, Granvilles, Bevilles, Fortescues, Bassets, St Aubyns, Glanvilles, etc., which do not concern us at present, fall into at least four classes.

---

130 Cf. the Arabic article *al* prefixed to place-names in Southern Spain, and to nouns of Arabic derivation in Spanish.

131 {*Noweth* 'new' does not occur in the name *Ponsanooth*, the qualifying elements of which are either *an woodh* 'the goose' or, perhaps more likely, *an wooth* 'the stream'.}

2.16.5.1. Names derived from places.

"By Tre, Pol, and Pen,
Ye shall know Cornishmen."

or as Camden more correctly expands it at the expense of metre:

"By Tre, Ros, Pol, Lan, Car, and Pen,
Ye shall know the most Cornishmen."

And he might have added many more prefixes. It is probable that many of these names originated in the possession of the estates of the same names.

Of this class are such names as *Trelawny*, *Rosevear*, *Polwhele*, *Lanyon*, *Carlyon*, and *Penrose*. To the ordinary Saxon they sound highly aristocratic, and are introduced into modern "up country" novels in a way that is often amusing to a Cornishman, and no doubt many of them do represent the names of families of past or present gentility, for in Cornwall, as in the Scottish Highlands, armigerous gentry were and are very thick on the ground, and a very large number of Cornishmen of every class and occupation might write themselves down "gentlemen" in the strict heraldic sense if they only knew it. But some names of this class are derived from very small landed possessions, and some probably, as similar names in England, from mere residence, not possession.

2.16.5.2. Patronymics. These are the equivalents of the English names ending in -*son* or -*s*, of the Welsh names beginning with *ap* (= *mab* 'son'), and the Irish and Scottish beginning with *Mac* or *O'*. They fall into five classes.

2.16.5.2.1. The Christian name used as a surname without alteration, as *Harry*, *Peter*, *John*, *Rawle*, *Rawe* or *Rowe* (for *Ralph* or *Raoul*), *Gilbart* and *Gilbert*, *Thomas* or *Thom*, *Davy*, *Bennet*, *Harvey*, *Tangye*, etc.

2.16.5.2.2. The diminutive of the Christian name, as *Jenkin*, *Hodgkin*, *Rawlin*, *Tonkin*, *Eddyvean* (= 'Little Eddy'), *Hockin* (= 'Hawkin', i.e. 'Harrykin'), etc.

2.16.5.2.3. The Christian name or its diminutive in its English possessive form, as *Peters*, *Johns*, *Rogers*, *Jenkins*, *Rawlings*, *Roberts*, etc.

2.16.5.2.4. Patronymics formed as in English, German, Dutch, and the Scandinavian languages by adding *-son*, as *Johnson*, *Jackson*, *Wilson*, etc. When these occur in Cornwall they are probably often of English origin.

2.16.5.2.5. Patronymics formed with the prefix *ap* (for *mab* 'son'), apocopated (as in the Welsh names *Probert*, *Pritchard*, *Price*, *Bevan*, *Bowen*) to a *p* or *b*. It is possible that to this class may belong *Prowse*, *Prawle* (*Ap Rowse*, *Ap Rawle*), *Bown* (*Ap Owen?*), *Budge* (*Ap Hodge?*), *Pezzack* (*Ap Isaac*).

The Christian names from which patronymics are formed are not as a rule very peculiar. There are the usual names of the well-known saints, *Peter*, *Paul*, *Mitchell* (*Michael*), *John*, *James* (or in its Cornish form, *Jago*), *Thomas*, *Matthew*, *Francis*, *Dunstan*, *Bennet*, *Andrew*, *Martin*, and the rest, the common general Christian names, *Harry*, *William*, *Robert*, *Roger*, etc., and some less common ones, such as *Julyan*, *Vivian*, *Nicholas* (*Nicol*, *Nicholl*, etc.), *Colin*, *Jeffry*, *Jasper*, *Gilbert*, etc., and names of Cornish saints *Keverne*, *Key*, *Gluyas*, *Ustick* (probably adjectival form from *Just*). Besides these there are a few from old British, or of Breton or Norman introduction, *Harvey* (*Hervé*), *Dennis*, *Rawle*, and *Rawlin* (*Raoul*, *Raoulin*, *Rivallen*), *Tangye* (*Tanguy*, a quite common name in Brittany, from St Tanguy, one of the entourage of St Pol of Leon), *Arthur*, *David* or *Davy* (as representing the Welsh saint, not the King of Israel), *Sampson* (representing the Bishop of Dol, not the Israelite hero), *Jewell* (Breton *Judicael* or *Juhel*). Some names take a variety of forms. Thus *Clement* is found as *Clemens*, *Clemments*, *Clements*, *Clemo* or *Clemmow*, *Climo*, *Climance*, etc., *Ralph* (*Radulphus*, *Rudolph*, *Randolph*, *Rollo*) is found as *Ralph*,

Rapson, *Rawe*, *Rawle*, *Rawlin*, *Rawling*, *Rawlings*, *Rabling*, *Randall*, *Rowe*, *Rowling*, *Rowse*, etc. There are also certain names which have a resemblance to Spanish names, *Pascoe*, *Varcoe*, *Jago*, *Crago*, *Manuel*, etc., but no theory of Spanish influence is necessarily to be built upon them, as they are otherwise explainable. As the Cornish had got beyond the matriarchal stage of culture before historic times, we do not find family names derived from names of women, but no chapter on Cornish nomenclature can omit that very remarkable and peculiarly Cornish name *Jennifer*, which is beyond any doubt a local form of the name of *Guenivere*, the wife of Arthur. A more Frenchified form is still found in Brittany, and the Cornish form goes back to time immemorial. At one time the name of an equally celebrated Queen of Cornwall was used as a Cornish Christian name, for *Ysolt* de Cardinham possessed the advowson of the church of Colan in the thirteenth century, but except as a modern revival, of which the present writer knows only one case connected with Cornwall, this name is no longer found. Another not infrequent Christian name is *Hannibal*, from which possibly may come the surnames *Hambly*, *Hamley*, and *Hamblyn*. The name is too old in Cornwall to have originated in any theory about the Phoenicians and the tin trade of the Cassiterides, for it is found in times when no one troubled himself about either, but its origin is decidedly a puzzle.

2.16.5.3. Names derived from trades or occupations. Some of these are only English—*Smith*, *Wright*, *Carpenter*, *Brewer*, *Paynter*, etc.—but others are real Cornish, as *Marrack* 'knight; *Angove* 'the smith'; *Drew* 'druid', 'magician' (and perhaps *An-drew* 'the druid', when it is not merely a patronymic);[132] *Tyacke* 'farmer'; *Sayer* and

---

132 {Jenner's interpretations of the surnames *Drew* and *Andrew* are very doubtful. They are most probably variants of the Biblical name *Andrew*.}

199

Sara, possibly *Saer* 'carpenter'; *Hellyar* 'hunter'; *Cauntor* (Latin *Cantor*), 'singer'.

2.16.5.4. Nicknames or names derived from personal peculiarities, such as *Black*, *White*, *Brown*, *Grey*, *Green*, which are mostly found in English, though one finds *Angwin* 'the white', and *Winn* 'white'; *Glass* and *Glaze* 'blue'; *Couch* 'red'; *Floyd* (cf. Welsh *Lloyd*) 'grey'; *Glubb* 'moist', 'wet'; *Coath*, *Coad*, and its English *Olde* or *Ould*; *Baragwaneth* 'wheat-bread', etc. Also names derived from names of animals, *Bullock*, *Cock*, *Fox*, or its Cornish *Lewarne* (unless that is *Le-warne* 'the place of alders'), *Mutton* (though this may be a place-name also), etc. One does not see why a man should have been called *Curnow* 'the Cornishman', in a country in which such an epithet could not have been very distinguishing, but that name is not at all uncommon, nor is *Andain* or *Endean* 'the man', which is still less distinguishing.

This is only a slight sketch of a considerable range of investigation, but the subject would require a book to itself, so that it is impossible here to do more than indicate the direction in which students of Cornish nomenclature should work. But in the investigation of place-names in any language one must always allow for corruption and alteration in the course of centuries, and in a Celtic country for the Celticizing of names of non-Celtic derivation. Thus the well-known Welsh name *Bettws* is probably the old English 'bede-house' ('prayer-house'), *Gattws*, less common, is 'gatehouse'. The terminations *aig*, *sgor*, *bhal*, *dail*, *ort*, so common in the Hebrides and West Highlands, are Gaelic forms of the Norse *vik*, *skjær*, *val*, *dal*, *fjord*, and many names in those parts are altogether Norse, spelt Gaelic fashion, and have no meaning whatever in Gaelic. Probably the Cornish place-name *Bereppa*, *Barrepper*, *Brepper*, *Borripper*, of which instances occur in Gunwalloe, Penponds, Mawnan, and elsewhere, is only the French *Beau-Repaire*, and there are probably many other names of French derivation.[133] Dr Bannister's Glossary of Cornish Names is of so eminently uncritical a character as to be of little use. Though he had a wide knowledge of separate Cornish words, he was no philologist, and did not seem to understand how to put his words together. Had he only given the situation of the places—the name of the parish would have been something towards it—he would have left a basis for future work. As it is, the whole work needs to be done over again. Of course one need hardly say that out of such a large collection of names a considerable number of the derivations are quite correctly stated, but those are mostly the easy and obvious ones, and even easy ones are often wrong, and it was quite useless to encumber the glossary with the hopeless derivations of eighteenth-century writers. But the interpretation of place-names is not so simple as it looks, and it is easier to criticize other people's derivations than to find better ones, so that one may admire Dr Bannister's industry while one deprecates the recklessness of many of his conclusions.

---

133 {*Bareppa, Barrepper*, etc. are confirmed as deriving from the French *beau repaire* 'pleasant retreat'.}

2.17. The days, months, and seasons in Cornish

2.17.1. The Days of the Week. *Dedhyow an Seithan.*

Dê Zîl	'Sunday'	*Dê Yew*	'Thursday'
Dê Lîn	'Monday'	*Dê Gwener*	'Friday'
Dê Mergh	'Tuesday'	*Dê Sadarn*	'Saturday'
Dê Marhar	'Wednesday'.		

It will be seen that, like the Welsh and Bretons as well as the Latin nations, the Cornish derived the names of the days directly from Latin, and did not, like the Teutonic nations, translate them in accordance with primitive ideas of comparative mythology.

2.17.2. The Months of the Year. *Mîsyow an Vledhan.*

Mîs Genver	'January'	*Mîs Gorefan*	'July'
Mîs Whevral	'February'	*Mîs Êst*	'August'
Mîs Mergh	'March'	*Mîs Gwengala*	'September'
Mîs Ebral	'April'	*Mîs Hedra*	'October'
Mîs Mê	'May'	*Mîs Deu*	'November'
Mîs Efan	'June'	*Mîs Kevardheu*	'December'.

2.17.3. The Four Seasons of the Year. *Pajer Termen an Vledhan.*

Gwainten	'Spring'	*Kidniav*	'Autumn'
Hav	'Summer'	*Gwav*	'Winter'.

2.17.4. Festivals and Holy Days. *Dêdh Goilyow ha Dedhyow Sans.*

Nadelik	'Christmas'
Bledhan Nowedh[134]	'New Year's Day'
Degl an Stêl[135]	'Epiphany'
An Dawdhegvas Dêdh	'Twelfth Day'
Pask	'Easter'
Pask Bîan	'Low Sunday'
An Askenyans[136]	'Ascension Day'
Zîlgwidn	'Whitsunday'
Pencast	'Pentecost'
Dê Zîl Blejyow	'Palm Sunday'
Dê Marhar an Losow	'Ash Wednesday'
Dê Yew Hamblys[137]	'Maundy Thursday'
Dê Gwener an Grows	'Good Friday'
Seithan Sans,	'Holy Week'
Seithan Mêr	
Degl Maria an Golow	'Purification', 'Candlemas'
Degl agan Arledhes	'Annunciation'
Degl Maria en Mîs Mergh	'Lady Day'
Degl Maria en Gorefan	'Visitation'
Degl Maria en Hanter-Êst	'Assumption'
Ewhelyans Maria	

---

134 {Also *Dê Halan an Vledhen.*}
135 {The correct form is *Stûl*; this seems to be a typographical error.}
136 {Also *An Assencyon.*}
137 {Also *Dê Yow Habblys.*}

Genesegeth Marîa	'Nativity of the Blessed Virgin Mary'
Golowan[138]	'Midsummer Day'
Genesegeth Jûan Bejedhyor	'Nativity of St John'
Degoledh ŷs[139]	'Lammas Day' 'Harvest Home'
Halan Gwav[140]	'All Saints Day'
Dêdh an Enevow	'All Souls Day'
An Pajer Termen	'Ember Days'
Dê Lîn Pencast	'Whit Monday'
Dê Zîl an Drinjes	'Trinity Sunday'
Degl Corf Crîst	'Corpus Christi Day'
Degl Sans Myhal hag ŏl an Eleth	'Michaelmas Day'.

138 'The Lights', or 'Midsummer Fires'.
139 Pronounced *dĕgŭldŷz*, meaning 'Corn Feast'. {Jenner has transcribed [ˌdeːɡəlˈdɔɪz]. The word survived in dialect as *gulthize*.}
140 'The Kalends of Winter'. {The correct form is *Dê Halan Gwav*. All Saints is also *An Hollsens*.}

2.18. List of some modern books and articles relating to Cornish

1. *The Ancient Cornish Drama*. Edited and translated by Mr Edwin Norris. Oxford, University Press, 1859. 2 vols. 8vo. [This contains the Trilogy known as the *Ordinalia* (see §1.2.6), followed by notes and a most valuable "Sketch of Cornish Grammar", and the Cottonian Vocabulary, arranged alphabetically.]

2. *Pascon agan Arluth*: the Poem of the Passion (see §1.2.5). [With a translation and notes by Dr Whitley Stokes.] *Philological Society's Transactions*, 1860–1861. 8vo.

3. *Gwreans an Bys*: the Creation of the World, a Cornish Mystery. Edited, with a translation and notes, by Whitley Stokes. *Philological Society's Transactions*, 1864. 8vo.

4. *Lexicon Cornu-Britannicum*: a Dictionary of the ancient Celtic language of Cornwall, in which the words are elucidated by copious examples from the Cornish works now remaining; with translations in English. The synonyms are also given in the cognate dialects of Welsh, Armoric, Irish, Gaelic, and Manx, showing at one view the connection between them. By the Rev. Robert Williams. Roderic, Llandovery, 1865. 4to.

5. A Collection of hitherto unpublished Proverbs and Rhymes in the ancient Cornish Language: from the MSS of Dr Borlase. By William Copeland Borlase. *Journal of the Royal Institution of Cornwall*, 1866. 8vo.

6. A Cornish Glossary. By Whitley Stokes. [Additions of about 2000 words to Williams's *Lexicon*, with some corrections.] *Transactions of the Philological Society*, 1868–9.

7. *Beunans Meriasek*: the Life of St Meriasek, Bishop and Confessor. A Cornish Drama. Edited, with a translation and notes, by Whitley Stokes. Trübner & Co., London, 1872. 8vo.

8. The Cornish Language. A Paper read before the Philological Society, March 21st, 1873. By Henry Jenner. *Philological Society's Transactions*, 1893.

9. Traditional Relics of the Cornish Language in Mount's Bay in 1875. By Henry Jenner. *Philological Society's Transactions*, 1876. 8vo.

10. The History and Literature of the Ancient Cornish Language. By Henry Jenner. A Paper read before the British Archaeological Association at Penzance, August 19th, 1876. *British Archæological Journal*, 1877. 8vo.

11. Copy of a MS in Cornish and English from the MSS of Dr Borlase. *Nebbaz Gerriau dro tho Carnoack*. By John Boson. Edited by W. C. Borlase. *Journal of the Royal Institution of Cornwall*, Nov. 1879. 8vo.

12. An English-Cornish Dictionary. Compiled from the best sources. By Fred. W. P. Jago. Luke, Plymouth; Simpkin, Marshall, & Co., London, 1887. 4to.

13. A Glossary of Cornish Names: ancient and modern, local, family, personal, etc. 2000 Celtic and other names, now or formerly in use in Cornwall... By the Rev. John Bannister. Williams & Norgate, London; J. B. Netherton, Truro, 1871. 8vo.

14. Articles in the *Revue Celtique*.

Vol. i. p. 332. "The Bodmin Manumissions." By Dr Whitley Stokes.

Vol. iii. p. 85. "Cornica." *Durdala, Dursona*; Cornish in the Vatican [John of Cornwall's *Merlin*]; Cornish Life of St

Columba [mention of a letter from Nicholas Roscarrock to Camden, referring to such a work]. By Dr Whitley Stokes.

Vol. iii. p. 239. "Le dernier écho de la Langue Cornique." By the Rev. W. S. Lach-Szyrma. [An account of the present writer's Paper on "Traditional Relics of Cornish in Mount's Bay," with additions.]

Vol. iv. p. 258. "Cornica." Fragments of a Drama. [Text and translation of the Add. Charter fragment (see §1.2.4).] Cornish Phrases. [From Andrew Borde (see §1.2.8).] By Dr Whitley Stokes.

Vol. xiv. p. 70. "Les Glosses de l'*Oxoniensis posterior* sont elles Corniques?" p. 301. "Les mots *Druic*, *Nader*, dans le Vocabulaire Cornique." By Professor J. Loth.

Vol. xviii. p. 401. "Études Corniques I." [On the pronunciation of *d*, *t*, *s*, *z*, *j*, etc.] By Professor Loth.

Vol. xxiii. p. 173. "Études Corniques II. Textes inedits en Cornique moderne." [Genesis 3, Matthew 4 and 2. From the Gwavas MS, with a French translation and notes.] By Professor Loth.

Vol. xxiii. p. 236. "Études Corniques IV. Remarques et corrections au *Lexicon Cornu-Britannica* de Williams." By Professor Loth.

Vol. xxiv. p. i. "Études Corniques V. Les Dix Commandements de Dieu." [The versions of Boson and Kerew in the Gwavas MS, with a French translation and notes.] By Professor Loth.

Vol. xxiv. p. 155. "Notes aux textes inédits en Cornique moderne." [Notes, in English, on Professor Loth's edition of Genesis 3, Matthew 4 and 2, in vol. xxiii.] By Henry Jenner.

Vol. xxiv. p. 300. "Some Rough Notes on the present Pronunciation of Cornish names." By Henry Jenner.

15. Articles in *Archiv für Celtische Lexicographie*.

Band i. p. 101. "Glossary to *Beunans Meriasek.*" By Dr Whitley Stokes,

Band i. p. 161. "Collation of Norris's Cornish Drama." By Dr Whitley Stokes.

Band i. p. 224. "Cornique Moderne." [The dialogues of Andrew Borde, and William Bodenor's Letter; with restored texts, translations, and notes.] By Professor Loth.

16. *Grammatica Celtica e monumentis vetustis tam Hibernicae linguae quam Britannicarum dialectorum Cambricae Cornicae Aremoricae comparatis Gallicae priscae reliquiis.* Construxit I. C. Zeuss. Editio altera. Curavit H. Ebel. Berolini, 1871. 4to.

THE END

Three early articles on Cornish

3.1. The Cornish language[141]

3.1.0. A good deal has been done by the Philological Society on the subject of the Cornish Language, and the present paper aims chiefly at supplementing this, to some extent, by a general survey of the grammar, literature, and history of the language.

3.1.1. The Cornish Language joins with the Welsh and Breton in composing the Cimbric branch of the Celtic family. It holds its place, philologically as well as geographically, about midway between the other two, inclining more if anything to the Breton than to the Welsh. In some points it differs from both of them, but these differences will mostly be found to arise, either from a greater contact with English, or from the fact of the language having been confined almost entirely to the lower and uneducated classes, and thus becoming more easily corrupted. The chief peculiarity seems to be a general tendency to soften down the hard and harsh sounds that still remain in the other Celtic languages. This tendency, preserving exactly the same form, may be traced from the earlier records of Cornish down to its last stages, the effects

---

141 Read before the Philological Society 21 March 1873. Published in *Transactions of the Philological Society*, 1873–72. Also issued as a pamphlet by the Philological Society.

thereof of course gradually increasing. Though very general, the changes may be easily reduced to a very small number.

a. Where in Welsh a word ended with *d* or *t*, in Cornish it ended with *s*, as *gwynt* 'wind', Cornish *gwyns*; *tad* 'father', Cornish *tas*; *nant* 'valley', Cornish *nans*. Eventually this change was extended to a *d* or *t* in the middle of a word, as *cresy* 'believe', Welsh *credu*; *dewsys* 'divinity', Welsh *duwdod*.

β. In later Cornish this *s* became *j* or soft *g*, as *cregy* for *cresy*; *carenja* for *carensa*; and this change of *s* or *z* to *j* is still prevalent in names of places in Cornwall. Thus there is a farm near St. Columb the name of which is always spelt and occasionally pronounced *Trebolzue*, but it is almost invariably called by the people of the neighbourhood *Trebijew*. Thus again *Carn-idjack* and *Carn-izeck* are used indiscriminately for the same place (a hill in Zennor parish near St. Ives).

γ. The guttural *ch*, particularly at the end of a word, becomes *h*, and eventually vanishes altogether. This belongs to the second stage of the language, and applies to other words besides those derived from Welsh. In the earlier books one finds *ch* and *gh* constantly. The word *bochodoc* 'poor' is a very good instance of this and the preceding change. In the Cottonian Vocabulary we find *bochodoc*, later on, *bochosoc*, *bohesoc*, and *bochesoc*, then a little later *bohajeck*, and lastly (in William Bodenor's letter of 1776) *boadjack*.

δ. Where in Welsh or Early Cornish an *n* or *m* occurred, later Cornish had *dn* and *bm*, as *pedn* for *pen*; *cabm* for *cam*; and this change was even applied to borrowed English words, for one finds *bargadnia* 'to bargain'. The earliest instance of this occurs in the beginning of the sixteenth century, but by the seventeenth it had become quite common.

ε. Occasionally an initial *t* becomes *ch* (pronounced as in the English word *church*). Thus the Welsh and Old Cornish *ty* 'a house' becomes *chy*. A similar change may be observed in the Manx language.

The Welsh *ll* is not known, unless the *thl* in the name *Beheathlan* may be looked upon as an attempt at representing it, and the initial *y*, so common in Welsh words derived from Latin ones beginning with an *s* followed by another consonant, as in *yscrifenu*, *yspryd*, etc., is never found, so that the Celtic dislike to pronouncing an initial *s* under such circumstances (as mentioned by Prof. Max Müller) does not apply to Cornish.

These are the chief differences that distinguish Cornish from Welsh. A few grammatical ones will appear in the following short sketch of the grammar.

The first thing that strikes one in the grammar of a Celtic language is the system of what is called *Initial Mutation*, that is to say, certain partly euphonic and partly grammatical changes of the first letter of a word. Those in Cornish incline rather more to the Breton than to the Welsh. The latter has three classes of mutation—

(1) The *Middle* (I use the names given to them in Rowland's Grammar), in which P, C, T become B, G, D; B, G, D become V (written F), G omitted, Dh (or *th* as in *thy*, written *dd*); M becomes V, and *ll* and *rh* respectively *l* and *r*. In Cornish and Breton the first mutation is the same as this, except that in both of them *ll* and *rh* are wanting, and in Breton D becomes Z, and G (unless followed by *w*, when it is omitted as in Welsh) becomes *c'h* (guttural).

(2) The second class in Welsh is called *Nasal*; in this P, C, T become *mh*, *ngh*, *nh*; and B, G, D, *m*, *ng*, and *n* (the other

letters do not take this form). This class is entirely wanting in Cornish and Breton, unless one may consider the solitary case of the mutation of *doar* 'the earth' to *noar*, which occurs in Cornish, to be an instance of it.

(3) The third class in Welsh is the *Aspirated*, in which P, C, T become *ph* (*f*), *ch*, *th* (the other letters remaining un-changed). In Cornish the only difference is that C becomes H, and in Breton T becomes Z.

(4) In addition to these mutations there occurs, in both Breton and Cornish, a form called by Zeuss, in his "Grammatica Celtica", *Provection*. By this B, G, D, take a sort of backward change into the corresponding surd forms, P, C, T. The only approach to this sort of thing in Welsh seems to be the change of *ll*, *rh*, to *l*, *r*, and *final* mutation in the case of compounds, as, from *teby**g*** is formed *teby**c**ach*; *gwly**b***, *gwly**p**ach*; *tlaw**d***, *tlo**t**ach*.

The rules for the use of mutations are almost identical in Cornish and Breton, but Welsh seems to differ considerably from both of them. In the later times of Cornish these mutations became very irregular, and it often happened that words were only known through one of their mutations, the radical form being never found.

The definite article in Cornish, as in Breton, is *an*. It is indeclinable, and when preceded by a particle ending with a vowel, always coalesces with it, as *than* for *tha an* 'to the', *han* for *ha an* 'and the'. In other cases the conjunction *ha* 'and' becomes *hag* before a vowel.

Substantives.—In later Cornish these were indeclinable as to case, cases being formed by means of prepositions; but in the earlier stages of the language there frequently appears a genitive formed by modifying the last vowel. Thus *marh* 'a horse', *rên verh* 'a horse's mane'. In later Cornish, and generally in earlier, the genitive was formed by placing the noun in apposition to the preceding word, as in Welsh, it being noted that the preceding noun does not take an article. The plural has several forms. Lhuyd enumerates five.—

1. The commonest in -*ow* (like the Welsh -*au* and Breton -*ou*), as *lyfyr* 'a book', pl. *lyfyrow*.

2. In -*i* or -*y*, as *arluth* 'a lord', pl. *arluthy*.

3. In -*ion* (Welsh -*ion*, Breton -*ien*), with the last vowel modified, as *mab* 'a son', pl. *mebion*.

4. In -*eth* (later Cornish -*es* or -*ez*), with the vowel modified (Welsh and Breton -*edd*), as *ail* 'an angel', pl. *eleth*; *floh* 'a child', pl. *flehes*.

5. By modification of the vowel, as *men* 'a stone', pl. *meyn*; *broder* 'a brother', pl. *breder*.

6. A few words originally English, as *honours*, *scriptours*, *persons*, etc., form the plural in -*s*.

7. There is also a dual, referring only (as in Welsh and Breton) to double parts of the body. This is compounded by prefixing the numeral *dyw* or *du* 'two'. Thus, *duscoth* 'shoulders', from *scoth*, *dewlagas* 'eyes', *deuglyn* 'knees', *dufron* 'breasts', etc.

Adjectives usually follow their substantives, and form their feminine by taking the middle mutation. Thus, *den braz* 'a great man', *benen vraz* 'a great woman'.

The comparative ended originally in -*agh*, which later became -*ah* and -*a*, as *tek* 'fair', *tekagh*, *tekah*, and *teka*. The superlative takes -*a*, as *uhel* 'high', *uhella* 'highest'.

In numerals the chief peculiarity is that the nouns following them are always in the singular, as *pemp lyfyr* 'five books', not **pemp lyfyrow*. The curious clumsy method of forming the numerals between fifteen and twenty in Welsh (*pymtheg, un ar pymtheg, dau ar pymtheg*, etc.) is not found in Cornish, these numbers being formed in the ordinary way. Andrew Borde, writing in 1542, has the following curious fact about Cornish numerals, but I have doubts about his accuracy. "No Cornyshman doth number above 30, and when they have told 30, they do begin agayne, one, two, three, and so forth, and when they have recounted to a hondred they say *kans*, and if they number to a 1000 they say *mil*."

The personal pronouns may be tabulated as follows:

		1	2	3	4
		Nominative.	Accusative, or as moi, tai, etc	Combined with a particle ending in a vowel	Combined with a preposition
Sing.	First Person	mi, me	vy, evi	'm	'f, 'm as *ynnof, thym*
	Second Pers.	ty	sy, gy, dy	'th, 'd	's as *ynnos, thys*
	Third (masc.)	e, ef	ef, o	'n	'o as *ynno, thotho*
	Third (fem.)	hi, hai	hy, y	's	'y as *ynny, thythy*
Plur.	First Person	nei, ny	ny	'n	'n as *ynnon, thyn*
	Second Pers.	why	why	's	'ough, 'eugh, as *ynnough, theugh*
	Third Pers.	gy, dshei	y	's, 'ns	'e, 'ns, as *ynne, thythyns*.

The possessive pronouns are:

Ma, ow 'my', taking the aspirate mutation, as *ma* or *ow thermyn* (*termyn*), my time.

Da, the, tha 'thy', taking the middle mutation, as *the dermyn*, thy time.

Y 'his', with the middle mutation, as *y dermyn*, his time.

Y 'her', with the aspirate mutation, as *y thermyn*, her time.

Agan, later *gan*, and *gen* 'our', without mutation, as *agan termyn*, our time.

Agas, later *gys*, and *gas* 'your', without mutation, as *agas termyn*, your time.

Aga, ge, and *gei* 'their', with the aspirate mutation, as *aga thermyn*, their time.

Frequently the noun with which these pronouns agree is followed by the second form of the personal pronoun, as *Agan tas ny* 'Our Father', in the Cornish version of the Lord's Prayer.

The ordinary relative pronoun is *a, neb* or *nep*. The latter seems to have become *leb* in later Cornish. A construction similar to the Hebrew use of אֲשֶׁר { *'ăšer*} when in the accusative is often found with these. Thus, *A thanfonas E*, 'whom he sent', (lit. 'whom he sent him', אֲשֶׁר שָׁלַח אֹתוֹ { *'ăšer šālaḥ 'ōtō*}).

The verb resembles the Breton rather than the Welsh in its arrangement, though in its personal terminations it inclines rather to the latter. It has three forms of conjugation, which may be termed the Inflected, the Impersonal, and the Compound.

1. The Inflected form is composed of the root with certain personal terminations, very similar in most instances to the third and fourth forms of the personal pronouns, suffixed.

The following is an example of the first tense (used for both present and future) of the verb *caré* 'to love' in Welsh, Cornish, and Breton.

Cornish.	*Caraf,*	*ceryth,*	*car.*	*ceryn,*	*carough,*	*carons.*
Welsh.	*Caraf,*	*cari,*	*car.*	*carwn,*	*carwch,*	*carant.*
Breton.	*Karann,*	*kerez,*	*kar.*	*karomp,*	*kerit,*	*karont.*

2. The Impersonal form is made up of the personal pronoun (first form) joined to the third person singular of the requisite tense of the verb by the particle *a*, the verb being in the middle mutation, as *mi a gar, ty a gar,* etc. I use the name generally given to it in Breton grammars, but *uninflected* would perhaps be a better word, for the pronoun is decidedly a *nominative*. This form was very common in the later stages of the language, and, with the compound, almost entirely superseded the inflected.

In Breton a precisely similar form is used, but in Welsh it seems to be confined chiefly to the passive and interrogative.

3. The Compound form is made up by means of the auxiliary verb *gurthil* 'to do'. The impersonal or inflected form of this is joined to the infinitive of the verb. It does not imply any emphasis, as in English, and is sometimes even found in the future; thus *guraf care* 'I will (do) love'; *mi a 'ura care* 'I love', etc. Besides this, there is a compound future made up of the verb *menni* 'to wish', used in much the same way as *gurthil*. This belongs to the later period of the language, for though the verb is found in the Ordinalia and Mount Calvary used in such a manner as that it might be translated as a future, still there is always some idea of emphasis upon the *will*. Thus in the Ordinalia, Pharaoh, referring to the Children of Israel, says, "*ME A VYN aga sywe, ha warbarth age lathe*" 'I will follow them and altogether kill them'. And again, "*Ni VENNAF onan sparye*" 'I will not spare one'. And in the second stanza of "Mount Calvary," "*Suel A VYNNO bos sylwys*" 'whoever will be saved', an exactly parallel instance to the use of *vult* in the first verse of the Athanasian Creed. In the later Cornish writings this form becomes simply a future, and entirely takes the place of the first tense, which, as I mentioned before, was originally used as a future. Thus in the story of John of Chyanhur, given by Lhuyd (see Appendix), we find, "*Mi VEDN laveral diz*" 'I will tell you', and in another 18th century specimen, "*Rag hedna VEDN bos cowsas*" 'for that will be spoken'.

In both these verbs, when used in the Impersonal, the *a* was dropped in later Cornish. Lhuyd gives *mi 'wrig guelaz* for 'I did see' (thence contracted into *mi riguelaz*), not *mi a 'wrig guelaz*;

and in the letter of William Bodenor (1776) we find *me 'rig deskys* for 'I learnt'.

Pronunciation and Accent.—Of course the spelling in the old MSS was very uncertain, the same word being spelt in all sorts of different ways; but this very circumstance makes it easier to judge of the pronunciation.

The vowels had much the same sounds as in Italian, with the addition of the sound represented in English by *aw*. This last was written variously, sometimes *o*, sometimes *aw*, and *oa*, and Lhuyd writes it by an inverted *a*. Thus.we find *môs*, *moaz*, *mawz*, *mɒz*, representing the same word. The consonants had much the Same value as in English, excepting the guttural *ch* and *gh* (afterwards softened into *h*), and a certain confusion between *s* and *th*, which seems to point to a lisping pronunciation of *s*. The accent, as in Welsh, was generally on the penultimate, never thrown further back, but sometimes, in dissyllables, on the *ultimate*—a tendency still to be found in the Cornish pronunciation of English.

3.1.2. The existing specimens of the literature of the Cornish language are not extensive. The earliest known MS is a Latin and Cornish Vocabulary, in the Cottonian Collection in the British Museum. Next to this come the Miracle Plays in the Bodleian Library; the Poem of the Passion, generally known as "Mount Calvary"; the Life of St. Meriasek, a play recently discovered among the Peniarth MSS by Mr Whitley Stokes; " The Creation of the World," by William Jordan; and a number of songs, proverbs, and smaller pieces collected by William Gwavas and others in the early part of the last century. I will now give a short sketch of each of these MSS.

3.1.2.1. *The Cottonian Vocabulary* (*Bibl. Cott. Vesp. A.* XIV.).

This MS was written a little anterior to the year 1200, as far as one can judge from the writing. It consists of about seven pages, preceded by a calendar containing the names of several Celtic saints, apparently in the same hand. The words are to a certain extent classified under various headings. It begins with heaven and earth, men and the various parts of the human body; then birds, beasts, and fishes, herbs, trees, and ecclesiastical terms; and lastly a number of adjectives. It has been claimed for both Welsh and Breton; but Lhuyd, in the Cornish preface to his Archæologia Britannica, shows it to be undoubtedly Cornish. The following is his criticism:—

"Besides these three MSS above mentioned (those in the Bodleian), Mr Anstis found in the Cottonian Library of London a British Vocabulary written many ages ago, and wrote to me about it. When I had seen the book, I knew very well that it was not a Welsh vocabulary, as it appeared by the Latin title, 'Vocabularium Wallicum' written at the end of it, but a Cornish vocabulary. This will be admitted, it seems to me, by any British reader who will look at the translation of these Latin words:—Angelus, *ail*; Stella, *steren*; Membrum, *esel*; Supercilium, *abrans*; Collum, *conna*; Palatum, *stefenic*; Mentum, *elgeht*; Tibia, *elescher*; Puer, *flogh*; Senex, *coth*; Bufo, *crinnoc*; Rana, *guilschin*, and many others which are not known among us Welsh folk." Then he goes on to dispose of the Breton theory, by giving examples of non-Celtic words which are undoubtedly of Early English or Saxon origin, thus:—Comes, *yurl*; Lector, *reddior*; Hamus, *hyc*; Fiala, *harfel*; Saltator, *Lappior*; Sartor, *sewyad*; Contentiosus, *strifor*; Fibula, *streing*; Raptor, *robbior*; and others, and by giving a few words which differ entirely from the Breton, as *glastannen* 'an oak', Breton *gwezen derô*, *eythinen* 'a bramble', Breton *lann*, *scovarnec* 'a hare', Breton *gâd*, *mîn* 'a kid', Breton *gavr bian*.

The greater part of the rest of the volume is taken up with lives of what are called in the modern index *Welsh* saints, but really in most instances *Cornish*, and clearly the work of a Cornish writer. In these occur occasionally names of places, the meanings of which are given in Latin, and these, as far as I have seen, are invariably Cornish. One of these lives, that of St. Cadoc, mentions what it pleases to call the *Punic* name of St. Michael's Mount, viz. *Dinsol*, but this it does not venture to interpret. The vocabulary has been printed by Zeuss in his Grammatica Celtica, as it stands in the original, and by Norris, with his Cornish Dramas, arranged alphabetically, and Lhuyd and Pryce have incorporated it with their vocabularies.

3.1.2.2. *The Poem of Mount Calvary (Harl. MS* 1782).

This is a versified account of the Passion of Christ, and consists of about 2000 lines divided into stanzas of eight seven-syllabled lines. The story begins with the Temptation, going on almost immediately to the week of the Passion. Most of the incidents are taken directly from the Four Gospels, but one or two (such as the legend of the holes bored in the Cross, and the curious account of the death of Judas) are taken from either the Pseudo-Gospel of Nicodemus or some similar work. There are five MS copies of this book in existence. One (probably the original) in the British Museum, two in the Bodleian Library, one in the Gwavas Collection of Cornish writings in the British Museum, and another in private hands (Mr Whitley Stokes, in his reprint of the poem for the Philological Society, states that he was unable to discover the present owner). The Museum copy is a small quarto on vellum, written in a by no means good hand of the fifteenth century. It is embellished with rude pictures, representing the Trinity, Adam and Eve, and the various incidents of the Passion, somewhat in the form of what are usually called the "Stations of the Cross," and in one instance there is an attempt at a translation at the bottom of the page. Besides these copies, there is a fragment of one with a Welsh and English translation (the latter being part of the translation made by John Keigwin) in Add. MS 14,934 in the British Museum. This is dated 1759, and forms part of Dr L. Morris's Welsh Collections. As the poem has been published for the Philological Society already, it will not be necessary for me to describe it more fully.

3.1.2.3. *The Ordinalia (Bodleian Library)*. These consist of three Dramas, collectively known under this title. The first play, called *Origo Mundi*, begins with the Creation of the World, the Fall of Man, Cain and Abel, etc., this being followed by the building of the Ark and the Flood, the story of the Temptation of Abraham closing the first act. The second act gives us the history of Moses, and the third represents the story of David and of the building of Solomon's Temple, curiously ending with a description of the martyrdom of St. Maximilla, as a Christian (!), by the Bishop placed in charge of the Temple by Solomon. Villemarqué, in the Preface to his translation of the Breton Miracle Play, *Barzud braz Jezuz*, conjectures that this last incident may refer to the death of Joan of Arc (particularly as the Bishop is made to speak a mixture of French and English), and this of course might tend to fix the date of the play. The second play represents the history of Christ from the Temptation to the Crucifixion, and this goes on without interruption into the third play, which gives an account of the Resurrection and Ascension, with the death of Pilate. As in the Poem of Mount Calvary, the Pseudo- Gospel of Nicodemus is largely drawn upon.

The metre of the three plays varies considerably. At first the stanzas consist of eight seven-syllabled lines rhyming alternately, the same pair of rhymes being continued throughout the whole stanza. Thus:

(Deus Pater loquitur)   Eñ tăs ā něf y'm gўlwўr
        Formўer pŭb trā a vўt guīys
    Onan ha try on yn gvyr
        En tas, ha'n map, ha'n spyrys
    Ha hethyw me a thesyr
        Dre ou grath dalleth an beys
    Y lavaraf nef ha tyr
        Bethens formyys orth ou brys

The next metre that appears consists of six-lined stanzas, rhyming AABAAB. Thus:—

(Deus Pater loq.) Nynsyw da, yn pur certan
    Bones un den y honan
      Heb cowyth py cowethes.
    Ke growet war an dor gulan
    Ha cosk byth na saf yn ban
      Er na fo cowethes gures.

Occasionally the third and sixth lines are only four-syllabled, as in the following:

(Lucifer loq.)   Ōv bănnēth theŭghwhȳ pŭb prȳs
                Mār thă ȳ wreŭgh ōw nȳgȳs
                   Prĕst ȳn pŭb lē
                Gorreugh an fals nygethys
                Gans Abel a desempys
                   The yssethe.

Some of the stanzas have eight lines, rhyming AAABAAAB, and there occurs one instance of five-syllabled verses.

                Aha Belsebuc aha
                On otte un purvers da
                   Lēmȳn whārfĕthȳs
                Awos ol roweth Adam
                Bys thy'n umma yn un lam
                   Ēf ă vȳth kȳrhȳs.

A few passages are written in a four-syllabled metre, generally with alternate rhymes, though sometimes rhyming.

The language of this play is very similar to that of the Vocabulary, very few words being much modified or corrupted, but the MS itself is of about the middle of the fifteenth century. The grammatical structure agrees almost entirely with the Poem of Mount Calvary, and the mixture of Saxon words is comparatively small, in fact, scarcely so great as in the Welsh of the present day, except of course where whole sentences of English occur.

3.1.2.4. *The Life of St. Meriasek.*

This play, which was written in the year 1504, as appears by the colophon, was discovered by Mr Whitley Stokes a year or two ago among the MSS of the Peniarth Library. It represents the life and death of Meriasek, called in Breton Meriadec, the son of a Duke of Brittany. The language of the play is later than that of the Ordinalia, the admixture of English being greater, while a few of the literal changes, such as the substitution of *g* (soft) for *s*, and in one instance (*bednath* for *bennath*) the change of *nn* to *dn*, begin to appear. The grammar has not changed much, but the use of the compound and impersonal forms is more frequent, and the verb *menni* has begun to be used as a simple future auxiliary. The metre is much the same as that of the Ordinalia, so it will be unnecessary to describe it more fully.

3.1.2.5. *The Creation of the World, with Noah's Flood,* *by William Jordan,* 1611.

This play marks the beginning of a new period in the language. The influence of English has been greater, as one sees by the increased number of borrowed words, and by the more frequent use of the before-mentioned verb *menni* or *medni* as a future auxiliary. The gutturals have mostly been softened down, the change of *nn*, *mm*, to *dn*, *bm*, has become general, and the substitution of *j* or soft *g* for *s* or *z* seems to be the rule. The plan of spelling has altered, and has very much conformed itself to the English use, as in the instance of mute final *e*'s for lengthening the preceding vowel, etc. The construction of the play is very like that of the first act of the Origo Mundi (the metres are exactly the same), and the author has sometimes borrowed whole sentences from it, but as a whole Jordan's play possesses far greater literary merit. Occasionally sentences of several lines in English are introduced, and it is curious to note that whenever this is the case they are invariably given to Lucifer or one of his angels, and in such a manner as to seem as if the author meant to imply that English was the natural language of such beings, and that they only spoke Cornish when on their good behaviour, relapsing into their own tongue whenever they became more than ordinarily excited or vicious. Four complete copies of this play are known, two of which are in the Bodleian, one in the British Museum (Harl. MS 1867), and a fourth in private hands, (bound up with the MS of "Mount Calvary" already mentioned). Besides these there is a fragment, in a similar hand to that of the complete Museum copy (probably that of John Keigwin, who translated the play in 1693 at the request of Sir Jonathan Trelawney {*recte* Trelawny}, then Bishop of Exeter), in the Gwavas collection in the British Museum. In a list of books published in *Welsh* (as it is expressed), given in one of Bagford's collections for a History of Printing (Lansdowne MS 808, British Museum), I find mention made of this play. No date is given, but the names of the books are arranged chronologically, and this comes between one of 1642 and one of 1662.

3.1.2.6. *The Gwavas Collection* (*Add. MS* 28,554).

William Gwavas, a gentleman living at Newlyn, near Penzance, in the beginning of the last century, collected a number of songs, proverbs, epigrams, etc., which (bound up in a volume with notes on the language and a few letters) were presented to the British Museum in 1870.

In this volume there are several short songs, some by one Jenkins, of Alverton, the last poet of the language; another (which Polwhele compares to the 27th Idyll of Theocritus, to which it certainly bears strong resemblance) may be easily recognized as the *original* of a well-known nursery-song, though an exact translation of its Cornish form would not be very edifying for nursery use, some of the verses being not exactly "proper." The first verse runs thus:

> Ple a wra why mos, môz, fettow, tek,
> Gen 'gas bedgeth gwin, ha 'gas blew melyn,
> Mos tha'n ventan, sarra whek
> Rag delkyew seve 'wra moyssy tek.

> Where do you go, pretty maid, he said,
> With your fair face and your yellow hair?
> Going to the well, sweet sir,
> For leaves of strawberries make maidens fair.

Then there are two or three versions of the Creed, Lord's Prayer, and Commandments, a translation of the first and third chapters of Genesis, and of the fourth and seventh of St. Matthew, of the Hundredth Psalm, Sternhold and Hopkins' version (almost literal), and of King Charles's Letter to the People of Cornwall, together with a few other scraps of no particular importance. The notes accompanying these are sometimes very good, and the whole volume is of the highest importance to a student of the language. Of course a great many of the pieces, being composed when Cornish was in a show a very conspicuous absence of anything like ...ical accuracy, and a considerable mixture of English. It is said that a Life of St. Columba of Cornwall, the patroness of the two parishes of St. Columb, once existed in Cornish, but no remains of it have as yet been discovered. These, then, represent the whole literature of the language.

3.1.3. Until the time of Henry VIII. we have no reliable information about the state or extent of the language. It is highly probable, from the number of names of places still retaining undoubtedly Celtic names, and retaining them in an undoubtedly Celtic form, that until at least the fifteenth century the Tamar was the boundary of English and Cornish. I n the reign of Henry VIII. we have an account given by Andrew Borde in his *Boke of the Introduction of Knowledge*, written in 1542, He says, "In Cornwall is two speches, the one is naughty Englysshe, and the other is Cornysshe speche. And there be many men and women the which cannot speake one worde of Englysshe, but all Cornyshe." He then gives the Cornish numerals and a few sentences of ordinary conversation. These are much mixed with English, and were probably such as might have been heard on the borders of Devon, for he probably did not penetrate very far, being doubtless deterred by the impossibility of obtaining drinkable beer, a circumstance which seems to have much exercised his mind in describing Cornwall.

Then we find, as mentioned by Carew, Polwhele, Davis Gilbert, Borlase, and others, that in the time of Henry VIII. Dr John Moreman, the parson of Menheniot (a small town near Liskeard) was the first to teach his parishioners the Creed,

Lord's Prayer, and Commandments in English, these having been "used in Cornish beyond all remembrance". This same Dr Moreman is mentioned in the petition (or rather *demand*) presented to Edward VI, by the Cornwall and Devon insurgents, in favour of the old form of worship. One paragraph of this is as follows:— "We will not receive the new service, because it is but like a Christmas game. We will have our old service of Matins, Mass, Evensong, and Procession as it was before; and we the Cornish, *whereof certain of us understand no English*, do utterly refuse the new service."

In Carew's Survey of Cornwall, written about 1600, we read, however, that the language had been driven into the uttermost parts of the county, and that very few were ignorant of English, though many affected to know only their own tongue. It seems, however, from what he says further on, that the *guaries*, or miracle plays, were then commonly acted in Cornish, and that the people flocked to them in large numbers, and evidently understood them.

In a survey of Cornwall, by John Norden, entitled, "Speculum Magnæ Britanniæ, pars Cornwall," addressed to James I., the following account of the language is given.

"The Cornish people for the moste parte are descended of British stocke, though muche mixed since with the Saxon and Norman bloude, but untill of late years retayned the British speache uncorrupted as theirs of Wales is. For the South Wales man understandeth not perfectly the North Wales man, and the North Wales man little of the Cornish, but the South Wales man much. The pronunciation of the tongue differs in all, but the Cornish is far the easier to be pronounced." (Here he goes on to compare the sound of it with the Welsh, to the disadvantage of the latter.) ... "But of late the Cornish men have much conformed themselves to the use of the English tongue, and their English is equal to the best, especially in the Eastern partes; even from Truro eastward is in a manner wholly Englishe. In the west parte of the county, as in the Hundreds of Penwith and Kerrier, the Cornishe tongue is mostly in use, and yet it is to be marvelled that though husband and wife, parents and children, master and servauntes, doe mutually communicate in their native language, yet there is none of them but in manner is able to converse with a stranger in the English tongue, unless it be some obscure persons that seldom converse with the better sort."

The next account we find in a diary of the Civil War, written by Richard Symonds, one of the Royalist army in Cornwall in 1644. He gives a short vocabulary of common words, together with four short sentences. To these he appends the following note:

"The language is spoken altogeather at Goonhilly (in Meneage, not far from the Lizard), and about Pendennis and the Land's End they speak no English. All beyond Truro they speak the Cornish language."

Much about the same time the Vicar of St. Feock, near Falmouth, Chaplain to Pendennis Castle during its siege by the rebel troops, was in the habit of using Cornish for the words of administration of the Sacrament, because the old people did not understand English.

Writing in the latter part of the reign of Charles II., William Scawen, a Cornish antiquary, gives a long account of the state of the language in his time, in a treatise in which he laments the decline thereof (accounting for it by no less than sixteen elaborate reasons). According to this the inhabitants of the western promontories of Meneage and Penwith, or the Lizard and Land's End peninsulas, were in the habit of speaking the language, so much so that the parson of Landewednack, Mr Francis Robinson, used to preach in Cornish, as being the only tongue well understood by his parishioners. Scawen also mentions one or two Cornish MSS that have since disappeared, one of which he calls a "Matins," which I conjecture to have been an attempt to translate the service of the Prayer Book into Cornish.

The next authority is that excellent Celtic scholar, Dr Edward Lhuyd, sometime Librarian of the Bodleian, who published his Archæologia Britannica in the year 1707. He gives the following list of the parishes in which the language was spoken (I give the present usual spelling of their names):—St. Just, Paul, Buryan, Sennen, St. Levan, Morva, Sancreed, St. Madron, Zennor, Towednack, St. Ives, Lelant, Ludgvan, and Gulval, and along the coast from the Land's End to St. Keverne (this would include St. Breage, Germoe, Mullion, Gunwalloe, Ruan Major and Minor, Landewednack, Grade, and St. Keverne), adding that many of the inhabitants of these parishes, especially the gentry, do not understand it, "there being no need, as every Cornishman speaks English."

Then the language quickly receded, until, in 1735, there were only left a few old people at Mousehole, Paul, Newlyn, St. Just, and other parishes along the coast between Penzance and the Land's End, who even understood any of it. It was about this time that Gwavas and Tonkin made their collections on the subject, and the language they found was a most irregular jargon, the chief peculiarity of which was a striking uncertainty of the speakers as to where one word left off and another began.

In 1746 Captain Barrington, brother of Daines Barrington the antiquary, took a sailor from Mount's Bay, who spoke Cornish, to the opposite coast of Britanny, and found him fairly able to make himself understood; and in 1768 Daines Barrington himself writes an account of an interview with the celebrated Mrs Dolly Pentreath, popularly supposed to have been the last person who spoke the language. Daines Barrington also mentions a letter received in 1776, written in Cornish and English, from William Bodenor, a fisherman of Mousehole. The writer states that not more than four or five people in his town, and these old folk of 80 years of age, could speak Cornish (see Appendix). Dolly Pentreath died in 1778 {*recte* 1777}; but both Pryce, in his Archæologia Cornu- Britannica (1790), and Whitaker, Vicar of Ruan-Lanihorne, in his Supplement to Polwhele's History of Cornwall (1799), mention the fact of two or three people still living who were able to speak Cornish, though theirs is only hearsay evidence. Some time ago I came upon a letter in the British Museum, addressed to Sir Joseph Banks, dated 1791, in which the writer mentions his own father as the only living man who could speak it.

Thus the old language died, but its ghost is still lingering about in the names of places and people, and in a few words here and there mixed up with the talk of the common people, more especially in mining terms. Its influence, too, is clearly visible in the accent and pronunciation of the people, and in various idioms and expressions. The curious use of the verb *to do* as an ordinary auxiliary, and without any sign of emphasis, in fact quite unaccentuated, is, I think, certainly a relic of the use of *gurthil* described above, as "they dŏ sáy," for "they say," etc. Again, one finds phrases literally translated into English, as "French nuts" for 'walnuts' (Cornish *cnyfyn Frenc*), "whitnack" for 'weasel' (Cornish *codna gwidn* = white neck), "black-head" for 'a boil' (Cornish *pedn du*), and sometimes mixed expressions, such as "cheeld vean" ('little child', vocative), and others. I have also noted down a few words in common use which are undoubtedly Cornish, and I have no doubt many more might be found in the extreme west, these being mostly from the neighbourhood of St. Columb, and almost all of them words which I have myself heard used: *cowal* 'a basket', *bowjey* 'a sheepfold' (*bow-chy* = 'cow-house'), *quoit* 'a druidical stone', *gweens* 'periwinkles', *croggans* 'limpets', *guilskin* or *wilkin* 'a frog', *bal* 'a collection of mines' (*to go to Bal* = 'to go to work in a mine'), *Wheal* 'a mine' (from *huela*, 'to work'), *stean* 'tin', *kibbal* 'a mine bucket' (Breton *kibal*), *pryan ore* 'loose ore mixed with *pryu*' (i.e. 'clay'), *ore* (from *an noar* 'the earth', an irregular mutation of *doar* 'earth', which ultimately was spelt *an oar*), *tomals* or *tummuls* 'heaps' (probably originally from the Latin *tumulus*), *soce* (a sort of vocative equivalent to 'old fellow', probably originally from *socius*), *sew* (in the expression 'gone to sew', = 'gone dry', applied to a cow, 'dry' in Cornish being *segh*, or *seh*), *pure* (used in the sense of 'very').

In local names Cornish words are the rule, those beginning with the well-known *Tre* 'a house or town' (or perhaps more exactly what is now called in Cornwall a "town-place", i.e. a farm with its outbuildings), *Pol* 'a pool', *Rose* 'a valley', *Car* 'a fortress or city', *Lan* 'a church', *Pen* 'a head', greatly predominating. In making researches for a glossary of Cornish names, Dr Bannister, of St Day, near Gwennap, Cornwall, collected upwards of 2000 names beginning with Tre, and various large numbers, ranging from 1000 to 200, with each of the other prefixes.[142] Many names have been curiously corrupted into similar sounding English ones, often thereby giving rise to strange and far-fetched legends. Thus the rocks off St. Keverne, now called the *Manacles*, were once *Mên eglos* 'the church rocks' (probably from their shape). *Brown Willy* (a hill near Camelford) was *Bryn uhella* 'the highest hill'; *Marketjew* was *Marghasiow* 'the markets' (another plural being *Marhasion* or *Marazion*[143]); *The Nine Maidens* (a row of Druidical Stones, giving a name to a hamlet in St. Columb parish) was *Naw Medn* 'the nine stones'; *Penny come quick* (another name for Falmouth, about the origin of which a very improbable story is told) was *Pen an cwm cuic* 'the head of the creek valley'; *Come to good* (near St. Mawes) was *Cwm ty coed* 'the valley of the wood house'; *Mousehole* (a place I have already had occasion to mention more than once) was *Môz hayle* 'the Maiden's brook'. In the Scilly Isles there is a rock called the *Man of War*, where they even go so far as to point out what, by a stretch of imagination, may be called the three masts, but there is little doubt that this was originally only *Men an Vor* 'the great rock'.[144] Then there is another class of names, in which the Cornish and an English translation thereof have been combined, but these are not common. Such are *Castle-an-dinas* (a British encampment near St. Columb). the *Main Stone* or *Men Stone*, the *Hayle River*, *Pentire Point* or *Headland* (*pen tir* = 'head land'), and a few others. To

---

142 Max Müller's *Chips from a German Workshop*.
143 Max Müller.
144 {It is in fact *Men ar Voth* 'stone facing the hump' (the hump being Round Island).}

show how very general the use of Cornish names is, I may mention that in the large parish of St. Columb (I give this one because I know it best), out of the twenty or more names of hamlets and farms, I do not remember a single one of other than Cornish origin. There is, however, a great tendency to alter the names to English ones; and looking at the Ordnance Survey, I find many places, that I have known of all my life by Cornish names, figuring under some new appellation.

The pronunciation of Cornish names has been very well preserved, particularly in the case of compounds, where the compounded character is kept clearly visible, so as to make the component parts appear almost like two words. In such names as *Tregurrian, Penryn, Trekening, Nanswhydden, Nanskivel, Carloggas, Bosworgy, Bedruthan, Halvear, Coswarth, Carworgy, Lanhengy*, and many others, the prefixes, *Tre, Pen, Car, Cos, Nans*, etc., are clearly regarded as separate words, and accentuated accordingly.

There is one curious indirect effect of the former existence of the Cornish language. The English spoken by the lower classes, instead of being a dialect derived straight from Saxon, and growing up side by side with classical English, as is the case with most provincial English, is remarkably good and pure, and this is easily accounted for by the fact that English was introduced at a comparatively modern period by the upper classes. I was particularly struck by this when visiting the Lizard last summer. The English spoken there, where Cornish had prevailed until so very lately, is, as far as *words* are concerned, particularly good, though the accent and tone are peculiar. In the translations of the Song of Solomon into various English dialects, made under the direction of Prince

Louis Lucien Bonaparte, the Cornish version differs less than any from the Authorized Version, indeed the chief peculiarity of Cornish-English is the constant use of words in the sense that they had in the time that our translation of the Bible was made.

This, then, is all that can be found at present on the subject of the Cornish language. I have done much more in the way of *compiling* than of originating anything, for the subject has been pretty well exhausted by other writers; and unless some new book should turn up, very little of any importance remains to be done.

I ought, perhaps, to mention that I have been greatly indebted to the following books for a great deal of information upon this subject, and they will certainly prove very useful to future students of the Cornish language:—

The Cornish Drama, with a sketch of Cornish Grammar. By Edwin Norris. Oxford, 1859.

Lexicon Cornu-Britannicum. By the Rev. R. Williams, of Rhydycroesau (Llandovery and London, 1865). This is a most excellent work, and invaluable to the student of Celtic languages in general.

Dr Whitley Stokes's editions of "Mount Calvary," Jordan's "Creation," and the Life of St. Meriasek.

Dr Edward Lhuyd's *Archæologia Britannica*, 1707. This is a very useful book, though somewhat marred by an eccentric system of spelling.

3.1.4. Appendix. Specimens of the Cornish language at various periods.

15th century (the end of the play, Origo Mundi).

Y vennath theugh yn tyen	His blessing to you wholly
Keffrys gorryth ha benen	As well to men and women
Flogholeth	(And to) children;
An guare yu due lymmyn	The play is done now,
Ha the welas an passyon	And to see the passion
A Jhesus hep gorholeth	Of Jesus without delay
A worthevys Crys ragon	Which Christ suffered for us,
A vorowe deug a dermyn	To-morrow come in time;
Hag eus pub dre	And go all (of you) home.
A barth a'n Tas, Menstrel a ras	In the name of the Father,
Pebough whare.	minstrels, I pray,
	Pipe at once.

Early 17th century (the end of Jordan's "Creation").

Dewhe a vorowe a dermyn	Come to-morrow in time,
Why a weall matters pur vras	You shall see matters very great
Ha redempcon grauntys	And redemption granted
Der vercy a Thew an Tase	Through the mercy of God the
Tha sawya neb es kellys	Father
Menstrels, growgh theny peba	To save him who is lost.
May hallan warbarthe downssya	Minstrels, do to us pipe,
Del ew an vanar ha'n geys.	That we may together dance,
	As is the manner and the sport
	(guise).

Circa 1700 (*from a Cornish story given by Lhuyd and Pryce*).[145]

Ha pa tera diuad an vledan e vester a disquedaz daedo an trei pens. "Mîr, Dzhuan," med e vester, "ybma de guber; bez mar menta rei dem arta, me a deska dîz ken pointa skians." "Dreu hedna," med Dzhuan. "Na," med e vester, "rei dem, ha me a vedn laveral dîz." "Kemeren dan," med Dzhuan. "Nanna," med e vester, "Kamer with na rey gara an vor goth rag an vor noweth." Enna dshei a vargidniaz rag bledan moy rag pokar guber.

And when the year was done, his master showed to him the three pounds. "See, John," said his master, "here is thy pay; but if thou wilt give it to me again, I will teach thee a point of wisdom." "Bring it here." said John. "No," said his master, " give it to me, and I will tell thee." "Take it to thee," said John, "Then," said his master, "take care not to leave the old road for the new road." Then they bargained for a year more for the same pay.

---

145 {It is worth giving both Lhuyd's version and Pryce's version for comparison. Two differences are underlined in Pryce's on the right:

[5]Ha pa ɕera diųað an vleðan, e vêster a ðisɜueðaz ðɐðo an trei pens. Mîr *Dzhûan* með e vêster; ẏbma ðɐ ɜûber: Bez mar menta rei ðem arta, me a ðeska ðîz kên point a skîans.

[5]Ha pa ɕera diųað an vleðan, e vêster a ðisɜueðaz ðɐðo an trei pens. Mîr *Dzhûan* með e vêster; ẏbma ðɐ ɜûber: Bez mar menta rei ðem arta, me a ðeska ðîz kên point a skîans.

[6]Dreu hedna með *Dzhûan*: Na með e vester rei ðem, ha me a vedn laveral ðîz: kemereu' ðan með *Dzhûan*. Nenna með e vêster: *Kemer uîth na 'rey gara an vòr' gôth rag an vòr noueth.*

[6]Dreu hedna með *Dzhûan*: Na með e vester rei ðem, ha me a vedn laveral ðîz: kemereu' ðan með *Dzhûan*. Nenna mẹð e vêster: *Kemer uîth na 'rey gara an vòr' gôth rag an vòr noueth.*

[7]Nenna an dzhei a varʒìniaz rag bleðan moy, rag pokâr ɡụber.

[7]Nenna an dzhei a varʒìniaz rag bleðan moy, rag pokâr ɡụber.}

1776 (*the Letter of William Bodenor*).

Bluth vee ewe try egance ha pemp Theatra vee dean boadjack an poscas, me rig deskys Cornouack termen me vee maw. Me vee de more gen sara vee a pemp dean moy en cock, me rig scantlower clowes eden ger Sowsnack cowes en cock rag sythen war bar. No rig a vee biscath gwellas lever Cornouack. Me deskey Cornouack mous da mor gen tees coath. Nag es moy vel pager pe pemp en dreau nye ell classia Cornish leben, poble coath pager egance blouth. Cornouack ewe all neceaves yen poble younck.

My age is threescore and five, I am a poor fisherman, I did learn Cornish when I was a boy. I was at sea with my father and five men more in a boat, I did scarcely hear one word of English spoken in the boat for a week together. I have not ever seen a Cornish book. I learnt Cornish going to sea with old folk. There are not more than four or five in our town can speak Cornish now, old people of fourscore years. Cornish is all forgotten by young people.

3.2. Traditional relics of the Cornish language in Mount's Bay in 1875[146]

3.2.0. In this paper I shall not attempt to discuss the question how far Old Cornish words are still used in conversation by the people of West Cornwall. Such words are undoubtedly used; but they are not known to be Cornish by those that use them, and cannot be said to belong to a tradition of a former language, except in the sense of their having been handed down therefrom. The words with which I have now to deal are not used in conversation, but are known, by those who can repeat them, to bare formed part of the old language of their ancestors. The words are but few, and almost all of them are known on paper, but they deserve to be pat on record as the very last relics of the language that have been handed down by word of mouth without having been incorporated with English.

Some while ago I received information from the Rev. W. S. Lach-Szyrma, Vicar of Newlyn, Penzance, to the effect that he had found in his parish some old people who could repeat the numerals and knew a few other words of Cornish. In July,

---

146 Read before the Philological Society 4 February 1876. Published in *Transactions of the Philological Society*, 1875–76. Also issued as a pamphlet by Asher & Co., London, 1876.

1875, I went to West Cornwall, and, in company with Mr Lach-Szyrma, I visited these old people, and afterwards made an expedition to the little village of Mousehole, in the parish of St. Paul, well known to students of Cornish as the home of the celebrated Mrs Dolly Pentreath, and, in still earlier days, of John Keigwin. The result of our investigations I have now to put forward. Such as it is, it may be divided into three classes:—A. *The Numerals*. B. *Detached words*, C. *Three complete sentences*.

The names of our informants are as follows:

1. John Kelynack, of Newlyn, fisherman, and his wife, the latter of whom had learnt the words from her father, John Tremethack, who died in 1852, aged 87 (a contemporary, therefore, of Dolly Pentreath, who died in 1778).

2. Mrs Soady, of Newlyn, a widow of past 80. She had also learnt of her father.

3. Stephen Richards, of Newlyn, Captain in the merchant service, aged about 70.

4. Benjamin Victor, of Mousehole, fisherman, aged about 70.

5. Mrs Tregarthen, of Newlyn, aged about 60.

3.2.1. *The numerals.*—We obtained two sets of numerals, differing in a few slight points, one from the Kelynacks and one from Mrs Soady. The best way to show these will be to tabulate them with those given by Dr Norris in his *Sketch of Cornish Grammar*, and by Pryce in his *Archæologia Cornu-Britannica*, the latter being those in use in the last century.

[I have adopted Mr A. J. Ellis's system of "Glossic" for the spelling of all the words obtained by me. See Appendix. All other words are spelt as I find them in print in the authorities cited.][147]

	The Kelynacks	Mrs Soady	Price, 18th c.	Norris[148], 15th c.
1	on	on·un	wonnan	un, onan
2	doo	deu	deau	deu
3	trei	trajy	try	try
4	paj	paj·u	padzher	peswar *m.*, pedyr *f.*
5	pemp	pemp	pemp	pymp, pym
6	weth	eth	wheh	whe
7	saa·yth	saa·yth	seith	seyth
8	eith	eith	eath	
9	noun	nou	naw	naw
10	deg	deg	deag	dek
11	ig·nak	ig·unak	ednack	
12	dau·dhak	dau·dhak	dowthak	dewthek
13	tau·dhak	tau·dhak	tarthak	
14	bizwau·dhak	bizwau·dhak	puzwarthak	
15	pemp·thak	pemp·thak	pemdhak	pymthek
16	wedh·ak	wedh·ak	huettag	
17	saa·ydhak	saa·ydhak	seitag	
18	ei·dhak	ei·dhak	eatag	
19	noun·jak	noun·jak	nawnzack	
20	ig·uns	ig·uns	igans	ugens, iganz

---

147 {I give here an IPA transcription Jenner's Glossic of the Kelynacks' examples followed by those of Mrs Soady: [ɔn, duː, trɔɪ, pædʒ, pɛmp, wɛθ, sɑɪθ, ɔɪθ, naʊn, dɛg, ˈɪgnæk, ˈdɒðæk, ˈtɒðæk, bɪzˈwɒðæk, ˈpɛmpθæk, ˈwɛðæk, ˈsɑɪðæk, ˈɔɪðæk, ˈnaʊndʒæk, ˈɪgɔns]; [ˈɔnɔn, dɪʊ, trædʒi, ˈpædʒɔ, pɛmp, ɛθ, sɑɪθ, ɔɪθ, naʊ, dɛg, ˈɪgɔnæk, ˈdɒðæk, ˈtɒðæk, bɪzˈwɒðæk, ˈpɛmpθæk, ˈwɛðæk, ˈsɑɪðæk, ˈɔɪðæk, ˈnaʊndʒæk, ˈɪgɔns]. For a note on Glossic, see pp. 251–252}

148 In the cases in which numerals are unrepresented in this column, Dr Norris has borrowed from Pryce, having failed to find the equivalents in the Cornish dramas.

Now this set of numerals is of value in determining the pronunciation of the vowels in the last stage of the language. It would not be difficult to discover from these what Lhuyd, in his *Archæologia Britannica*, meant by his elaborate system of Cornish orthography, adopted when the language was actually spoken.

I account for the survival of the numerals on this wise. Pilchards, the great branch of trade in Mounts Bay, are counted in the following manner. Take three in each hand, and say "one," another three and say "two," and so on up to twenty, by which means the "long hundred" (or one hundred and twenty) is arrived at, after which begin again. Now it is easy to see that those who learned English as a new language would find it easier to count in Cornish, and would count their fish in that tongue, and their children would hear them do so, and would do so themselves, and so for that purpose the numerals as far as twenty would survive long after the death of the rest of the language. This, of course, is merely conjectural, for I have no evidence of fish having been counted in Cornish, but the analogies of the mutilated Welsh numerals used in the Yorkshire "sheep scoring," and of the present use of Manx numerals for counting herrings in the Isle of Man by even the English-speaking Manx-men, as well as the coincidence of twenty being the limit, give an air of probability to the notion.

3.2.2. *Detached words.* Some of these were obtained from more than one of our informants. In many of them the rules of changes mentioned at the beginning of my paper on the Cornish Language (*Transactions of the Philological Society*, 1873–4,

p. 165),[149] are noticeably carried out. I have arranged them in alphabetical order, giving to each the name of our informant.

Aaree·u {[ɑ'riːə]} (Mrs Tregarthen). An expression of surprise. This is the present form of the old expletive *re-varia* 'by St Mary' mentioned by Scawen (*circ.* 1670), and by Lhuyd. It is still used occasionally.

Baa·gus {['bɑgəs]} (Captain Richards). 'A kite or hawk'. *Baa·gus vee·un* {'viːən} 'a little kite', *baa·gus brou* {'brɑʊ} 'a great kite'. This word is found in the play of *Origo Mundi* under the form of *bargos*, in the account of the naming of the animals by Adam. Welsh *barcud*, Breton *barced* or *barged*. {Revived Cornish *bargos*.}

Boo·bun {['bubən]} (Richards). 'A wick for a lamp'. The nearest analogy is the Breton *poulc'hen* (*méche*). As Cornish it is a new word. {Revived Cornish *bûben*.}

Chil {[tʃil]} (Richards). 'A lamp'. {Revived Cornish *chylla*.}

Chib·lz {['tʃibəlz]} (Richards). 'Young onions'. Welsh *sibwl*, Breton *sibolez*, French *ciboule*, Italian *cipolla*, Latin *cepulla*. Not found otherwise in Cornish. {Revived Cornish *chybol* 'spring onion; scallion'; cf. *chyvel* chives.}

Chei {[tʃəɪ]} (Richards). 'A house'. Originally *ti* or *ty*, under which form it appears in the Cottonian vocabulary and in the earlier plays. As a prefix in names of places West of Truro this word (spelt *chy*) is very common, but in the only instance in which I know of its occurring in East Cornwall (Chytan, near St Columb), it is sounded *chee* {[tʃiː]}; but the older form *ty*, which is occasionally found, is sounded (Glossic) *tu* {[tə]} (as in

---

149 Reprinted at p. 211 above.

the name *Tywardreath*), Welsh *ty*, Breton *ti*, Irish and Scotch Gaelic *tigh*, Manx *thie*.{Revived Cornish *chy*.}

Deu {[diʊ]} (Richards, Kelynack and Victor). 'Black'. Cornish vocabulary (13th century) "*duw* niger", Welsh *du*, Breton *du*, Irish and Scotch *dubh*, Manx *doo*.{Revived Cornish *du*.}

Dou·u {['daʊə]} or *dowr* (Richards). 'Water'. This was given with *chei* as the meaning of the name *Chy-an-dowr* (a place adjoining Penzance). The vocabulary gives it *douer* and *dofer*, Welsh *dŵr*, *dwfr*, Breton *dour*, Old Irish *dobhar*,[150] Old Scotch *dobhar* (preserved in the word *dobhran* 'an otter'), Manx *dubbyr* 'a pond'. {Revived Cornish *dowr*.}

Frag·un {['frægən]} (Richards). 'Dirt'. This was given as the meaning of the name of a field near Newlyn. The Breton *frigas* 'mud', appears to be an analogous word. {Revived Cornish *frajen* 'dirty place'.}

Gijoa·ltu {[gɪ'dʒoːltə]} (Kelynack and Richards). 'A spar used to push out the sail of a fishing boat'. Also called a *vaa·goo·ud* {['va'guːəd]}. A notched board to keep this in its place was called a *timunog·i* or *trimunog·i* {[t(r)mənɔ'gi]}. These words are not used now, and are unknown to fishermen from other coasts, but I can find no derivations for them, though my informants believed them to be Cornish words. {Evidently English dialect words *gijoalter*, *gudgawlter*; *vargord*, *timmynoggy*, *trimmynocky*' cf. Nance's *Glossary of Cornish Sea-Words*, 1963.}

---

150 "*Bior is An agus Dobhar*
 Tri hanmann d'uisce an domhain."
 Bior and An and Dobhar
 Three names for water in the world.
 —The "Forus Focail" of John O'Dugan.

Krog·un {['krɔgən]} (Richards). 'A limpet'. In the vocabulary this is found as "*crogen* concha," in which form it also occurs in the Ordinalia and in the Poem of the Passion. Lhuyd writes it *crogan*. Welsh *cragen*, Breton *crogan*. {Revived Cornish *crogen*.}

Krou {['kraʊ]} (Richards). 'A pigsty'. Lhuyd gives this as 'a hovel', and *crow moh* 'a pigsty'. The word is still used in West Cornwall, usually in the form "a pig's crow," but is known to those who use it as a peculiar word. Welsh *craw*, Breton *craou*, Irish and Scotch *cro*, Manx *croe*. {Revived Cornish *crow*.}

Meenol·as {[mi'nɔləs]} (Kelynack). 'A hearth-stone'. (Richards and Victor). 'A caboose'. From *men*, 'a stone' (Welsh *maen*, Breton *men* or *maen*), and *ollas* 'hearth' (Welsh *aelwyd*, Breton *aoled*. This word has a curious history. Kelynack gave it to us as a Cornish word that he had been told of in his youth, and gave its literal meaning; but Victor said that he remembered when a *meenol·as* was used on the fishing boats. It was, he said, a sort of box with stone and clay in the bottom, in which fishermen cooked their food before the invention or introduction of iron stoves. This accounts for the survival of the word. When first used, it was called by the name of the nearest thing to it—a hearth-stone; but since the namers spoke Cornish, they called it *meenol·as*, and, there being no English word for this ingenious makeshift, the original name stuck to it till the thing itself went out of use.[151] {Revived Cornish *men olas*.}

Min·us {['mɪnəs]} (Richards). A small stone used to drive the fish, otherwise known as a *kuboo·li-stone* {[kə'buli]} I would conjecture that the original word was *men minys* a little stone,

---

151 This word, in the form *myn olla*, is mentioned in a paper by J. H. Nankivell, of Penzance, in the Gentleman's Magazine of September, 1865.

and that the word *men* was dropped. {Revived Cornish (*men*) *munys*; *cabûly*.}

Pee·th {[pi:θ]} (Richards). 'A well'. This is a new word in Cornish, doubtless from the Latin *puteus*; Welsh *pydew*, Breton *puñs*, French *puits*. {Revived Cornish *pith*.}

Pedn {[pɛᵈn]} (Richards). 'A head'. Given with names of places. This is the common later form of *pen*, which is too well known a Celtic word to need discussion. {Revived Cornish *pedn*.}

Vee·un or *vee·n* {['vi:(ə)n]} (Richards). 'Little'. This is a common late form of *bechan* or *bihan* (with the first mutation). The vocabulary gives it as "*bochan* parvus," Welsh *bach* and *bychan*, Breton *bihan*, Irish, Scotch and Manx *beg*. It is still used in the expression *cheeld vee·n* or *vaiyn* = 'little child' (a common vocative), and Mrs Kelynack remembered a girl who used in her younger days to be called "*Jenny vee·un*". {Revived Cornish *bian*.}

The following additional words were supplied by W. J. Rawlings, Esq., of Hayle, who remembered their use many years ago. They are undoubtedly Cornish, and, with the exception of the first, are quite obsolete.

Skou or *skeu* {[skaʊ, skiʊ]}. 'An elder-tree'. This I have heard used myself, though the impression of the users was clearly that the tree was called a *skew*-tree because it was crooked, Welsh *ysgawen*, Breton *skaw* and *scawen*, Latin *scobies*. {Revived Cornish *scaw*.}

Pun·yun. {['pənjən]} 'A gable'. Latin, *pinnium*, (see Ducange), French *pignon*, Welsh *piniwn*, Breton *pinoun*. {Revived Cornish *pùnyon*.}

Guldaa·yz and *diguldaa·yz* {[gəl'daɪz, ˌdɪgəl'daɪz]}. 'A harvest feast'. Lhuyd gives *degl* as meaning a holiday, and derives it from *dedh goil* 'the day of feast'. Welsh *dydd gwyl*, Breton *de gouil*. The *daa·yz* is perhaps the English word "tide" with the first initial mutation of *t* to *d*, and the usual corruption of *d* to *z*. {Revived Cornish *goldheys, degol deys*.}

3.2.3. *The Sentences.*

3.2.3.1. (Supplied by Kelynack and Richards), *Breeŭl meeŭt* (Kolynack *met·u*) *troo·ja bizwau·dhu pem·pez* (Kelynack *tem·pez*) *wheth·ez* (the rest is English) *all ascrowd all along the line oh.* {['briːəl 'miːət ('mɛtə) 'truːdʒæ bɪz'wɒðə 'pɛmpɛz 'ʌɛθɛz]} This used to be sung out by fishermen in hauling in the mackerel nets. My informants could not translate it, but Kelynack knew that when they came to the words "all ascrowd," the fish were coming in too thick to count. The translation is this, *Bree·ul* is a late form of *brithel*, or as the vocabulary gives it, "*breithel mugil*" 'mackerel', from *brith* 'streaked' or 'variegated' (Welsh *brith*, Breton *briz*). The Welsh equivalent is *brithyll* 'a trout', and the Breton *brezel* 'mackerel'. *Mee·ut* or *met·u* is simply the English word *mate*, *Troo·ja*, *bizwau·dhu*, *pem·pez*, *weth·ez*, are 'third', 'fourth', 'fifth', and 'sixth'. I will just tabulate these with Norris's and Pryce's Cornish, and with the Welsh and Breton.

1875	NORRIS	PRYCE	WELSH	BRETON
troo·ja	tressa	trega	trydydd	trived
	trega	(g soft)		trede
	tryge			
bizwau·dhu	peswere	peswarra	pedwerydd	pevarved
	pyswere			pevara
pem·pez	pympes	pempaz	pummad	pemved
weth·ez	whefes	wheythas	chweched	c'houec'hved
			chwechfed	

Kelynack's *tem·pez* is of course a mistake. The presence of the *dh* in *bizwau·dhu* is curious. Possibly a form *peswarva* or *peswarves* once existed, and the *v* (as the *f* in the case of *weth·ez* changed into *th*) became *dh*.[152]

3.2.3.2. *Lag·en en dou·u* {['lægɛn ɛn 'daʊə]} (Richards). This was explained as meaning 'splashing backwards and forwards in the water' (speaking of fish). *Lag·en* is probably the same as *logan* in the name of the Logan (or rocking) stone. It is not Celtic, but seems to have been adopted into Cornish. *En* is *in*. *Dou·u* is *water* (see above). {Revived Cornish *lagedna in dowr*.}

3.2.3.3. *Paj·i kulaa· tuvee·unpolee·un dumoi·jonaa·y.* {['pædʒi kə'la tə'viːənpɔ'liːən də'mɔɪdʒɔ'nɑɪ]} This sentence was supplied by Benjamin Victor. His account of it was that it used to be said to an old man called Tom Becaleck, and that it meant 'Tom Becaleck, lend me your stick to go to Penzance.' The general meaning of this translation is probably right. I think the sentence may be divided in the following way, though two of the words are as yet unintelligible to me.

Paj·i kulaa· tu vee un (or *tu vee·un*) *polee·un du moi·j onaa·y.*

Paj·i is *pigy* or *pesy*, meaning *pray* or *please*.

kulaa I cannot translate—perhaps it means *lend*.

tu vee is *dho vy*, to me.

un is *an*, the.

(or *tu vee·un* is *do vean*, thy little.)

polee'un is similar to the Welsh *polyn*, a pole or stick.

---

152 In Mr Nankivell's paper, before alluded to, this sentence is given, but with the cardinal numbers from one to six, instead of these ordinals.

du moi·j is *dho mos*, to go; the *s* being corrupted into *j* according to the common rule.

onaa·y I cannot translate.

Thus the English of the sentence would be,

Please lend (?) *to me the stick to go* (*onaa·y*).

or *Please lend thy little stick to go* (*onaa·y*).

This then is the result of our investigations. It is not much, but I believe that there is more to be found. The great district of the Lizard or Meneage peninsula has not been searched yet, but there are several workers in the field, and before long we shall perhaps know for certain exactly how much tradition remains. The outlying districts of Zennor, Morvah and Towednack, in the Land's End peninsula, seem to contain no memories whatever of the old language; but that may bo owing to the scattered nature of these parishes, which would have made it difficult for old people to have kept up their knowledge of Cornish by conversing with others of their own age.

Perhaps it may not be out of place here to give a short account of what now remains to be done with regard to the Cornish language before every remaining fragment of it is carefully put into print.

1. There are several proverbs, songs and sentences of late Cornish to be found in the Gwavas MSS (Add. 28,554) in the British Museum, and in the MSS of Dr Borlase at Castle Hornick, Penzance. These should be printed and annotated, and such of them as have been already printed by Pryce and Davies Gilbert should be done over again, as those editions, especially the latter, are almost worthless.

2. Then a supplement should be made to the excellent Cornish Lexicon of the Rev. Robert Williams, which should contain every word or form of a word (not already recorded therein) that is to be found in the aforesaid MSS, in Andrew Borders Cornish dialogues in his *Boke of the Introduction to Knowledge*, in Symonds' diary of the Civil War, in Richard Carew's "Survey of Cornwall," in the Drama of St Meriasek, and even (with judicious selection) in Hals' History of Cornwall. No one could do this better than Canon Williams himself, if his valuable work in the way of editing Welsh Romances should leave him time to undertake it,

3. Lastly, perhaps a grammar should be made, based upon Dr Norris's *Sketch of Cornish Grammar*, and that in Lhuyd's *Archæologia Britannica*, only bringing in *every* period of the language.

When these things are done, one at least of the world's languages will have been thoroughly worked out.

APPENDIX.

Table of Glossic Letters used in the Foregoing Paper.

Vowels.

A	{[æ]}	as *a* in *hat*.
AA	{[ɑ]}	as *a* in *father*.
AA·Y	{[ɑɪ]}	as the word *aye* (moaning *yes*) broadly sounded.
AI·Y	{[eɪ]}	as *ay* in *tray*.
AU	{[ɒː]}	as *aw* in *law*.
E	{[ɛ]}	the ordinary short *e*, as in *men*.
EE	{[i]}	the ordinary long *e*, as *ee* in *seen*.

EE·Ŭ	{[iə]}	a fracture of the preceding, as in the word *ear* with the *r* perfectly untrilled.
EI	{[aɪ] or [əɪ]}	as *y* in *my*.
EU	{[ju] or [iʊ]}	as *ew* in *dew*.
I	{[ɪ]}	as *i* in *tin*.
O	{[ɔ]}	as in *not*.
OA	{[o:]}	as in *smoke*.
OI	{[oɪ]}	as *oy* in *boy*.
OO	{[u:]}	as *oo* in *pool*.
OO·Ŭ	{[uə]}	a fracture of the preceding, as *oor* in *moor* with the *r* untrilled.
OU	{[aʊ]}	as *ow* in *now*.
U	{[oɪ]}	common short *u* as in *until*, or like the second *e* in the German *meine*.

The consonants have their usual English value. The following only call for any remark. *Ch* is always soft {[tʃ]}, as in *church*. G always hard {[ɡ]}, as in *go, get*. *J* always sounded {[dʒ]}, as in *James*. *Dh* represents *th* {[ð]} as in *thy*, *th* being always sounded {[θ]} as in *thin*.

For more minute description of the value of Glossic letters, and for their comparison with Palæotype and with Mr Melville Bell's Visible Speech letters, see the Appendix to Mr Elworthy's paper on the "West Somerset Dialect in the *Transactions of the Philological Society* for 1875–6, Part I. pp. 218–272.

3.3. The history and literature of the ancient Cornish language[153]

3.3.0. Though most people know of the former existence of the Cornish language, it is very curious what a vague and confused notion prevails, even in Cornwall, as to what it was or when it ceased to exist. I remember not very long ago being told as a fact, and that by a Cornish man, that the last old woman who spoke Cornish, walked up to London in the Exhibition year of 1851 to see the Queen, and when I expressed a doubt on the subject, I was assured that the fact was well known; to which I could only reply that she must have been at least 180 years of age. But, for all that, the Cornish language has been, I will not say thoroughly *worked* out, for much yet remains to be done, but very considerably *talked* out. Every one who has written upon Cornwall, even down to the authors of magazine articles on summer tours, has had something to say upon the subject, more or less correct. So I am afraid that I have nothing very new to put forward in this paper, and what originality it may possess will be rather in the

---

153 Read before the British Archaeological Association at Penzance 19 August 1876. Published in the *Journal of the British Archaeological Association*, vol. 33, 1877. Also issued as a pamphlet by the British Archaeological Association, vol. 33, 1877.

way of omitting oft-repeated nonsense than of adding to facts already put forward. As the subject is, perhaps, an out-of-the way one, I shall speak as though my hearers knew nothing at all about it (though I am sure such is not the case with them all), and shall begin at the beginning, and tell you what the Cornish language was.

I hear that something has been said during this Congress of the connection of Cornish with Hebrew, and that a learned Hebraist had taken some pains to show that by a judicious manipulation of the letters, a Cornish word might be made to look something like a Hebrew word, which either had or had not (generally the latter) a somewhat similar meaning. Now any philologer, who has not gone back into the eighteenth century for his system, would have no hesitation in saying that Hebrew and Cornish are about as much connected as English and Arabic. They belong to two totally distinct classes. Cornish is one of the three members of the Cymric division of the Celtic languages, which form a branch of the great Aryan or Indo-European family. The other division of the Celtic languages is generally known as Gaelic, and contains the three dialects of Irish, Scotch Gaelic, and Manx; but with these we have nothing to do at present. The Cymric branch includes Welsh, Breton (in the four dialects of Leon, Treguier, Cornouaille, and Vannes), and the now dead Cornish. There is great reason to suppose that the ancient Gaulish belonged to this branch; and if that is so, it is probable that the language of the Galatians, alluded to by St Jerome, was also a dialect of Cymric. Judging from the Cymric glosses in early MSS, such as those in the Luxemburg folio (which I consider to be Breton, though they are generally claimed as Welsh) and in the

Cambridge Juvencus, or even from early specimens of Welsh literature, it would seem that Cornish, in its undecayed state, represented more exactly the ancient British than the more cultivated Welsh does. It is especially noticeable that a firm vowel-sound is retained in Cornish, where in Welsh it has become diphthongalized, as in such cases as *men*, for the Welsh *maen* 'a stone', *mill* or *mol* 'bare' for *moel*, etc., but in both languages many inflections have been dropped, and certainly in practice, by reason of the customary impersonal form of the verbs, Cornish was less inflected than Welsh. Want of space will not allow a minute discussion of this question, which certainly belongs rather to the domain of philology than of archaeology, so I will not pursue the subject further: suffice it to say that it is highly probable that Cornish and Breton are the modern representatives of the languages of the Southern and more civilised of the ancient Britons.

Except for the existence of the Cornish names in the Bodmin Gospels, and as alternative names of places in one or two early charters,[154] and of the Cornish vocabulary in the Cottonian Library (of which I shall have something to say presently), the earliest mention of the Cornish language that I have yet discovered occurs in Cott. MS Vesp. a. xiv, in the British Museum (the volume in which the said vocabulary is included), in a Latin life of St Cadoc. This speaks of St Michael's Mount as being called "in the idiom of that province," *Dinsol* (or the Mount of the Sun). Next in date to this comes a passage in the register of Bishop Grandison, of Exeter (1327–1369), quoted

---

154 E.g., in Cott. Aug. ii. 44, charter of Edrcd, 949, "Welegford... quæ sita est iu Cornubia... ubi ruricolæ illius pagi barbarico nomine appellant Pendyfig."

by Dr Oliver in his *Monasticon Diocesis Exoniensis* (p. 11), which, in an account of the submission of the parish of St Buryan to the bishop, after a certain quarrel between them, states that a formal submission was made by the principal parishioners in French and English (the names are given, thirteen in number), and by the rest in Cornish, interpreted by Henry Marseley, the rector of St Just, and that after this the bishop preached a sermon, which was interpreted by the same priest for the benefit of the Cornish-speaking members of the congregation. From this it would appear (as might naturally be supposed from the history of the county) that the gentry were Normans and Saxons (though mostly bearing Cornish names), and did not speak Cornish, but that that language was confined to the peasantry. If this was so at St Buryan, within six miles of the Lands End, the same would no doubt be the case throughout the county.

But until the time of Henry VIII we have no trustworthy information about the state or extent of the language. It is highly probable, from the number of names of places still retaining undoubtedly Celtic names, and retaining them in an undoubtedly Cornish form, that until at least the fifteenth century the Tamar was the boundary of English and Cornish. In the reign of Henry VIII we have an account given by Andrew Borde in his *Boke of the Introduction of Knowledge*, written in 1542. He says, "In Cornwall is two speches, the one is naughty Englysshe, and the other is Cornysshe speche. And there be many men and women the which cannot speake one worde of Englysshe, but all Cornyshe." He then gives the Cornish numerals and a few sentences of ordinary conversation. These are much mixed with English, and were, no doubt, such as might have been heard on the borders of Devon, for he probably did not penetrate very far, being doubtless deterred by the impossibility of obtaining drinkable beer—a circumstance which seems to have much exercised his mind in describing Cornwall.

Then we find, as mentioned by Carew, Polwhele, Davis Gilbert, Borlase, and others, that in the time of Henry VIII Dr John Moreman, the parson of Menheniot (a small town near Liskeard) was the first to teach his parishioners the Creed, Lord's Prayer, and Commandments in English, these having been "used in Cornish beyond all remembrance". This same Dr Moreman is mentioned in the petition (or rather *demand*) presented to Edward VI by the Cornwall and Devon insurgents, in favour of the old form of worship. One paragraph of this is as follows: "We will not receive the new service, because it is but like a Christmas game. We will have our old service of Matins, Mass, Evensong, and Procession as it was before; and we the Cornish, *whereof certain of us understand no English*, do utterly refuse the new service."

In the early part of the reign of Elizabeth, during the course of the many discussions on church matters, a number of articles were drawn up, to judge by their general tone, by the extreme Protestant party, and a copy of these, taken from a MS in Corpus Christi College, Cambridge, occurs in Egerton MS 2350, f. 54, in the British Museum. They are entitled "Articles drawn out by some certaine, and were exhibited to be admitted by authority, but not so admitted," and their date, to judge by accompanying letters, etc., is about 1560. The last article is "A punishment for such as cannot say the Catechisme", and in it there occurs the following sentence:

"Item that it may be lawfull for such Welch or Cornish children as can speake no English to learne the Præmises in the Welch tongue or Cornish language."

It is a pity that this article did not pass, for if the said "Catechisme", as might have been probable from the decidedly North British tone of theology in the articles, resembled that called the "Shorter" (because "it's no athegither as lang as the Bible"), the whole Cornish language might have been preserved to us.

In the same reign, but somewhat later, a report on England, addressed to Philip II of Spain by an Italian agent, speaks thus of Cornwall: "Li habitante sono del tutto differenti *di parlare*, di costume et di leggi alli Inglesi; usano le leggi imperiale così como fa ancola li Walsche loro vicini; quali sono in prospettiva alla Irlanda et sono similmente tenuti la maggior parte Cattolici." However, since the agent insists that the *Severn* divides Cornwall from England, he can hardly have known much about the county. The report occurs among a number of Spanish state papers in Add. MS 28,420, in the British Museum.

In Carew's Survey of Cornwall, written about 1600, we read, however, that the language had been driven into the uttermost parts of the county, and that very few were ignorant of English, though many affected to know only their own tongue. It seems, however, from what he says further on, that the *guaries*, or miracle plays, were then commonly acted in Cornish, and that the people flocked to them in large numbers, and evidently understood them. Carew adds that the principal love and knowledge of the language died "with one Dr Kennall, a civilian".

In a survey of Cornwall, by John Norden, entitled, "Speculum Magnæ Britanniæ, pars Cornwall", addressed to James I, the following account of the language is given.

> The Cornish people for the moste parte are descended of British stocke, though muche mixed since with the Saxon and Norman bloude, but untill of late years retayned the British speache uncorrupted as theirs of Wales is. For the South Wales man understandeth not perfectly the North Wales man, and the North Wales man little of the Cornish, but the South Wales man much. The pronunciation of the tongue differs in all, but the Cornish is far the easier to be pronounced.

Here he goes on to compare the .sound of it with the Welsh, to the disadvantage of the latter.

> But of late the Cornish men have much conformed themselves to the use of the English tongue, and their English is equal to the best, especially in the Eastern partes; even from Truro eastward is in a manner wholly Englishe. In the west parte of the county, as in the Hundreds of Penwith and Kerrier, the Cornishe tongue is mostly in use, and yet it is to be marvelled that though husband and wife, parents and children, master and servauntes, doe mutually communicate in their native language, yet there is none of them but in manner is able to converse with a stranger in the English tongue, unless it be some obscure persons that seldom converse with the better sort.

The next account we find in a diary of the Civil War, written by Richard Symonds, one of the Royalist army in Cornwall in 1644 (Brit. Mus., Add. MS 17,052). He gives a short vocabulary of common words, together with four short sentences. To these he appends the following note:

The language is spoken altogeatber at Goonhilly, and about Pendennis and the Lands End they speak no English. All beyond Truro they speak the Cornish language.

Much about the same time the vicar of St Feock, near Falmouth, chaplain to Pendennis Castle during its siege by the rebel troops, was in the habit of using Cornish for the words of administration of the Sacrament, because the old people did not understand English.

In 1662 and 1667 John Ray, in his *Itinerary*, mentions one Dickan Gwyn (evidently his real name was Dick Angwin) of St Just as the only man who could write Cornish. Ray adds that few of the children could speak it, "so that the language is like in a short time to be quite lost."

Writing in the latter part of the reign of Charles II, William Scawen, a Cornish antiquary, gives a long account of the state of the language in his time, in a treatise in which he laments the decline thereof (accounting for it by no less than sixteen elaborate reasons). According to this, the inhabitants of the western promontories of Meneage and Penwith were in the habit of speaking the language, so much so that the parson of Landewednack, Mr Francis Robinson, used to preach in Cornish down to the year 1678, as being the only tongue well understood by his parishioners.

The next authority is that excellent Celtic scholar, Dr Edward Lhuyd, who published his *Archæologia Britannica* in the year 1707. He gives the following list of the parishes in which the language was spoken (I give the present usual spelling of their names): St Just, Paul, Buryan, Sennen, St Levan, Morva, Sancreed, St Madron, Zennor, Towednack, St Ives, Lelant,

Ludgvan, and Gulval, and along the coast from the Lands End to St Keverne (this would also include St Hillary, Perran Uthno, St Breage, Germoe, Mullion, Gunwalloe, Ruan Major and Minor, Landewednack, Grade, and St Keverne), adding that many of the inhabitants of these parishes, especially the gentry, do not understand it, "there being no need, as every Cornishman speaks English." Then the language quickly receded, until, in 1735, there were only left a few old people at Mousehole, Paul, Newlyn, St Just, and other parishes along the coast between Penzance and the Lands End, who even understood any of it. It was about this time that Gwavas and Tonkin made their collections on the subject, and the language they found was a most irregular jargon—a peculiarity of which was a striking uncertainty of the speakers as to where one word left off and another began.

At this time there seems to have been a little coterie of antiquaries at Penzance and the neighbourhood who busied themselves much with the remains of the old language. The patriarch of these was old John Keigwin, of Mousehole, the translator of the poem of *The Passion* and the play, of *The Creation*. He was born in 1641, and died in 1710, and, according to Lhuyd and Borlase, his knowledge of Cornish was "profound and complete". However, that did not prevent him from making some extraordinary mistakes in his translations, which should perhaps be set down to the archaic form of the language with which he had to deal. He seems to have been a considerable linguist, being acquainted with Latin, Greek, French, and even Hebrew, and in a translation into Cornish of the letter of King Charles to the people of Cornwall, he makes use of his Hebrew knowledge when he foiled to remember the exact Cornish word, writing "milcamath" for "war".[155] Among the other members of this little party maybe mentioned William Gwavas, John Boson and his brother Thomas, Thomas Tonkin, the historian, Oliver Pender, and last (as probably the youngest) Dr William Boriase, the author of the well known history of Cornwall. It does not seem that any of these, except perhaps Keigwin, troubled themselves much about Cornish literature, but they did good service in the way of preserving words, proverbs, colloquial sentences, etc., and seem to have found great enjoyment in translating various passages of Scripture, songs, etc., into the Cornish that was current in their own day. These being spelt phonetically (as far as the writers could manage to do so in the days before "glossic" and "palæotype"[156]), and therefore varying a good deal in orthography, are now of great value in determining the sound of the latest Cornish. It is curious to note that, like Manx, but unlike other Celtic dialects, the sounds of the vowels had in their changes kept pace with those of English, and had not at that period retained the "foreign" or "Italian" sound. This is evident from a comparison of words as they appear in the earlier dramas, etc., with the form that they took in the writings of these men when the modern English system of spelling was applied to them. When Lhuyd was at work upon his Cornish grammar, he received considerable assistance from Keigwin, Gwavas, and Tonkin, and a vocabulary compiled by the two last was afterwards printed by Dr William Pryce in 1790, with Lhuyd's grammar, *as his own composition.* This fraud was exposed by Prince L. L.

155 {See p. 18 above.}
156 {For a note on Glossic, see pp. 251–252.}

Bonaparte, into whose hands the original MS fell; but though it certainly was not right of Pryce to act in this manner, he does deserve some credit for having published the vocabulary at all, and the service that he did in so doing may be the better estimated by a knowledge of the fact that it was very considerably through the medium of Pryce's publication that Dr Edwin Norris obtained the acquaintance with Cornish necessary to enable him to bring out his valuable edition of the early Cornish dramas. It is strange that so much abuse has been heaped upon Pryce, while Davies Gilbert has escaped with comparative freedom, in spite of a villainously careless edition of a number of scraps of Cornish (printed at the end of his copy of the play of The Creation), gathered entirely from Gwavas' MS, now in the British Museum, and inserted, with notes and all, without a word of acknowledgment, and in such a manner as to lead one to think that the translations and notes at any rate were his own doing. Pryce certainly took the trouble to correct his proofs, and Davies Gilbert could hardly have attempted to do so.

In 1746 Captain Barrington, brother of Daines Barrington the antiquary, took a sailor from Mount's Bay, who spoke Cornish, to the opposite coast of Britanny, and found him fairly able to make himself understood; at least, so he said, but I doubt it very much. In 1768 Daines Barrington himself writes an account of an interview with the celebrated Mrs Dolly Pentreath, popularly supposed to Lave been the last person who spoke the language. He also contributed to the *Archæologia* a letter received in 1776, written in Cornish and English, from William Bodenor, a fisherman of Mousehole. The writer states that not more than four or five people in this town, and these old folk of eighty years of age, could speak Cornish. Dolly Pentreath died in 1778; but both Pryce, in his *Archæologia Cornu-Britannica* (1790), and Whitaker, vicar of Ruan-Lanihorne, in his Supplement to Polwhele's *History of Cornwall* (1799), mention the fact of two or three people still living who were able to speak Cornish, though theirs is only hearsay evidence. Some time ago I came upon a letter in the British Museum addressed to Sir Joseph Banks, dated 1791, in which the writer mentions his own father as the only living man who could speak it.

Then, as a spoken language, Cornish died out entirely, and there only remained various traditions thereof in the shape of words, sentences, etc., handed down among the inhabitants of the districts where it was last current. Even these have very much diminished of late years, and, though there are many people still living who have heard such things as the Creed, Lord's Prayer, etc., repeated in Cornish by the old folk many years ago, when I made some investigations last year at Newlyn and Mousehole (the results of which may be read in a paper contributed by me to the Philological Society), I only found that a few people of great age could repeat the numerals as far as twenty, and one or two knew a few detached words and two short sentences. But, though Cornish is dead, its ghost still haunts its old dwelling, in the form of idioms, provincialisms, words, and phrases, and still more apparently in the names of every hill, farm, river, rock, stream, or well, and of the descendants of those who once spoke it. And this brings me to a most important point in my paper. I believe that the Ordnance Survey is being made at present, and though, as a *map*, the last survey was most excellent, the constructors thereof were not so successful in one important matter—*the spelling of Cornish names*. Some of these were apparently spelt phonetically, others according to a curious idea of assimilating Cornish to Welsh, and others after a wildly affected plan, with accents and strange philological tricks, based upon the system adopted (very usefully in *that* case) in Canon Williams' Cornish Lexicon. The phonetic plan is too liable to variations, and too arbitrary to be good for much. The Welsh plan is founded on an erroneous conception of the nature of Cornish, which is not Welsh, never was Welsh, and never spelt itself like Welsh in its life, though of course it was a kindred language. The philological plan is all very well for philologists, but utterly useless to the very large majority of people who, though able to read, are not scientific. Now, what I want considered is this. Let a committee be formed which shall decide all questions relating to Cornish spelling, and let the form which the names should take be settled by them on principles consistent with the *present sound*, the *derivation*, and the *meaning*, taking care in all cases in which the spelling has been already settled by anything like common usage, to preserve it as so settled. I would suggest that the system should be based upon modern English, avoiding all scientific affectations, such as the foreign or so-called "Italian" vowel sounds (as tending after awhile to alter the pronunciation), and all use of accents, or of the *dh* for the broad sound of *th* (as tending to puzzle all but scientific people). If any such plan should be adopted, I shall be very willing to give any assistance that my time will allow, but I give notice that 1 shall violently oppose any antiquated vagaries or unnecessary deviations from established usage, and shall try to get the spelling settled in accordance with practical common sense, and not with any design for cramming a smattering of ancient Cornish down the throats of a number of people who do not in the least want to be bothered with it.

And now, as far as time will allow, I will attempt to describe the literary remains of the Cornish language.

These literary remains are but scanty. For the most part they consist of plays on Scriptural or hagiological subjects, and these plays appear to have been acted down to at least the seventeenth century. As an account of the manner of acting the plays will probably form part of another paper to be read at this Congress, I shall not occupy time with any words on that subject. Such performances were very common during the middle ages, and there is no doubt that this manner of setting forth religious truths, strange and even profane as it may appear to modern minds, was both popular and profitable to the more simple-minded Christians of pre-reformation days. This is not the place to discuss the question of the propriety of such exhibitions, but I think anyone who studies the subject fairly and carefully, not from the point of view of a nineteenth century Englishman, but by putting himself, in imagination, in the place of the devout but uneducated peasants of the middle ages, will find in these pageants not profanity, but a devout identification of religion with the details of daily life. The custom is a very early one. The first known Scriptural play is one by St Gregory Nazianzen, entitled Χρίστος Πασχῶν, in which the events of the Passion are given in the form of a Greek tragedy of the classical type, and a very beautiful one it is too, quite as worthy of the attention of scholars as those of the recognized tragedians.

From that time down to the present day there have been numberless instances of such plays in almost every European language. Probably the most recent performances occurred a few weeks ago in Wales, when, according to the *Western Mail*, the plays of "Joseph a'i Frodyr" (Joseph and his Brethren) and "Moses Bach" (Little Moses) were performed to the edification of a large audience at a Baptist Chapel at Briton Ferry, Glamorganshire.

The following is a list of the known remains of Cornish:

1. The manumissions of slaves in the Bodmin Gospels. (Add. MS 9381, in the British Museum.)
2. The Cottonian Vocabulary. (Brit. Mus., Cott. Vesp. A. XIV.)
3. The Poem of Mount Calvary. (Brit. Mus., Harl. 1782.)
4. The *Ordinalia* plays, entitled *Origo Mundi*, *Passio Christi*, and *Resurrectio Domini*. In the Bodleian Library.
5. The Life of St Meriasek, with the Life of St Sylvester the Pope. A play. In the Peniarth Library.
6. The Creation of the World, with Noah's Flood. A play. In the Bodleian Library and in the British Museum. (Harl. 1867.)
7. The Gwavas collection of songs, translations, etc. (Brit. Mus., Add. MS 28554.)
8. The Borlase Collection, similar to the preceding. In the library of W. C. Borlase, Esq., F.S.A., of Laregan, Penzance.
9. The grammar, etc., of Messrs. Gwavas and Tonkin. In the library of H.I.H. Prince Louis Lucien Bonaparte.

This list contains the names of all that have been as yet discovered. It is known from various sources, among others from a letter to William Camden, by Nicholas Roscarrock (7 August 1607), that a life of St Columba of Cornwall, the patroness of the two parishes of St Columb, once existed in Cornish; and William Scawan, whom I mentioned just now, alludes to two or three other MSS that have since disappeared. Having given this list, I will take each of the MSS in their order and describe them shortly.

3.3.1. *The Bodmin Gospels.* This is a quarto MS on vellum, written apparently in France during the tenth century. The greater part of the book is taken up with the four Gospels in Latin, but at the beginning and end occur a large number of manumissions of slaves, almost all the names being Cornish, while the accompanying text is either Latin or Saxon. About two hundred Cornish words can be gathered from this book.

3.3.2. *The Cottonian Vocabulary* (see Plate 1). This forms part of a MS of the end of the twelfth century, and consists of about seven pages, preceded by a calendar containing many Celtic names, and followed by lives of Welsh and Cornish saints. The words are classified under various headings, such as heaven and earth, different parts of the human body, birds, beasts, fishes, trees, herbs, ecclesiastical and liturgical terms, and at the end occur a number of adjectives. It has been printed by Zeuss in his *Grammatica Celtica*, by Dr Norris with the *Ordinalia*, and has been incorporated into Canon Williams' Cornish Lexicon.

3.3.3. *The Poem of Mount Calvary* (see Plate 2).—There are five MSS of this in existence. One is in the British Museum (Harl. 1782), and is probably the original, said to have been found in the church of Sancreed. It is a small quarto, on rough vellum, written very badly in a fifteenth century hand, and embellished with very rude pictures. Of the other copies two are in the Bodleian, one in the Gwavas collection of Cornish writings in the British Museum, with a translation by William Hals, the Cornish historian, and one is in private hands. It has been twice printed, once with a translation Ivy John Keigwin of Mousehole, edited by Davies Gilbert in 1826, and by Dr Whitley Stokes for the Philological Society in 1862. There is very little in this poem beyond a versified narrative of the events of the Passion, from Palm Sunday to Easter morning, taken directly from the four Gospels, preceded by an account of our Lord's fasting and temptation. The only peculiarities and additions are the following:

3.3.3.1. In the account of the death of Judas it is said—

"Eneff Judas ny allas dos yn mes war y anow
Rag y anow a ammas the Jhesus leun a rasow
Dywolow yfarn a squerdyas corf Judas ol the tharnow
Hag a notho a gerhas y eneff the dewolgow."

The soul of Judas could not come out by his mouth,
For his mouth had kissed Jesus full of grace.
Devils of Hell tore the body of Judas all to pieces,
And thus they bore away his soul to darkness.[157]

---

157 A similar idea is to be found in an English poem of the early fourteenth century, called *Vita Jude Cariote* (Harl. MS 2277), wherein it is said,

"Him silf he heng vp a treo, for such deþ he schulde to
His wombe to-berste a-midde a two, þo he schulde deye,
His guttes fulle to grounde, menie men hit iseye,
Þer wcnde out a liþer gost, atte mouþ hit ne miȝte,
For he custe er oure louerd þerwiþ mid unriȝte."

3.3.3.2. Pilate is spoken of as "Pen Justis", the chief justice.

3.3.3.3. The finding of the beam for the cross is described as in the play, of which I shall speak presently.

3.3.3.4. The well-known story of the smith and his wife, who made the nails, is given.

3.3.3.5. The legend of the holes for the nails being bored too far apart, and of the means used to set right the mistake, is told.

3.3.3.6. A curious interpretation is given of the words of Our Lord, "The Son of Man hath not where to lay his head":

> "Rag gwan spyr{n} hag ef yn ten caman na ylly gwythe
> Warnans na basse y ben rag an arlont a ussy
> Mar posse an neyll tenewen rag y scoth by an grevye
> Ha whath gwetha wre an pren war thellargh mar an gorre.

> "Na war rag ef ny ylly pose rag own bos megis
> Yn erna del redyn ny y{n} lyffrow y thew scrifys
> Then ethyn gwyls rag nyethy tellyryow esa parys
> The Crist y ben py sensy teller vyth nyn go kefys."

> For weakly he breathed, and was constrained; he could not
>   keep any way.
> On nothing could he lean his head, for the garland that he
>   wore.
> If he leant on the one side, for his shoulder it pained him;
> And yet worse did the tree, if he put it backwards.

> Nor could he lean forward for fear of being choked.
> Then as we read in books as it is written;
> For the wild birds to make nests, places were prepared;
> For Christ, where he may lay his head no place was found.

3.3.3.7. The centurion is called "den henwys sentury" (a man called Century).

3.3.3.8. According to the usual legend the soldier with the spear is represented as being blind, and is called Longis (Longius or Longinus).

3.3.3.9. At the end is a statement of the number of the wounds in Christ's body, which is estimated at 5,475, and the following declaration:

"Pub tetholl neb a vynne leuerel pymthek pater
A leun galon rag gorthye pascon agan Arluth ker
Yn blythen y a vye ha bederow keneuer
Hag a owleow ese yu corf Jhesus worth neuer."

He that would every day say fifteen paternosters
With a full heart to worship the passion of our dear Lord,
In a year there would be as many paternosters
As there were wounds in the body of Jesus by number.

The metre consists of eight-lined stanzas (written as four lines) of seven-syllabled trochaic lines. There are about two hundred and sixty of these stanzas.

3.3.4. *The Ordinalia.* These consist of three dramas collectively known under this title. The first play, called *Origo Mundi*, begins with the Creation of the World, the Fall of Man, Cain and Abel, etc.; this being followed by the building of the Ark and the Flood, the story of the temptation of Abraham closing the first act. The second act gives us the history of Moses, and the third represents the story of David and of the building of Solomon's Temple, curiously ending with a description of the martyrdom of St Maximilla, as a Christian (!), by the Bishop placed in charge of the Temple by Solomon. Villemarqué, in the preface to his translation of the Breton miracle-play *Barsud braz Jezuz*, conjectures that this last incident may refer to the death of Joan of Arc (particularly as the Bishop is made to speak a mixture of French and English); and this, of course, might tend to fix the date of the play. The second play represents the history of Christ from the Temptation to the Crucifixion; and this goes on without interruption into the third play, which gives an account of the Resurrection and Ascension, with the death of Pilate. As in the poem of *Mount Calvary*, the pseudo-Gospel of Nicodemus is largely drawn upon.

But interwoven with the Scriptural narrative comes the beautiful and curious Legend of the Cross. The legend is this. When Adam found himself dying, he sent bis son Seth to the Gates of Paradise to beg of the angel that guarded them the oil of mercy, that his father might live. The angel let him look into Paradise, where he saw many strange and beautiful fore-shadowings of things that should be upon the earth; and the angel gave him three seeds from the Tree of Life, and he departed. When he came to where his father was, he found that he was already dead, and he laid the three seeds in his mouth, and buried him therewith on Mount Moriah; and in process of time the three seeds grew into three small trees, and Abraham took of the wood thereof for the sacrifice of Isaac his son; and afterwards Moses' rod, wherewith he smote the rock and divided the sea, was made from one of their branches. And soon the three trees grew together into one tree, whereby was symbolized the mystery of the Trinity; and under its

272

branches sat King David when Nathan the prophet came to him, and there he bewailed his sin, and wrote the Miserere psalm. And Solomon, when he would build the Temple on Mount Sion, cut down the tree, which was then as one of the chiefest of the cedars of Lebanon, and bid men make a beam thereof; but it would in no wise fit into its place, howsoever much men cut it to its shape. Therefore Solomon was wroth, and bid men cast it over the brook Cedron as a bridge, so that all might tread upon it that went that way. But after awhile he buried it, and over where it lay there came the Pool Bethesda with its healing powers; and when our Lord came on earth the beam floated up to the surface of the Pool, and the Jews found it, and made thereof the Cross whereon Christ died on Calvary.

The metre of these plays is very much the same as that of the numbers of English and Latin miracle-plays that existed in the middle ages. It has been used also in that beautiful imitation of a mediaeval play in Longfellow's *Golden Legend*, as well as in another imitation less beautiful in its idea, though perhaps more so in its language, called *The Masque of Queen Bersabe*, by Mr A. C. Swinburne. As a specimen of the style of thing, I will give the following short passage from one of the well known Chester miracle-plays (that of the Drapers' Guild). The words are addressed by the Creator to Adam:

"Here, Adam, I give thee this place,
Thee to comforte and solace,
To keepe it well while thou yt hast,
    And done as I thee saye.

Of all the trees that be herein
Thou shalt eate, and nothing synne;
But of this tree, for wayle or wynne,
    Thou eate of by noe waye.
What time thou eatest of this tree
Death thee behooves, beleeve thou me;
Therefore this frute I will thou flee,
    And be thou not too boulde.
Beestes and foules that thou maye see
To thee obedient aye shall be;
What name they be given by thee,
    That name they shall houlde."

3.3.5. *The Life of St Meriasek.* This play, which was written in the year 1504, as appears by the colophon, was discovered by Mr Whitley Stokes a few years ago among the MSS of the Peniarth Library. It represents the life and death of Meriasek, called in Breton Meriadec, the son of a Duke of Britanny, and interwoven with it is the legend of St Sylvester the Pope and the Emperor Constantine, quite regardless of the circumstance that St Sylvester lived in the fourth century or so, and St Meriasek in the thirteenth. The language of the play is later than that of the *Ordinalia*, the admixture of English being greater, while a few of the literal changes, such as the substitution of *g* (soft) for *s*, and in one instance (*Bednath* for *Bennath*) the change of *nn* to *dn*, begin to appear. The grammar has not changed much, but the use of the compound and impersonal forms is more frequent, and the verb *menni* has begun to be used as a simple future auxiliary. The metre is much the same as that of the *Ordinalia*, so it will be unnecessary to describe it. As an account of this play will form part of a paper by the Rev. W. S. Lach-Szyrma, I shall not describe it more fully.

3.3.6. *The Creation*, by William Jordan, A.D. 1611. The construction of this play is very like that of the first act of the *Origo Mundi* (the metres are exactly the same), and the author has sometimes borrowed whole sentences from it; but as a whole Jordan's play possesses far greater literary merit. Occasionally sentences of several lines in English are introduced, and it is curious to note that whenever this is the case, they are invariably given to Lucifer or one of his angels, and in such a manner as to seem as if the author meant to imply that English was the natural language of such beings, and that they only spoke Cornish when on their good behaviour, relapsing into their own tongue whenever they became more than ordinarily excited or vicious. Four complete copies of this play are known, two of which are in the Bodleian, one in the British Museum (Harl. MS 1867), and a fourth in private hands (bound up with the MS of *Mount Calvary* already mentioned). Besides these there is a fragment in a similar hand to that of the complete Museum copy (certainly not that of John Keigwin, who translated the play in 1693 at the request of Sir Jonathan Trelawney {*recte* Trelawny}, then Bishop of Exeter, though with his translation on the opposite pages to the text) in the Gwavas collection in the British Museum. In a list of books published in Welsh (as it is expressed), given in one of Bagford's collections for a History of Printing (Lansdowne MS 808, British Museum), I find mention made of this play. No date is given, but the names of the books are arranged chronologically, and this comes between one of 1642 and one of 1662. The play has been printed (with Keigwin's translation) by Davies Gilbert in 1827, and with a translation by Dr Whitley Stokes in the Philological Society's volume for 1864.

3.3.7. *The Gwavas MS.* This valuable collection was made at the beginning of the last century by William Gwavas of Newlyn. The following is a brief abstract of the Cornish part of its contents (a fuller description of which may be seen in the catalogue of Additional MSS acquired by the British Museum in 1870, under "Add. MS 28,554").

3.3.7.1. Five songs of various lengths, mostly unpublished.

3.3.7.2. The story of "John of Chy-an-Hur" (printed by Pryce).

3.3.7.3. Translations of Genesis 1 and 3, Matthew 2 and 4, the Old Hundredth Psalm (literal), King Charles I's Letter to the People of Cornwall, and various fragments and verses from the Bible.

3.3.7.4. Several versions of the Apostles' Creed, the Lord's Prayer, and the Ten Commandments.

3.3.7.5. A large number of epigrams, mottoes, and other scraps.

3.3.7.6. Portions of letters of William Gwavas and others. Besides these the MS contains the poem of *Mount Calvary*, with a translation by William Hals, the historian, and a fragment of the play of The Creation, with part of what I believe to be Hals' Cornish Vocabulary (alluded to by Pryce in his grammar), and a number of notes, lists of words, etc. The greater part of this has never been printed, and it is hoped that, if the proposed "Cornish MSS Society" should be started, this MS will furnish matter for its first number. The collection passed to Mrs Veale, daughter of Gwavas, and to her son, the Rev. H. Veale, from whom it came to the Rev. W. Wingfield, vicar of Gulval, Penzance, who presented it to the British Museum.

3.3.8. *The Borlase MSS.* This collection, made about 1748 by the Rev. William Borlase, D.C.L, F.R.S, contains very similar matter to the preceding. The following is a list of its contents:

3.3.8.1. Notes, etc., on the language, with an abstract of Lhuyd's grammar.

3.3.8.2. Vocabularies, etc., partly printed in the "Antiquities of Cornwall".

3.3.8.3. Sentences of Cornish, colloquial phrases, proverbs, etc., a large number hitherto unpublished, some being taken from a play called "The Duchess of Cornwall's Progress", probably by John Boson {*recte* Nicholas Boson}.

3.3.8.4. Songs, translations, etc., many unpublished.

3.3.8.5. "Nebbaz Gerriau dro the Carnoack" (*i.e.*, a few words about Cornish), being a short treatise in Cornish and English, probably by John Boson, in the handwriting of the Rev. H. Ustick, vicar of St Breage. This important collection will also furnish materials for the "Cornish MSS Society."

3.3.9. *The Grammar of Tonkin and Gwavas.* This contains little besides the grammar, vocabulary, etc., printed by Pryce as his own in 1790, so it needs no further description.

This, then, completes the literary remains of Cornish, and brings my paper to a close. I have omitted any discussion of the grammatical peculiarities, etc., of the language, and may refer any one who would like to read a short sketch of these to a paper read by me before the Philological Society of London in March 1873, and printed in the Society's Transactions for that year (Part I, p. 165).[158] The following list of works useful for the study of Cornish may be of interest:

3.3.9.1. *Archæologia Britannica*, by Edward Lhuyd, 1707.

3.3.9.2. *Archæologia Cornu-Britannica*, by William Pryce, 1790.

3.3.9.3. Antiquities of Cornwall, by William Borlase, 1754.

3.3.9.4. *The Cornish Drama, with a Sketch of Cornish Grammar*, by Edwin Norris, Oxford, 1859.

3.3.9.5. *The Poem of the Passion (or Mount Calvary) and Jordan's Play of the Creation*, edited by Whitley Stokes for the Philological Society, 1860, 1864.

3.3.9.6. The same, with additional matter in the way of proverbs, etc., edited by Davies Gilbert, 1826, 1827.

3.3.9.7. *The Life of St Meriasek*, edited by Whitley Stokes, 1872.

3.3.9.8. *Lexicon Cornu-Britannicum*, by the Rev. Robert Williams, 1868.

---

158 Reprinted at p. 211 above.

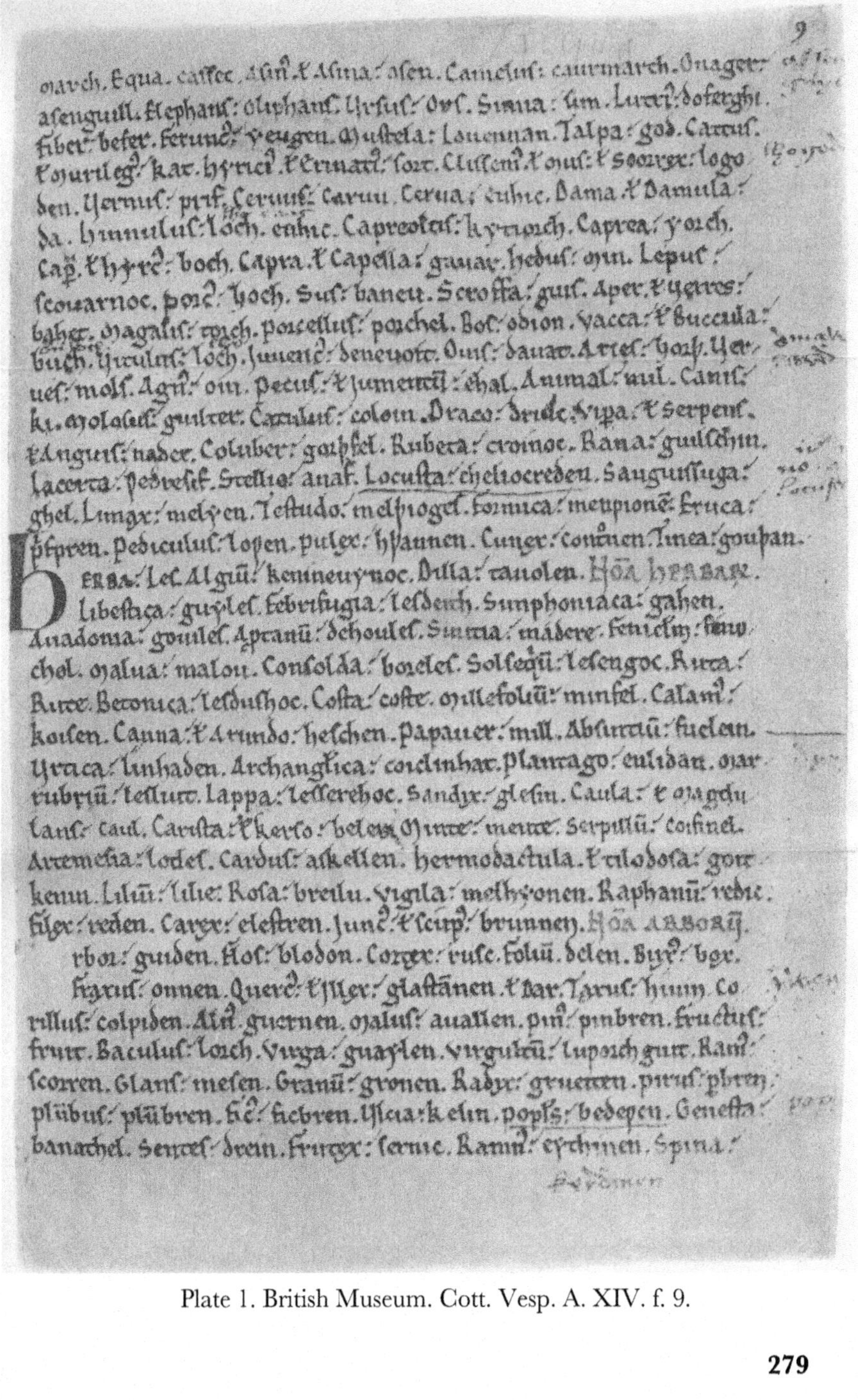

Plate 1. British Museum. Cott. Vesp. A. XIV. f. 9.

LATIN-CORNISH VOCABULARY
OF THE LATTER PART OF THE TWELFTH CENTURY.

[N.B. The words are arranged in columns for the sake of greater convenience. Those that occur in brackets are interlinear and marginal glosses in Welsh added by a later hand. The first and last words are supplied by the preceding and succeeding pages.]

Equs. march
Equa. cassec
Asinus. vel asina ⁚ asen
Camelus ⁚ caurmarch
Onager ⁚ asenguills [assenguyl]
Elephans ⁚ oliphans
Ursus ⁚ ors
Simia ⁚ sim
Lutrius ⁚ doferghi
Fiber ⁚ befer
Feruncus ⁚ yeugen
Mustela ⁚ loucnnan
Talpa ⁚ god
Cattus vel murilegus ⁚ kat
Hyricius vel Erinatius ⁚ sort
Clissemus vel mus ⁚ vel sorex ⁚ logoden
  [lhogod]
Uermis ⁚ prif
Ceruus ⁚ caruu[158]
Cerua ⁚ euhic
Dama vel damula ⁚ da
Hinnulus ⁚ loch euhic [lho ewic]
Capreolus ⁚ kytiorch
Caprea ⁚ yorch
Caper vel hyrcus ⁚ boch
Capra vel capella ⁚ gauar
Hedus ⁚ min
Lepus ⁚ scouarnoc
Porcus ⁚ hoch
Sus ⁚ baneu

Scroffa ⁚ guis
Aper vel uerres ⁚ bahet
Magalis ⁚ torch
Porcellus ⁚ porchel
Bos ⁚ odion
Vacca ⁚ vel Buccula ⁚ buch [buwch]
Vitulus ⁚ loch [llo]
Iuuencus ⁚ deneuoit
Ouis ⁚ dauat
Aries ⁚ horþ
Uerues ⁚ mols
Agnus ⁚ oin
Pecus vel Iumentum ⁚ ehal
Animal ⁚ mil
Canis ⁚ ki
Molosus ⁚ guilter
Catulus ⁚ coloin
Draco ⁚ druic
Vipera. vel serpens. vel anguis ⁚ nader
Coluber ⁚ gorþfel
Rubeta ⁚ croinoc
Rana ⁚ guilschin
Lacerta ⁚ wedresif
Stellio ⁚ anaf
Locusta ⁚ cheliocreden
Sanguissuga ⁚ ghel
Limax ⁚ melyen
Testudo ⁚ melþioges
Formica ⁚ menwionen[160]
Eruca ⁚ prifpren

---

159 Omitted by Zeuss, Norris, and Williams.
160 Mistake of the copyist for *meurionen*.

Pediculus : lowen
Pulex : hwannen
Cimex : contronen
Tinea : gouþan

NOMINA HERBARUM
HERBA : les
Algium : kenineuynoc
Dilla : tauolen
Libestica : guyles
Febrifugia : lesderth
Simphoniaca : gahen
Auadonia : gouiles
Aprotanum : dehoules
Sinitia : madere
Feniculum : fenochol
Malua : malou
Consolda : boreles
Solsequium : lesengoc
Ruta : rute
Betonica : lesdushoc
Costa : coste
Millefolium : minfel
Calamus : koisen
Canna vel arundo : heschen
Papauer : mill
Absintium : fuelein
Urtica : linhaden
Archangelica : coidenhat
Plantago : enlidan
Marrubrium : lesluit
Lappa : lesserehoc
Sandix : glesin
Caula : vel magdulans : caul
Carista : vel kerso : beler
Minte : mente
Serpillum : coifinel
Artemisia : lotles
Cardus : askellen
Hermodactula. vel tilodosa : goitkenin

Lilium : lilie
Rosa : breilu
Vigila : melhyonen
Raphanum : redic
Filex : reden
Carex : elestren
Juncus : vel scupus : brunnen

NOMINA ARBORUM
Arbor : guiden
Flos : blodon
Cortex : rusc
Folium : delen
Buxus : box
Fraxus : onnen
Quercus : vel ilex : glastanen vel dar
Taxus : hiuin
Corillus : colwiden
Alnus : guernen
Malus : auallen
Pinus : pinbren
Fructus : fruit
Baculus : lorch
Virga : guaylen
Virgultum : luworch guit
Ramus : scorren
Glans : mesen
Granum : gronen
Radix : grueiten
Pirus : perbren
Plumbus : plumbren
Ficus : ficbren
Ulcia : kelin
Populus : bedeven [kerdinen]
Genesta : banathel
Sentes : drein
Frutex : sernic
Ramnus : eythinen
Spina : drain

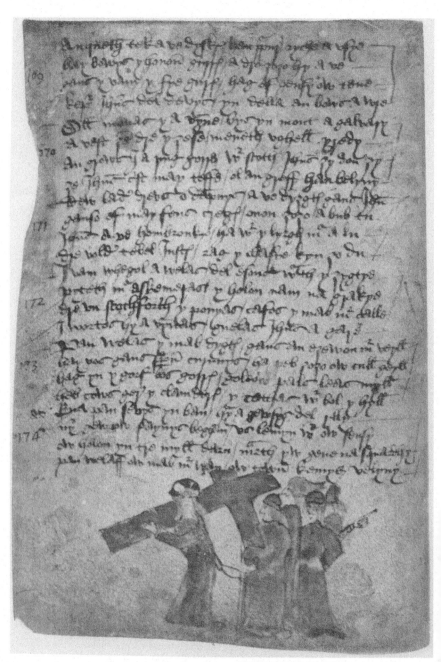

Plate 2. British Museum. Harl. M S. I 782. f. 14 b.

POEM OF THE PASSION, OR "MOUNT CALVARY",
LATE FIFTEENTH CENTURY

[N.B. The letters in italics are extensions of the abbreviations used in the text. *dh* is used to represent the *ʒ* of the original, with the sound of *th* in *the*.

An queth tek a ve dysk*is* | han p*ur*pur ryche a vsye
hay bowys y honon gurr*is* | a dro dhodho hy a ve
gans y vam y fye gur*is* | hag ef gensy ow tene
kepar Ih*e*sus del devys | yn della an bows a wre
Oil monas y a vy*n*ne | bys yn mont a galvary
a vest dhe*n* dre y dhese | meneth vghell yredy
an grows I a rug gorre | w*ar* scoth Ih*e*sus dhy don dhy
dhe Ih*e*sus cr*i*st may teffe | ol an greff ban belyny
Dew lad*er* drevs o da*m*pnys | a ve dy*ʒ*gt*is* gans Ih*e*su
ganso ef may fens creg*is* | onon dliodho a bub tu
Ih*e*sus a ve hombronk*is* | ha w*ar* y lyrgh m*ur* a lu
dre vold*er* tebel Iust*is* | rag y chasye kyn dho du
I vam whegol a welas | del esons w*or*th y dhygtye
pyteth m*ur* askemeras | y holon nam na grakye
dre vn scochforth y ponyas | cafos y mab m*ar* calle
I w*or*tos hy a vy*n*nas | quelas Ih*e*sus a gare
Pan welas y mab dygt*is* | gans an edhewon m*ar* veyll
hay vos gans sp*er*n curunys | ha peb dhodho ow cull geyll
hag yn y gorf bos gorr*is* | goleow pals leas myll
heb cows ger y clamder*is* | y cothas w*ar* bol y hyll
Ena pan sevys yn ban | hy a gewsys del ylly
ny*n* gew ow faynys beghan | vs lemyn w*ar* ow sensy
ow holon yn tre myll darn | marth yw gene na squardhy
pan welaff ow mab mar wan | ow town kemys velyny

Translation. Chiefly taken from that of Dr Whitley Stokes in the Philological Society's Transactions for 1860.

The fair cloth was stript off, and the rich purple that he used,
And his own coat it was put around him;
By his Mother it was made while he was with her as a babe,
And as Jesus grew up so she made the coat.
All would go to the Mount of Calvary.
Outside the town it was, a mountain high indeed.
The cross they put on the shoulder of Jesus to bear thither,
That to Jesus Christ might come all the grief and villainy.
Two bold thieves that were doomed were dighted with Jesus,
That they might be hanged with him, one on either side of him.
Jesus was led on, and much people after him,
By order of an evil judge, to chase him though he were God.
His sweet Mother saw how they were dighting him;
Great pity took her; her heart all but broke.
Through a cross road she ran, if she could get her Son.
She wished to wait for him, to see Jesus whom she loved.
When she saw her Son dighted so vilely by the Jews,
And that he was crowned with thorns, and all to him doing guile;
And that in his body were put plenteous wounds, many thousands.
Without speaking a word she fainted; she fell on the back of her
    head.
There, when she rose up, she said as she could
Not little are my pains which now are holding me.
It is a marvel to me that my heart does not tear into a thousand
    pieces,
When I see my Son so weak, suffering so much villainy.

Some ephemera

{While preparing this edition, I acquired a copy of the offprint of the preceding article. When it arrives, I found that not only had I received the offprint, but four Christmas cards which Jenner had sent out in 1903, 1904, 1905, and 1906. These contained original poetry in Cornish with translations. They have been published elsewhere, but it seemed right to take advantage of this fortune, and republish them here.}

OFFEREN CRIST.

CAN NADELEK YN TAVAS KERNUAK.

(GANS TREYLYANS YN SOWSNEK.)

SCRYFYS GANS

GWAS MYHAL

BARDH A WORSEDH GORENYS BRYTON-ISAL.

HA DANFONYS, GANS DYNNERGH A'N GWELLA

DHEWORTH _____

DHO _____

DEGL NADELEK,
YN BLEDHEN AGAN ARLUTH, 1903.

Offeren Crist

The Christ-Mass

(An keth can-ma yn Sowsnek.
The same English'd by H. J.)

Otteve genys hedhyu
Bara Beunans, glan y lyu,
   Yn Bethlem, Chy an Bara.
Can an Eleth hemma yu,
"Meur wordhyans re bo dha Dhew
   Yn Uhella!"

Lo, this day is born for thee
Living Bread, so bright of blee,
   In Bethlem, the House of Bread.
Hearest thou the Angels sing?
"High in Heaven God our King
   Be worshipped."

Hedhyu ny a dhe tergweth,
Hanter-nos, deth-tarth ha deth,
   Mab Maria dha wordhya
Yn y drigva, ple a dheth
Drewyon, Bugaly, Eleth,
   Dhy honora.

Thrice to-day we take our way,
Midnight, dawn and shining day,
   Blessed Mary's Son to greet
In His dwelling, whither went,
Sages, Shepherds, Angels bent
   On service meet.

Lu an Eleth a wruk mos
Dha gana yn hanter-nos,
   Yn deth-tarth an Vugaly
Drewyon, a bell bro ow tos,
Eth yn golow deth dha vos
   Y servisy.

Quires of Angels, full of light,
Sing their praises at midnight,
   Shepherds in the morning grey;
Sages from a distant land
Come by day with laden hand
   Homage to pay.

Yn gwav yen gwyn o an bys,
Pan ve Jhesus dynythys,
   Offryn glan, a Wyrhes lan.
Mab den warnodho megys
Hav an jevyth, gwyn y vys,
   Aberth Nef splan.

Cold was winter, white was earth,
On the day of Jesus' Birth,
   Virgin-born, pure Sacrifice.
Fair their lot on Him who feed,
Endless summer is their meed
   In Paradise.

Agan Arluth, Jhesus whek,
Roy lowender Nadelek
   Dhyso ha dheth gosgar dy.
Re'th witho Maria dek
Ha Myhal El colonnek,
   Gans oll dhe chy.

Jesus sweet, the Lord of all,
Grant that Christmas Joy befall
   Thee and all thy company.
Mother Mary, Maiden bright,
And Saint Michael in his might
   Guard thine and thee.

Yn della pysaf Gwas Myhal.

STEREN BETHLEM.

CAN NADELEK SCRÎFES EN TAVAS KERNÛAK

GANS

GWAS MYHAL.

GANS TRAYLYANS GER-RAG-GER EN SOWSNAK

GANS

H. J.

" MA GWELLEZ GEN A NI E STERAN EN EST, HA THO
NI DEVETHEZ THA GORTHIA THOTHA."
Awayl S. Mathew, ii., 2.
(Herwedh dorn-scriven Gwavas).

Steren Bethlem

The Star of Bethlehem

(Traylyans ger-rag-ger.
A Literal translation.)

Steren splan en tewalgow!
Seveugh, deugh, a Vaternow.
  Ple hombronky hy a wra,
  Own na bertheugh dhô sewya;
Gwreugh holya Steren Golow.

A gleaming Star in the darkness!
Arise, come, O Kings.
  Whither it will lead,
  Have no fear to follow;
Follow the Star of Light.

Naunek, sehes, sqwîth ha gwan,
En yender pe tomder tan,
  Dres gwerwels pe menedhyow,
  Dre'n diveyth pe lowarthow,
Gwreugh holya an Steren splan.

Hungry, thirsty, weary and weak,
In the cold, or fiery heat,
  Over pasture-land or mountains,
  Through the wilderness or gardens,
Follow the gleaming Star.

A dhiragough y wheler
Crows golow formyes a ster,
  Deulav, Treys, ha Colon Sans,
  Pen golyes Arleclh Bewnans;
Gwreugh holya an Grows mar glêr.

Before you shall be seen
A Cross of light formed of stars,
  The Hands, the Feet, the Sacred Heart,
  The wounded Head of the Lord of Life;
Follow the Cross so bright.

En bowjy pan welough why
Lês rial 'gan Arledh ny,
  E Honan war dron sedhes,
  Deulin agan Arledhes,
Gordhyeugh gens an Vîgely.

In the cattle-shed when you see
The royal palace of Our Lord,
  Himself seated on a throne,
  The knees of Our Lady,
Worship with the Shepherds.

Gordhyeugh, 'Dhrewyon a, bel bow,
Reugh dhodho ages roow,
   Reugh owr rîdh, encoys ha mer,
   Dhô servya 'gan Arledh ker;
Gordhyeugh Matern Maternow.

Worship, Druids from a distant land,
Give Him your gifts,
   Give red gold, incense and myrrh,
   To serve our dear Lord;
Worship the King of Kings.

Sav, golow, a Dhinas Dew,
Ottensa, gennes hedhew,
   Dha Wolow yu devedhes,
   Gordhyans Dew yu dreheves
Warnas dî, a Dhinas Dew.

Arise, shine, O City of God,
Behold Him, born to-day,
   Thy Light is come,
   The Glory of God is risen
Upon thee, O City of God.

Deugh, a dîs; Golow an Bes,
Agas Matern, at dhê nes;
   Lugarnow teg a dhisqwedh,
   Berth an Eglos, an Arledh,
Barra Bewnans en E Lês.

Come, O People; the Light of the World,
Your King, draweth nigh;
   Fair lights make known,
   Within the Church, the Lord,
The Bread of Life in His Palace.

Oe Hothman, dre dha dhedhyow
Sew an Steren caradow;
   En Eglos, par del en Nev,
   Tî a, vedn E drovya Ev,
A re fethas an Ankow.

My Friend, through thy days
Follow the beloved Star;
   In the Church, as in Heaven,
   Thou shalt find Him,
Who hath overcome Death.

Crîst, Myhal, ha Marîa,
Re wrellens dha venigya;
   Bledhan Nowedh lowenek
   Rens y dhes, ha Nadelek
Fest en lowen maga ta.

Christ, Michael and Mary,
May they bless thee;
   A Happy New Year
   May they give thee, and a Christmas
Right merry as well.

Danvones, gans dinerhyans a'n gwella.

Dhort..

Dhó..

En Degl Nadelek, 1904.

CAN AN PESCADOR KERNÚAK.

SCRIFES EN TAVAS KERNÚAK
GANS
GWAS MYHAL,
BARDH A WORSEDH GORENYS BRETAN-ISAL.

GANS TRAYLYANS EN GWERS SOWSNAK
GANS
H. J.

THE CORNISH FISHERMAN'S HYMN.

WRITTEN IN CORNISH
BY
GWAS MYHAL,
A BARD OF THE GORSEDD OF BRITTANY.

WITH A TRANSLATION IN ENGLISH VERSE
BY
H. J.

Can an Pescador Kernûak

TON: *Palmoryon an Nos* (Niv. 623 en Canow Coth ha Nowedh)

Adro'n Lethowsow ma an mor ow crîa,
　Rag corfow ûs Carrek an Bleidh a wol;
Gwren môs en rag, dre weres Mab Marîa,
　Dhô beryl mor ha carrek heb own ol.
Burdhen:　Crîst, Mab Marîa, Steren an Mor,
　　　　Golsow ha gortheb pesadow pescador.

Crîst, tî elwas pescadoryon a'n kensa
　War drêth Mor Galilêa dhô'th holya;
Ol agan gwaith haneth rag dha garensa
　Dheso en lên offrenny ny a wra.
Burdhen:　Crîst, Mab Marîa, Steren an Mor,
　　　　Golsow ha gortheb pesadow pescador.

The Cornish Fisherman's Hymn

TUNE: *The Pilgrims of the Night* (No. 623 in Hymns Ancient and Modern)

All round the Longships mighty waves are crying,
　For lives of men the howling Wolf doth call;
Forth let us fare, on Mary's Son relying,
　Fearless of rock and flood, whate'er befall.
Chorus:　Christ, Son of Mary, Star of the Sea,
　　　　Listen and answer a fisher's cry to Thee.

Fishers were they whom first Thy Name confessing
Thou calledst by the Sea of Galilee ;
For Thy dear sake, and mindful of Thy blessing,
This our night's toil we dedicate to Thee.
Chorus:　Christ, Son of Mary, Star of the Sea,
　　　　Listen and answer a fisher's cry to Thee.

293

Adrês an mor, Arledh, yu dha gamennow
  Ha'th fordhow dî war bejeth dowrow down
Gwren dha holya, herwedh dha worhemennow,
  Pan leverta, "Mî yu, na bertheugh own."
Burdhen: Crîst, Mab Marîa, Steren an Mor,
        Golsow ha gortheb pesadow pescador.

Tî a wrîg gwîl an lor ha'n steren golow,
  Ordnes en Nev dhô rowlya termen nos,
Golow an Bês, pan sewyen ny dha olow,
  Splan warnan ny ple pennak gwren ny môs.
Burdhen: Crîst, Mab Marîa, Steren an Mor,
        Golsow ha gortheb pesadow pescador.

Marsyu dha vodh, dha servisy mar pedhyn,
  Ro en 'gan russow pesk ha megyans lour.
Tî a wrîg gwîl puscas an mor ha'n edhyn,
  Ha pa pennak a gerdh en fordhow dowr.
Burdhen: Crîst, Mab Marîa, Steren an Mor,
        Golsow ha gortheb pesadow pescador.

Marsyu dha vodh, pan wra an houl derhevel,
  Ny dhô wrowedha en dan tonnow mor:
Gwra 'gan enevow en dha wîth dhô sevel;
  Dre'n mor ythos ky ogas vel dre'n nor.
Burdhen: Crîst, Mab Marîa, Steren an Mor,
        Golsow ha gortheb pesadow pescador.

En dha dheulav ny a gemmen an lester;
  Ro gwensow mas hag awel deg dhen ny,
Myhal an Arh-El, marrek agan Mester,
  Danvon dhen ny rag dhô 'gan hombronky.
Burdhen: Crîst, Mab Marîa, Steren an Mor,
        Golsow ha gortheb pesadow pescador.

Over the sea, O Lord, Thy paths are guiding,
  On the deep waters Thou Thy ways hast laid;
We follow Thee, in Thy commands abiding;
  For Thou hast said: "'Tis I, be not afraid."
Chorus: Christ, Son of Mary, Star of the Sea,
           Listen and answer a fisher's cry to Thee.

Thou, who didst form the moon and stars, that gleaming
  Stand in the sky to rule the time of night,
Light of the world, do Thou upon us beaming,
  When in Thy steps we follow, give us light.
Chorus: Christ, Son of Mary, Star of the Sea,
           Listen and answer a fisher's cry to Thee.

If Thou wilt deign to grant Thy servant's wishes,
  Fill Thou our nets with wealth that comes of Thee
Thine are the fowls, and Thou hast made the fishes
  And whatsoever moveth in the sea.
Chorus: Christ, Son of Mary, Star of the Sea,
           Listen and answer a fisher's cry to Thee.

If, ere the sun rise, we should lie a-sleeping
  Under the waves, we die at Thy command;
Have Thou our souls in Thine eternal keeping;
  Thou art as near by water as by land.
Chorus: Christ, Son of Mary, Star of the Sea,
           Listen and answer a fisher's cry to Thee.

Into Thy hands our vessel now commending,
  Grant us, we pray Thee, wind and weather fair;
Michael of might, Thine own Archangel, sending
  To be our guide and guardian everywhere.
Chorus: Christ, Son of Mary, Star of the Sea,
           Listen and answer a fisher's cry to Thee.

Gwren môs en rag, ow trestya en dha weres:
  En dha dhorn dî yu bewnans hag ancow.
Gordhyans re vo dhô Das ha Mab ha Speres,
  Try en Onen, Gwithyas 'gan enevow.
Burdhen: Crîst, Mab Marîa, Steren an Mor,
      Golsow ha gortheb pesadow pescador.

GWAS MYHAL

Scrifes hag offrennes dhô Vr PEDER JACKA, an Cotha,
a Newlyn, Pescador, en termen Pask, 1905.
Argrafes en termen Nadelek, 1905.

————

Let us go forward, trusting in Thy merit;
  Both life and death Thy loving hand controls.
Worship be done to Father, Son, and Spirit,
  God Three in One, the keeper of our souls.
Chorus: Christ, Son of Mary, Star of the Sea,
Listen and answer a fisher's cry to Thee.

H. J.

Written, and dedicated to Mr PETER JACKA, Senior,
of Newlyn, Fisherman, Easter-tide, 1905.
Printed at Christmas-tide, 1905.

DANVONES, GANS DINERHYANS A'N GWELLA
RAG NADELEK HA'N VLEDHAN NOWEDH,

DHORT ....

DHÔ ....

En Degl Nadelek, 1905.

{The sender and recipient of this card are erased in contemporary ink; the erasure is deleted below. Mary Beazley confirms that the handwriting is Henry's.}

DANVONES, GANS DINERHYANS A'N GWELLA
RAG NADELEK HA'N VLEDHAN NOWEDH,

DHORT ...... H. + K. Jenner ....

DHÔ ... Miss M. Murray ....

En Degl Nadelek, 1905.

DEVEDHYANS AN MATERN.

Can Nadelek

Scrives en Kernuak ha Sowsnak.

gans

GWAS MYHAL,

(Hedna yu H. J.)

Bardh a Worsedh Bretan-Isel.

Sav aman, golow, Hierusalem, dreven bos dha
Wolow devedhes. —*Esay*, lx. 1.

Levereugh en mesk an dîs : An Arledh a vedn
roulya a'n Pren. — *Ps.* xcv. 9.

THE COMING OF THE KING.

A Christmas Carol,

Written in Cornish and English

by

GWAS MYHAL,

(i.e. H. J.)

A Bard of the Gorsedd of Brittany.

Surge, illuminare, Jerusalem, quia venit
Lumen tuum.—*Esaias* lx. 1.

Dicite in nationibus : Dominus regnabit a
Ligno.—*Ps.* xcv. 9 *(Versio Mozarabica.)*

Devedhyans an Matern

Sav aman, Dinas Dew, devedhes yu
    Dha Wolow, an roul coth yu tremenes,
Fethes an Escar, taw an Tuller deu,
    An Matern gwir a dhe wostewedh dhes.

Tewlder a wressa kîdha fas an bes,
    Trom warnen ny drog-allosow an Nos.
En splander sans Ev a ve denethes;
    Golow yu'n bes, ha'n Matern ny ow tos.

An Vaternes a'n sens war î deulin;
    Matern Maternow, heb brîs yu Dha Drôn!
Mîreugh, coyn rîal rag E vegyans gwin,
    Ha'n Werhes worth E vaga a'i deuvron.

The Coming of the King

City of God, arise, thy Light is come,
    Now is the ancient usurpation past,
Vanquished the Foe, the Dark Deceiver dumb,
    Thy true King cometh to His own at last.

Darkness had covered all the face of earth,
    Heavy on us the wrongful powers of night.
Now in the holy splendour of His Birth
    Our King is come and all the world is light.

Lo, the Queen Mother holds Him on her knee;
    Priceless the throne whereon the King doth rest!
A royal feast for His blest banquet see,
    When as she feeds Him at her virgin breast.

Kensyu saw beugh hag asen ol adro,
   Ha bîgely 'ga Matern dho wordhya,
Omblegya wra Maternow prest dhodho,
   E vîgely gans roow dhô servya.

'Wren E gorona lemmen? Nynsyu gwres
   E ober; tanow yu E servisy.
En dadn E dreys pan vedh pebtra settyes,
   Coron adro dhoy dal y whorrans y.

'Wren E gorona gans owr? Nynsyu'n êr;
   Garlons a dhevnedh aral rag E ben,
Pan wel tîs ol an bes en gordhyans mêr
   Agan Matern ow roulya a'n Grows-Pren,

Lowenen; ottama 'gan Matern ny.
   Hedhew a'n dra a wharfo na woleugh.
Ogas dhoy Stevel-Trôn heb own deugh why;
   Marîa'n Vaternes a elow dheugh.

What though but ox and ass are kneeling nigh?
   What though but shepherds recognize their King?
Kings shall bow down before Him by and by,
   And serve His shepherds with their offering.

Crown Him? Not yet, the work is not complete;
   Only a few His loyal subjects now.
When He shall put all things beneath His feet,
   There shall be set a crown upon His brow.

Crown Him? Not now, and not with crown of gold?
   Of other ware His diadem shall be,
When all the nations of the earth behold
   The King of Glory reigning from the Tree.

Let us rejoice because our King is here;
   Reck not to-day of what shall else betide,
Come to His Presence Chamber, nothing fear;
   Mary the Queen doth call you to His side.

Danvones gans denerhyans a'n gwella
rag Nadalek an Vledhan 1906, ha'n
Vledhan Newedh 1907,

Sent, with the best greetings, for
Christmas, 1906, and the New Year
1907,

Dhort }
From } H. & K. JENNER.

Dhô   }
To   } ....

The Old House,
    Bushey Heath,
        Herts.

The Song of the Western Man	Can Tîs West (Jenner 1905)
A good sword and a trusty hand!	Ma lêl an lêv, ma'n cledha mas,
A merry heart and true!	Ma'n golon lowen, gwir!
King James's men shall understand	Tîs Matern Jams 'wra convedhas
What Cornish lads can do!	Pandro all' Kernow sîr!
Chorus:	*Burdhen*
And shall Trelawny live?	'Verow Trelawny brâs?
And shall Trelawny die?	'Verow Trelawny brâs?
Here's twenty thousand Cornish men	Mez igans mîl a dîs Kernow
Will know the reason why!	A woffeth ol an câs.
And have they fixed the where and when?	Yu ornes lê ha prês ankow?
And shall Trelawny die?	'Verow Trelawny brâs?
Here's twenty thousand Cornish men	Mez igans mîl a dîs Kernow
Will know the reason why!	A woffeth ol an câs.
Chorus	*Burdhen*
Out spake their Captain brave and bold:	'Medh aga Hapten crev ha drews,
A merry wight was he:	Gwas lowen ev a vê,
"If London Tower were Michael's hold,	"Mar pê Tour Loundres Carak Lûz,
We'll set Trelawny free!	Ny a'n kergh mes a'n lê."
Chorus	*Burdhen*
"We'll cross the Tamar, land to land:	"Ny â dres Tamar, tîr dhô dîr,
The Severn is no stay:	A pê 'vel Havren down,
With 'one and all' and hand in hand;	Onen hag ol, dhô'n den es fîr
And who shall bid us nay?	Dhô gan lettya vêdh own."
Chorus	*Burdhen*
And when we come to London Wall,	"Pan wrellon dôs dhô Foss Loundres,
A pleasant sight to view,	Dhô wel a blek dhen ny;
Come forth! come forth! ye cowards all:	Ownegyon ol, gwreugh dôs a ves
Here's men as good as you.	Dhô dîs es gwell es why!"
Chorus	*Burdhen*
'Trelawny he's in keep and hold;	"En carhar kelmes rag ankow
Trelawny he may die:	Mîreugh Trelawny brâs!
Here's twenty thousand Cornish bold	Mez igans mîl a dîs Kernow
Will know the reason why	A woffeth ol an câs."
Chorus	*Burdhen*

CAN TÎS WEST (CAN TRELAWNY)

Can Tus West (Unified Cornish)

'Ma lel an lef, 'ma'n cledha vas,
'Ma'n golon lowen, gwyr!
Tus Myghtern James 'wra convedhes
Pandr' allo Kernow, sur!
Burdhen
  'Verow Trelawny bras?
  'Verow Trelawny bras?
  Mes ugans myl a dus Kernow
  A woffyth ol an cas.

Yu ornes le ha prys ancow?
'Verow Trelawny bras?
Mes ugans myl a dus Kernow
A woffyth ol an cas.
Burdhen

'Meth aga Hapten cref ha drus,
Gwas lowen ef a ve,
"Mar pe Tour Loundres Carak Lus,
Ny a-n-kergh mes an le."
Burdhen

"Ny a dres Tamar, tyr dhe dyr,
A pe 'vel Havren doun,
Onen hag ol dhe'n den es fur
Dhe 'gan lettya vyth own."
Burdhen

"Pan wrellen dos dhe Fos Loundres,
Dhe wel a blek dhen-ny:
"Ownegyon ol, gwreugh dos yn mes
Dhe dus es gwell es' why!"
Burdhen

"Yn carghar kelmys rag ancow
Myreugh Trelawny bras!
Mes ugans myl a dus Kernow
A-woffyth ol an cas."
Burdhen

Cân Tus West (Standard Cornish)

'Ma lel an leuv, ma'n cledha mas,
'Ma'n golon lowen, gwir!
Tus Mytern Jams 'wra convedhes
Pandr'yll Kernow sur!
Bùrdhen
  'Verow Trelawny brâs?
  'Verow Trelawny brâs?
  Mès ugans mil a dus Kernow
  A woffyth oll an câss.

Yw ornys le ha prës ancow?
'Verow Trelawny brâs?
Mès ugans mil a dus Kernow
A woffyth oll an câss.
Bùrdhen

'Medh aga Hapten, crêv ha dreus,
Gwas lowen ev a veu,
"A pê Tour Loundres Carrek Loos,
Ny a'n kergh mes a'n le."
Bùrdhen

"Ny â dres Tamar, tir dhe dir,
A pe 'vell Havren down,
Onen hag oll, dhe'n den eus fur;
Dh'agan lettya y fëdh own."
Bùrdhen

"Pan wrellen dos dhe Fos Loundres,
Dhe wel a bleg dhyn ny;
Ownegyon oll, gwrewgh dos in mes
Dhe dus eus gwell esowgh why!"
Bùrdhen

"In carhar kelmys rag ancow
Mirowgh Trelawny brâs!
Mès ugans mil a dus Kernow
A woffyth oll an câss."
Bùrdhen

Lightning Source UK Ltd.
Milton Keynes UK
UKOW05n1829280617
304296UK00005B/23/P